ALLAN
LAMB

ALLAN LAMB

MY AUTOBIOGRAPHY

CollinsWillow

An Imprint of HarperCollins*Publishers*

To my dear loving wife, Lindsay,
to Katie-Ann, Richard and the rest of
my family, my friends and the
cricket fans who have supported me
throughout the years. Also to all
children suffering from cystic fibrosis.

First published in 1996
by CollinsWillow
an imprint of HarperCollins*Publishers*
London

A CIP catalogue record for this book is
available from the British Library

ISBN 0 000 218525 3

Printed and bound in Great Britain by
Caledonian International Book Manufacturer

PICTURE ACKNOWLEDGEMENTS
The publisher would like to thank the following sources:
Press Association p 4 (top); Patrick Eager pp 4 (bottom), 5 (centre),
6 (top and bottom right), 7 (top and bottom), 10 (top, centre and
bottom), 12 (top left and bottom), 13 (top), 14 (top and centre),
15 (top), 15 (bottom); Graham Morris pp 5 (top), 6 (middle left),
9, 10 (top); David Munden p 8; Popperphoto pp 11 (top and
bottom), 14 (bottom left and right), 15 (centre right), 16 (top left);
Allsport pp 12 (top right and centre), 13 (bottom right), 15 (centre
left), 16 (top right); Robin Matthews p 16 (bottom).

Contents

Acknowledgements

My thanks go first to Lamby's mother, Joan, and to his wife, Lindsay, for a magnificent set of scrapbooks and cuttings that have recorded everything printed about the cheeky chappy since the age of seven. There has been no censorship, and the scissors and paste must have been pretty painful tools at times, but their loving diligence made it unnecessary for me to explore the normal sources of research.

Alan Herd has been a tower of strength in providing a wealth of detail about Lamby's brushes with the law and the cricket authorities that has added so much to the telling of those episodes.

Wendy Wimbush is also high on my thank you list, for her splendid and accurate statistical breakdown of a fine career, both at county and international level.

And a final thank you to mum and daughter, Lindsay and Katie-Ann, for making my overnight trips to Scaldwell so memorable. Lindsay for her hospitality, her frankness when she did not have to be and for her important contribution to the book.

And Katie-Ann? A thank you for writing in her school essay that Daddy was writing a book and he was paying me to help him with the spelling.

I hope she agrees that the munny was not waisted!

Jack Bannister

Preface

Wisden will record my 79 Tests for England, another 122 appearances in one-day internationals – the last of which was the now infamous Texaco Trophy match at Lord's in 1992 against Pakistan – and the rest of a career which I can look back on with pride.

I am one of sixty batsmen in the history of the game to score over 30,000 first-class runs, and fewer than half in that list have scored more than my 89 first-class hundreds. I captained England three times and was vice-captain for two years, while at county level I led Northamptonshire for seven years, which just goes to show that I must have convinced a few people in the last twenty years that I could be trusted on and off the field.

I have demonstrated that it is possible to have a successful career and at the same time enjoy life in the fast lane. By that I mean I have always been one to let my hair down at the drop of ... well, fill in your own words. How else to explain that I have walked the tightrope with some of my antics, but have usually been able to deliver the goods on the field?

My brushes with authority started back in my schooldays, like the time I was reprimanded for taking the teachers' car-parking spaces, or when our cricket team came to lose its entire stock of beer in Graaff Reinet because of the local drought. These skirmishes continued into my late teens, when, for example, I was disciplined in my first two games for Western Province at the age of eighteen; and when, on my stag night in Cape Town, I was separated from my clothes but somehow managed to stay on the right side of prison bars. I have experimented with soft drugs, both as a kid and as a cricketer, but only briefly, and despite some close shaves I have only ever been locked up once, and that was for being drunk one night during my National Service. That was a fun period in my life: I even recall the consequences for the platoon of my attempt to become an Artful Dodger in order to avoid drill exercises on a hot day … and how the water I got into with my mates was even hotter!

I was brought up in a hard cricketing school, where sledging was part and parcel of growing up. Most of it was fun, including the best bit of silent sledging I have ever seen which involved – how shall I put it – some unusual revelations, and it worked even though the batsman claimed he shouldn't have been given out because we were 'incommoding the striker'.

But more of that later. This is my book and therefore my view on my life and career. All sorts of people have had a major influence, especially my family, and most of all, my wife Lindsay. Only I know how much she has helped our relationship through thick and thin, which is why I think it right that she has a chapter in the book to herself to explain some of the difficulties we have had to deal with. As she makes clear, there was a time we could have split up, but her determination and character enabled us to come through that and to re-establish a sound base for our partnership. She is a strong person, and she doesn't mince her words here.

Whether at school, doing military service, playing cricket, and even going to court, I have enjoyed life to the full. After all, isn't that why we're all here?

1
The Beginning

The day was 20 June 1954. The place was Langebaanweg, about an hour's drive up the west coast from Cape Town. I was the fourth child of Joan, my Mom, and Mickey, my Dad, who were both born in England although Dad had some Irish in him. That could explain a lot, as could the fact that Mom 'declared' after I was born, perhaps because I argued with the mid-wife.

My arrival squared up the family 2–2, helping brother Mike to stand up to sisters Barbara and Brenda even though I was the youngest. Mike is eight years older than I am, Brenda six years and Barbara three. Until I was four, we lived on the Air Force station in Langabaanweg, but then moved to Cape Town when Dad, who was in the South African Air Force, was posted to Ysterplaat, close to Milnerton, five miles west of Cape Town.

Mike was out of my age group as a kid, as was Brenda, so we didn't do all that much together outside the house. We have all gone our different ways since, with Mike involved in a furniture business in Cape Town, Barbara running a restaurant in Johannesburg, and Brenda living in England. She married Tony Bucknall, the England rugby international, and I bet there isn't another pair of brothers-in-law who share the unique record of captaining England three times and being on the losing side in every game.

Brenda always reckoned that I was the spoiled one of the family, perhaps because I was the youngest, but more likely because Mom and Dad saw that I might be a good cricketer one day and did everything to help me. To this day she says that I never used to pack my own cricket bag for matches and, whereas she and Mike

11

used to cop it from Dad, I always seemed to get away with everything.

I admit that in my middle teens, Dad didn't mind me having the odd beer. I was also reasonably free to do what I wanted, including staying away for the occasional night or weekend if my mates went fishing or boating. As for Brenda, once she started to go out with lads, she seemed to favour a United Nations approach, with boys of a bewildering variety of nationalities appearing on our doorstep on a regular basis.

I remember in particular this Portuguese bloke turning up once whose English was pretty non-existent. Dad gave Brenda a strict curfew time, but she went way past that and it was late when 'Eusebio' – I can't remember his real name – drove her back home and she sneaked up the stairs on tip-toes to the safe haven of her room … or so she thought.

Unfortunately, lover-boy blew her cover when he revved up in reverse and got stuck up against a mud wall! That woke up the old man, and next thing there was this real ding-dong outside, half of it in broken English. After the boyfriend had hastily driven off, there was silence until I heard Dad go to Brenda's room and utter: 'You little cow, you never moved through all that!' I recall that she tried to say that she'd been asleep, but it wasn't going to work that night.

My first pre-prep school was in a suburb of Cape Town, Pinelands, and I went there for two years before I joined Wynberg Junior School at the age of seven. Even at that age I was more concerned with anything but lessons and even in later years, though I never went out of my way to be different or to make trouble, somehow authority and I were always at odds.

Most of it was cheek, like when I used to drive to Wynberg Boys' High School, about six miles south of Cape Town, in the old family car and was punished for parking it in the teachers' spaces; or when I was made a deputy prefect, a sort of probationary appointment bestowed on me more in the hope that responsibility would quieten me down than for any other reason. As I was seventeen by then, I think they had left it a bit late!

Anyway, my new-found position in life didn't quite work out as planned by the school authorities, mainly because I lasted as long as it took the headmaster, Mr Blackbeard, to tell me that in order to show a good example to the younger boys, I had to stop going to the pub and having a few beers. Mr Blackbeard was quite a disciplinarian, but this was one pupil who was not prepared to back down. So when he made me this teetotal proposition, I said 'Thanks, but no thanks', and promptly handed back my prefect's badge.

Most of the sporting records I set at school have or will be beaten, but I bet nobody has ever been a prefect for a shorter period of time!

Another reason I didn't fancy being a prefect was because they used to inspect our hair at school. It was not allowed to be over our ears and the teachers had powers to make us have it cut, and also shave if our faces weren't smooth enough. I was always in trouble about my hair, and whenever I didn't rush off to the barbers, I'd get another dose of lines to write.

As a kid though, I think I was reasonably normal, although I never seemed far away from trouble. But I have never been one for the quiet life. Things might have been different if I had been born in England, because the climate in South Africa governs a lot, such as school hours, which start at 8 am and finish early afternoon so that sports can be played. The way of life over there is geared to the outdoors.

Dad encouraged us a lot, and he was a good club cricketer who first gave me the taste for the game above all the sports I was playing in at the time – rugby, tennis, athletics, swimming, badminton and even hockey. I've been sports mad all my life, partly to get out of extra lessons at school, but also to escape from my National Service military training. At school I always tried to dodge lessons and homework, as well as Friday afternoon cadets, which I usually managed to miss because those afternoons I was picked for coaching at the Western Province cricket nets.

Alan Oakman, then of Sussex, used to run those and I got up his nose because I always wanted to hit the ball out of the net. He warned me one day as I put my pads on, 'Make sure you practise properly. The first ball you hit out of the net will be your last'. I lasted two balls, missing the first but whacking the second for many a mile. That was the end of my net, but I always had that cocky streak that made me want to do things I was told not to.

I was also coached by another Sussex cricketer, Don Bates, who did a full season at our school, whereas Alan only made the odd visit because of his Western Province duties. Don always had a go at me

13

because he said I had too much bottom hand in my batting, but he was never one to throttle natural habits. You can't teach every kid by the book, and my technique was little different when I finished cricket after twenty years in the first-class game. Because of my dominant right hand, I could cut and pull as hard as anybody, and I made the rest of my game work in my own fashion. In sport, you've got to go with what you've got. That is not to say you must never listen, but the important thing is to work out for yourself what suits you best, and then play to your strengths.

Dad served in the South African Air Force for nearly forty years, during which time he saw action in World War II, in the Berlin Airlift, and in Korea. But he had to suffer a court martial which stopped his promotion gallop when he must have been a candidate to go to the top. What happened was, he was instructing a youngster who kept failing the exams for his wings, so there was no love lost between them. When the Prime Minister, Hendrik Verwoerd, was shot in 1966 and Dad heard the news, he said, 'I hope he doesn't bleed to death'.

But he was reported as saying that 'I hope he bleeds to death', and that's why there was a court martial hearing. He wasn't found guilty as such, but his promotion ceased until he retired in 1982 at the age of sixty as a Lieutenant-Colonel. So I'm not the first Lamb to be sheared for the wrong reasons.

Both my Mom and Dad's families went out to South Africa to live and it was there that my parents met. Dad was by then in the Air Force, and Mom's father in the RAF, having been posted from Malta.

That was in 1943 when Mom was nineteen and Dad twenty-one, but Dad's family had emigrated when he was five, so he did all his schooling and growing up in South Africa. After World War II, Mom's family went back to England but she stayed to marry Dad, and that decided my birthplace. I say this, because the only comment on my Test cricket career that I have ever taken exception to was that almost every mention of my name in the press was coupled with the two words 'South African'.

Even now, after nearly twenty years in England and having established house and home here for my family, my wife Lindsay and children Katie-Ann and Richard, journalists never seem to miss a chance to remind me of my roots. All I will say is that in the last few years, criticism has been expressed at the attitude of some England cricketers who were born abroad. Even the term 'flag of convenience' has been used. I have always shown my commitment to England, not just playing cricket but with my home and family, including education. Perhaps it's my accent? Which is why I often get asked, 'Are Katie-Ann and Richard really your kids? They speak so nicely.'

I can only speak for myself. I didn't make the rules that allowed me to play county cricket immediately because my parents were British. If such rules were not there in the past, how would 'Gubby' Allen, Ted Dexter, Colin Cowdrey, Bob Woolmer, Robin Jackman and many others have played county cricket and for England?

I decided to throw in my lot with Northamptonshire in 1978 when I was twenty-four, and I considered myself to be as British as anyone in their dressing-room.

I remember how I made the final decision. I'd been thinking about it for a long time, but it was such a commitment that I couldn't bring myself to take the plunge. My sister Brenda was the one who gave me the final push. It happened one day when we were sitting on some steps in the main Claremont shopping precinct near Newlands cricket ground.

When I told her what I was thinking of, she said to me, 'Go for it. You've got to, because it could be your only chance of international cricket'. Lindsay was also keen for me to go. We had first met in 1974 at the Forester's Arms about a mile from Newlands. We saw each other on and off for a couple of years without the relationship becoming serious because I was doing my National Service, mainly in the town of George in the Eastern Cape. After that finished, we started seeing a lot more of each other. She was then twenty-one, doing interior design at college in Cape Town, and knew me well enough to push me in the same direction as Brenda had.

It would be dishonest not to admit that a major factor was the thought that, even if I became good enough to play Test cricket, my chances of playing for South Africa, what with the international ban, were close to nil. I thought of players like Mike Procter, Eddie Barlow and Barry Richards and how they had been denied continuing in Test cricket through no fault of their own.

But what I want to make clear is that, having decided to cross over I didn't mess about. I went for it the whole way, and ever since then my first loyalties in cricket, as in other sports I've played, have always been to England. Just ask my family and friends. It is always 'we' when I talk about England, whether it be cricket or rugby. If that wasn't true, I would probably have thought seriously about going back there to South Africa to live when I retired, but that has never been mine nor Lindsay's intention.

When I joined Northamptonshire, it was impressed on me right at the start that I had to prove I meant business by buying a property for residence, and this I did. We are now settled in Scaldwell, near Kettering. So are our kids, and I consider myself a part of the scene there.

Furthermore, when I got an offer from Dr Ali Bacher, the head of the South African Cricket Board, to play against Graham Gooch's 'rebel' England side in 1982, I turned it down because of the danger of breaking my registration with Northamptonshire.

Also, ever since 1984, I have only twice wintered back in South Africa to play first-class cricket, with Orange Free State and Western Province, and I did so as their official *overseas* player. And the fact I was awarded the captaincy of my county, as well as a benefit and a testimonial, shows that the club accepted me for what I was – a whole-hearted county cricketer whose proudest moment came when I was selected for the first of my combined 201 international appearances for England.

I said Dad had Irish blood in him, which is possibly why I never ducked an argument, even after being warned about the consequences. Nobody will ever change me, not that a few haven't tried. It's not that I'm a so-called rebel, but rather that I've got a sense of fair play which I will not compromise. If I believe in something, I'm prepared to go all the way, never mind what trouble it causes me.

2
My Start in Cricket

After we all moved to Cape Town in 1958, I used to go with Dad to his club games and I was so keen that it seemed inevitable for me to start playing in teams at school. I had a go at everything, not just batting, but wicket-keeping as well until the age of ten. I then took the advice of my teacher, Mel Bohling. We used to play with a two-piece cricket ball and I found I could swing it for miles. After an untidy performance from me in one game, he suggested I gave up the gloves and tried to bowl. In one particular match we were a bowler short, and I took six wickets.

I don't remember too many of my early games at school, but I can quote scores because Mom religiously kept scrapbooks of everything that ever appeared in print about me – and after I got married and settled in England, Lindsay took over. Between them, they have a comprehensive collection of cuttings from almost every game I played in. I've always been a great believer in the family spirit, and I could not have managed or survived the worst times without their help and support. Some of the stuff they filed must have hurt them, but they have kept everything.

Mom's first scrapbook was a little exercise book with pages lined with squares, and she stuck the figure '1' on the brown paper cover, with the label 'Wynberg Junior School, Cricket Scores for Under-12 upwards, 1966-69'. And there was my first cutting – the scores of Wynberg Under-12s against Golden Grove. They got 41 and we won by five wickets with 'Lamb 23 n.o'.

Not a bad start, but what about the next two cuttings? We beat Paul Roos School by 55 runs, when I got 34 and took seven wickets

17

for 19 with my medium-pace nothings. The next team to think I was another Mike Procter was the Under-13s, when I had a golden couple of matches between 28 February and 18 March 1967. I scored 76 out of 189 against Christian Brothers College and then took four for 14 as we bowled them out for 36. Now I was the hero, and even more so against St Joseph's School in Rondebosch when I took nine for 4 and scored 51. I did so well that in 1968, I jumped a year straight into the Under-15s and took part in the first ever Under-15s Cricket Week to be held in Western Province. I played for Wynberg in a tournament consisting of eight schools, including Grey High School from Port Elizabeth and composite teams from Boland, Northern areas and the suburbs of Cape Town.

It was a three-day tournament, and my 66 against Boland got me into the big match on the final day between a Western Province Under-15 XI and a Western Province Invitation XI. Also playing for the Province was Stephen Muller, son of rugby Springbok Hennie, and he hit the highest score of the week, 141 not out.

I am a year older than Peter Kirsten – who played cricket for South Africa both at home and in England after the Test ban was lifted – but we started to play against each other in 1969 when he got into the South African College School side. By now, I was getting proper coaching from people like Tom Reddick, the former Nottinghamshire player and coach, and later from Don Bates and Alan Oakman. Tom was sufficiently impressed by my potential to mention me in a piece he wrote on club cricket in the *Cape Times*. He started writing about my brother, Mike, but then went on: 'For those who like to spot future winners, there is a younger Lamb at Wynberg Boys' High School with an abundance of natural talent. I am sure he will make his mark one day'.

I was only ten when I first came under Tom Reddick's coaching, and even now I remember what impressed me most was the way he dressed. Everything was always immaculate – he was what we would call a 'pukka dresser'. It was the same with his coaching. Everything had to be done by the book and in a completely correct manner, so some of my shots used to get him frowning and shaking his head. 'Keep the ball on the ground, lad, and they'll never get you out,' he must have said to me a hundred times. I respected him more than any other coach, because as I grew up I realised what a terrific knowledge he had. His views on discipline were a bit different from mine, but that's another story...

At that time I was also playing schools rugby, and Mom even pasted in a cutting about a try I converted in a 14–4 win for Wynberg against Paul Roos. On the cricket front, I was being considered for the Nuffield Schools Week, which in the past has thrown up so many top South African cricketers. Because I had jumped a year and was playing with older boys, I was asked if I would make myself available for the Under-15 section, but not for the Open-age teams. I told them that I was only available for the full Nuffield week, so I didn't get picked because they said I was too young. I know I was right for myself, but it only convinced people that I was too cocky. Even then, I would not compromise, because if I was good enough to score 84 in the final provincial trial at Rondebosch, then I thought I deserved full consideration.

As the *Cape Times* put it, 'Allan Lamb, the 15-year-old Wynberg BHS wicket-keeper batsman must have come very close to selection, but is only in Standard Six so will have another chance next year.'

The 1970-71 schools season started with a big game for us kids against a Wilfred Isaacs XI. You can compare Wilf with England's Derrick Robins, who put together so many sides of top cricketers to play all over the world. Wilf lives in Johannesburg, and has given a lot to South African cricket with his invitation teams made up of several first-class cricketers and some top club players.

He brought his side on a short tour of the Cape in September 1970, but rain spoiled most of the games. His side included two Test players, Denis Lindsay and Roy McLean, plus what could have been a third in Gary Watson. Watson, a promising young fast bowler from Transvaal, was picked for the 1970 tour of England which was called off because of the apartheid system that governed what was then my country.

It is all too easy to say that I didn't agree with apartheid; it is also easy to say that because I was born into the system, I never knew any better until I travelled abroad. What is not in doubt is that my folks were against it and they brought the four of us up to treat everyone the same.

Cricket did as much as it could, with the historic walk-off the field at Newlands on 3 April 1971 involving big-name players such as the Pollocks, Peter and Graeme, Eddie Barlow and Barry Richards. They had been playing in a Test trial before the South African party was picked for the coming tour of Australia (which was eventually cancelled) and decided to take action to bolster the policy of the South African Cricket Association to pick sides purely on merit. It may not have appeared a huge gesture to the outside world, but I knew what guts it had taken the individual players to stand up against the attitude of the South African government and police authorities at that time.

I've seen discrimination all over the world, and I've copped my fair share of public criticism, especially in England where some people have been reluctant to accept that I meant what I said when I qualified to play as an England cricketer after four years. I'll say it again, I did not do it as a temporary measure, and it is now nearly twenty years since I made the break and joined Northamptonshire. People have said that as soon as I finished on the Test scene, then I'd be off back to South Africa. Well, they've already had a long wait, and they've got a longer one coming.

The Wilfred Isaacs team which gave us up-and-coming kids such a thrill to play against also included four other Transvaal Currie Cup cricketers – Robbie Muzzell, Albie During, Patrick Flanagan and Clive Rice, as well as Andre Bruyns from our own Western Province. Robbie is now based in East London and is a top administrator who has already managed one South African side abroad; and 'Ricey' is a Test selector, which is quite a performance considering the rows he had towards the end of his career with the South African Cricket Board which led to him being left out of the squad for the 1992 World Cup.

As for Denis Lindsay, what a great wicketkeeper-batsman and what a character! He has always liked a glass or two, and he stays forever if there's an argument going on. It's worth paying admission money when he and Trevor Quirk get together. They both kept wicket for Northern Transvaal, and neither will ever admit that the other can 'keep'.

Against the Isaacs team, we lost easily of course and I was bowled by Gary Watson for eight, but it meant a lot to us to start the season against a side like that. We travelled straight after the match the four hundred miles to Graaff Reinet for a schools week. Even though I didn't get many runs, I'll never forget that trip because of what happened to the team's secret stash of beer.

To keep us out of trouble with the schoolmasters, we decided to hide it in some safe place. The open sluices on the outskirts of the ground appeared to be the best bet, but, unbeknown to us, because of the drought these sluices had been linked directly to all the gardens for watering purposes. So, far from being in safe storage, that was the first and last we saw of our precious drink once the sluices were switched on and the beer flushed away to oblivion. At least our beery efforts caused no damage – unlike a couple of other bits of mischief we got up to on that trip.

We stacked some cycle racks across the main road into town and almost immediately nailed a mini which crashed into them. That, plus an overturned ice-cream van, didn't exactly please the locals.

I seemed to have a thing about ice cream in those days, for another incident involved me in a streak through an ice cream parlour in Newlands. It was a hot day and a group of us decided it would be fun to do a quick streak. I was not only the smallest of our gang, it seems I was the slowest as well, because while the others nipped in and out safely, I failed to make good my escape and was locked in by the owner. What could I do? Order the biggest cornet he had for modesty purposes? This bloke seemed more likely to get me in a wafer grip, but a nice little rugby swerve got me around him with just enough space and time to unlock the door. My legs might have been short as a teenager – and still are – but they could twinkle when necessary.

So here was I sprinting up Main Road being chased by this man with most of my short life flashing (no pun intended) in front of me. My mates had gone, and so, nearly was I. I've never given up in life, even when things look hopeless, and suddenly I realised I was passing the big local swimming-pool opposite the old Newlands Sun Hotel.

That was it. In I went, ignoring the request from the attendant for my membership card or money – how did he think I was carrying either? – but just kept going and dived into the water. Brilliant. It rivalled Steve McQueen's getaway in *The Great Escape*; the pool was crowded and I reckon I broke the local record for underwater swimming, having swum at least a hundred yards and only coming up for air for a split second at a time.

I watched the ice-cream man, but he had no chance of picking me out from dozens of kids – unless I came out of the water with my non-existent trunks, and then what would he recognise? He gave up after ten minutes, and a borrowed towel and a telephone call for the cavalry with some clothes saved the day.

It had been quite a summer. It must seem I was one of a crowd of hooligans, and I suppose I'd lecture my kids if they tried the same things. All I can say is that I was young, bursting with life and energy and never set out to cause any real trouble. In that week in Graaff Reinet, both Kenny McEwan, who later played for Essex, and Peter Kirsten got a lot of runs, with Kirsy's 94 against Grey High School taking the headlines because, at fifteen, he was three years younger than Kenny.

I hardly got a run for my school, but still got picked for the final trial for the Western Province Nuffield side for the annual week which that year was held in Port Elizabeth. Having made myself unavailable the previous season for the Under-15s, thinking I was good enough for the open age team, I suppose it was 'sod's law' that my form disappeared the year after.

I was a bit lucky to get a final chance, but all I needed was a good score, and I would be in. Unfortunately, all my hopes disappeared out of the window when I was run out for a duck. Wynberg didn't get one player in the final squad of thirteen. Rondebosch had five representatives, and Peter Kirsten got in, although he was only fifteen years and six months. It was a body blow to me, but Kirsy deserved it. We played against each other in the last match of term, and I scored 20 to his 56 not out. He had a great first half-season, and I hadn't, but there was still the rest of the season to come.

I got better, with several thirties and forties, but my best match was one we lost at the end of March to Rondesbosch. I grabbed four wickets and top-scored with 60 out of 145, and that won me a bat presented by the *Cape Times* to the Schoolboy Cricketer of the week. I've still got the letter from the newspaper, dated 7 April 1971, telling me where and how to claim my award.

'Kindly present this letter and attached order form No 751 to Messrs Jack Lemkus Sports (Pty) 48 St George's St., Cape Town, and there choose a four star bat suitable for your size and height.'

I badly wanted Nuffield colours in 1971/72, having already missed out twice, and I started well with 83 and 35 in the first cricket week of the season. This was held in Cape Town and involved eight schools, including four from the Eastern Cape. My 35 came against

Grey College from Port Elizabeth, and I also took five wickets with, according to one reporter, 'medium-paced cutters with accuracy'…

I still needed a big score, and I finally got one, 137, in a friendly for the school against Wynberg Cricket Club. Then a fortnight later I scored 75 not out in a big win against Westerford. By this time, a very young and spindly Garth Le Roux was in our side, and I still get a chuckle out of the fact that I used to get on to bowl before him!

I made another hundred that term, but my most treasured picture is one my Mom pasted in my record book. It shows a batsman of Rondebosch and me, the bowler, with my hand raised in frustration as I beat him. It's the caption I treasure: 'J. Matthew has a narrow escape as a ball from Wynberg bowler A. Lamb whistles past his off stump'.

'Whistles', no less. How could Big Garth ever complain that I was a better bowler once upon a time?

I scored 66 and 21 in the trials, and that was enough. The party of thirteen was announced on 11 December, and my name was there, as was Peter Kirsten's.

The annual Nuffield Week was held in Johannesburg in early January, and it was the twenty-ninth such occasion. Other young hopefuls were Ray Jennings, that great wicket-keeper, who played for Transvaal schools and Paddy Clift and Kevin Verdoorn who also went on to play plenty of first-class cricket.

It was a rainy week, but I got a couple of 20s and five for 42 against Border. If Le Roux still had a problem with my bowling, I bet he choked over his body-building cornflakes when he read in the newspaper that 'Border could only manage 149 against hostile bowling from Allan Lamb'.

'Whistled past'. Now 'hostile'. It was nearly enough to persuade me that I was quite a tearaway with the ball. Nearly. But deep down I knew that, if ever I could bat for a living against my own bowling, I'd be rich in a month.

I enjoyed the atmosphere in Johannesburg and was hugely impressed by the Wanderers Club where a lot of the matches were played. Neither Kirsy nor I made the final Schools XI which played Transvaal, but I was just happy and thrilled to be part of a week which had produced so many great cricketers since its inception in 1940.

How many sides could you pick from these names? By January

1972, forty-four Nuffield schoolboys had gone on to play full Test cricket for South Africa, including Jackie McGlew, Hugh Tayfield, Roy McLean, Johnny Waite, Trevor Goddard, Clive van Ryneveld, Ken Funston, Paul Winslow, Peter Carlstein, Geoff Griffin, Eddie Barlow, Colin Bland, Peter Pollock, Graeme Pollock, 'Tiger' Lance, Peter van der Merwe, Denis Lindsay, Ali Bacher, Mike Procter, Barry Richards and Lee Irvine.

I have kept several souvenirs of my first big representative recognition, including a booklet which lists every player for each province. Included in that week in Johannesburg were Anton Ferreira from Northern Transvaal, Robbie Armitage from Eastern Province, and one other, the youngest of the lot. Remember, I had been considered too young at fifteen to play with the big boys, some of whom were well over eighteen here. In fact, Border picked a couple of lads who were over nineteen, but there, nestling at the bottom of the Orange Free State squad is K Wessels, aged fourteen years and three months.

It is the oldest saying in every cricketing country except England, that if you're good enough, you're old enough. The same week, another schools competition was staged in the country, and one which was organised by Ali Bacher, then only twenty-nine years old, and captain of South Africa in their last series against Australia before isolation.

When I tell you that the week was staged in Soweto, you'll get an idea of what happened. It was a national week involving one hundred African schoolboys from ten provinces who would play their matches on matting, as there were no grass pitches in Soweto until Ali Bacher, again, moved in about fifteen years later. I have said that cricket led the other sports into chipping away at apartheid, and one of the sponsors was South African Breweries, still one of cricket's biggest sponsors in South Africa.

Dr Ali Bacher was involved with the blacks and the coloureds in South Africa, not just in cricket but in medicine as well. When he qualified he went to work in Johannesburg hospital which treated all nationalities. Perhaps because of his own upbringing as a Lithuanian Jew, he has fought for equality in life, and, more than any other person in South Africa, he has never stopped working for the non-whites. He has a reputation as an opportunist and a wheeler-dealer, but only those qualities would have enabled him to integrate cricket as he did, particularly after the Gatting 'rebel tour' when his township scheme was threatened by the African National Congress. He rode out that crisis, and now has several people working for the United Cricket Board who in the 1980s were threatening his life. He ran domestic cricket almost single-handed at that time. Every decision was his, including the elbow-room he gave to Orange Free State when he wanted them to hold their own in the 'A' section of the Currie Cup. The overseas rule was flexible to say the least when I went there in 1987, and he juggled it around so that Alvin Kallicharran, Sylvester Clarke, Alastair Storie, Gordon Parsons and Jeremy Lloyds were all there in addition to me. Ali was the one who organised the big sponsorship deal, which resulted in the quickest ever pay-out when I got the best score of 294 for Orange Free State against Eastern Province in 1987.

In the meantime, I went back to Cape Town after the schools week wanting more representative cricket, and knew I just had to keep banging the scores into the score book. I was captain of Wynberg High now and had a couple of big hundreds under my belt, as well as keeping the bowling talents of Garth Le Roux under wraps. Garth still moans, but he weighed about ten stone dripping wet then, and was no quicker than I was. Wynberg won six out of eight matches that year and I set a new record with 1200 runs in the season.

The 1972/73 season was my last year at school and I enjoyed such a good first summer term that I not only was an automatic pick for Nuffield Week, held this time in Bulawayo, but I also made my debut for Western Province 'B'.

I was still giving myself plenty of bowling, but Big Garth was now starting to grow and I often shared the new ball with him. Mind you, it was no contest as to who was the better bowler. In two successive weeks against Westerford and Pinelands, he got none for 5 and none for 13, while I sneaked in with seven for 11 and eight for 19, gaining plenty of publicity along the way.

My 'B' team debut came against Eastern Province in a two-day game at Newlands, but my wickets clearly didn't impress the captain, Jack Burt, from my brother's club, Claremont, because he didn't give me a bowl. Things went my ways though, because I'd been picked as an opening bat and made 77 not out and 36, but I only played as a replacement when the regular opener dropped out for business reasons.

At least I'd put a marker down for a debut game in the senior provincial side in the Currie Cup, but first there was Nuffield Week, over the border in Bulawayo. I was desperate to make the final representative side to play Rhodesia, captained by Mike Procter, and everything came right for me. I hit two hundreds and a 96, but Kirsy missed out and was made twelfth man, so I was the only Western Province representative in a side that included Kevin Verdoorn, Ray Jennings and Kepler Wessels.

The Rhodesian attack was easily the best I'd ever faced, with Mike Procter and Robin Jackman taking the new ball, followed by Paddy Clift and Jacky Du Preez. Their batting line-up wasn't bad either, with Peter Carlstein and Brian Davison, although we didn't get past 'Procky' at five, because they hammered us for 332 for the loss of only three wickets off 61 overs. I got a bowl, but wished I hadn't, being hit for 40 runs off four overs, which is probably why my bowling was never taken too seriously after that.

I batted all right for 27, and was pleased at how I played Procky. He'd got our captain, Charles Middleton, lbw first ball, but I hit my first ball from him for four. I was given a stare and a mutter which became a lot louder when I hit another four. Schoolboy against Test cricketer it might have been, but that didn't stop me from getting the full verbal treatment. Mom and Dad could have disproved one remark, but not some of the others which were quite new, even to the son of a military man.

Mike Procter was one of my boyhood heroes, because I loved the way he played. Whether batting or bowling, he never held back and he convinced me that was the only way to play. Some top cricketers are the same on and off the field, but Procky was different. He was a real hard man until the close of play, but friendly and quieter when he had a few beers. I saw a lot of him as an opponent for Natal and Gloucestershire, and a colleague with Free State and Northants as manager and coach. I just wish he'd been able to express himself more freely to the players when they were having a rough time. But what a great cricket brain he had.

We were bowled out for 177, with Verdoorn batting brilliantly for 69 before he was run out. Still, I'd got my Nuffield Schools cap and tie and I had impressed a few people, including Robin Jackman, who wrote in the Bulawayo *Sunday News*, 'One name has been predominant during the Nuffield Week. That is Allan Lamb of

Western Province… He scores freely off both the front and back foot and I am sure he has a great future ahead of him'.

My scrapbook of that week includes several snapshots taken mostly off the field, including one with three of us smartly dressed in hat, jockstrap and shoes. In another is the odd bottle of beer, and I remember how we beat the official curfew time on the itinerary which said, 'Reveille, 6.15 am' and 'Lights out 10.30 pm'.

The lights did go out at 10.30 pm, but so did I and a few mates at 10.31 pm. We used the bail-out system with the help of sheets, and not just on one night either. I wanted to go out, mainly because it was written down that we shouldn't. Given no curfew, I probably wouldn't have bothered, but now I was eighteen and thought I knew everything. Happy days, they really were.

I left Bulawayo with a feeling of anti-climax. End of the Nuffield Week and end of school. So now what? I soon knew. On the train trip home, we stopped at Worcester for a few minutes and some of the boys bought a newspaper and came whooping back to tell me that I'd been picked for my first-class debut against Eastern Province at Newlands.

I could hardly believe it had come so quickly, but what had helped me was that Richard Morris and John Cheetham would not be available for the five remaining Currie Cup matches because of business and study commitments. The selectors had to decide whether to go for experience and pick the Somerset professional Roy Virgin, or take a punt with a youngster. The train trip from Bulawayo to Cape Town took three days, and I just hoped that the paper hadn't got it wrong.

It only sank in after we arrived. Some Western Province officials were at the station to tell me what I already knew, that I was going to play among players who were my heroes, such as Eddie Barlow, the captain, Hylton Ackerman, Peter Swart – now assistant groundsman at Newlands – Denys Hobson, Grahame Chevalier and the wicket-keeper Gavin Pfuhl.

More important, what about the Eastern Province side? Dassie Biggs was captain, and he had a lively new ball attack of 'Spook' Hanley and Etienne Schmidt, as well as a strong batting side which included Kenny McEwan, Chris Wilkins, who played for Derbyshire, and Lorrie Wilmot who was a big striker of the ball. Graeme Pollock was their big gun, but he'd broken his arm and missed most of that season.

'Spook' Hanley was a typical tearaway fast bowler, and you could have got 50–1 about what he would end up doing. He is now an artist who has painted for a living for many years and has a high reputation.

My name was in the headlines before the game, and Mom even spotted an advert which she pasted into the book: 'Price of Lamb jumps by 20c a kilo'. There is also a photo of Dad and me, with the one quote from me that pleased him. 'I owe it all to my Dad. He has been coaching me since I was two years old.'

It was Western Province's last home match of the season, and a win would put us top of the log at the halfway stage. I was to bat at no. 3, and I was snowed under with cards of good wishes, telegrams and a letter from the Wynberg High School Old Boys Union. I loved one sentence: 'I must commend you on the big match temperament and the fact that you were able to approach the Nuffield tournament with your usual quiet confidence and attacking style.'

Quiet confidence? Ask Eddie Barlow and the Eastern Province senior official, Geoff Dakin, about that. When I went in to bat in the second innings, I joined Eddie who had warned me before the start of the innings to watch what and who I hooked. In fact, I was known as the 'Happy Hooker', as I couldn't resist anything dropped short. So when Schmidty let me have one, I had a full go at it, missed it, and knew that I was about to get an ear bashing.

Down the pitch came 'Bunter', although even I would never have dared to call Eddie that. 'They've put a man out at deep square leg for the hook shot, so don't do it.' Good advice that, and I should have been grateful that a Test player wanted to help a novice. As kids we all looked up to Eddie. Not just because of his cricket, although he was our boyhood hero through the 1960s when he played for South Africa, but because his whole attitude grabbed me. As far as Eddie was concerned, the trouble was that the kid from Langebaanweg wanted to compete on equal terms, not just with the bat, but with the mouth as well.

I only had to wait a few minutes. Schmidty tried another bouncer next over – only to Eddie, not me. Bang. He middled it for a great hooked four, but I wasn't going to let the previous over's conversation pass without a comeback. Down the pitch I went and said, 'Eh, remember that man on the boundary? He's there to catch you as well'. I went back to my end, with Eddie, for once, silent in what the umpire told me was sheer disbelief.

I'm told that he was the same when he was my age, so perhaps that's why I didn't get a rocket. I batted well in both innings for 58 and 36 and collected a double first on my debut: my first 50 and my first hangover for Western Province. But that put me at odds with Geoff Dakin, who was managing Easterns.

I was 41 not out overnight and feeling full of myself in the bar of the Newlands Sun. I was having a few beers with Kenny McEwan when up came Dakin, who hadn't got the quietest voice you'd ever heard. Perhaps he thought I was trying to nobble his young batsman who had smashed us for 85 out of 200, including five sixes and four fours, but the manager wanted to crack the whip.

None of my business I suppose, except that I'd known Kenny for a few years and wanted to have another drink with him. The printable part of the conversation was a polite suggestion from me that Kenny take no notice, stay where he was and have another beer.

Next morning, before I went in to bat, I was called in front of Gerald Innes, our manager, who said that Dakin had accused me of swearing at him. I tried to tell him that if I called anybody anything, it was Kenny for listening to his manager. It didn't work, and I was told to apologise to Dakin, which I did with the same willingness that I'm told Mike Gatting showed to Shakoor Rana in Faisalabad.

First game, and my first taste of discipline – plus a warning about my future behaviour. I have to say that I was not at my freshest when I resumed my innings that morning, and was finally bowled by Keith Reid for 58. The *Cape Times* misread my batting on that second morning: 'Young Lamb, the Wynberg High School cricketer, seemed to lose his concentration after reaching his 50'.

Except that you can't lose what you didn't have, and all I could think of was that I'd been bounced in my first match, and I wished I hadn't been so insistent on those last few beers. We won the match and went to the top of the 'A' section table. I got a great press, with Tom Reddick saying, 'The eighteen-year-old Lamb, with 5000 spectators rooting for him, made a most auspicious debut. Apparently free of nerves, he used the hook, cut and drive with judgement and force. There are no frills or fancies in his cricket make-up and he watches the ball. We shall be watching him too, for here is a player with a future.'

He finished with a paragraph which showed I wasn't the only one who had a few too many beers during the match. 'I must congratulate the spectator from under the plane trees for his entertaining gravity-defying act. His attempted vault over the fence into the green rubbish bin reminded me of Buster Keaton at his best.'

Michael Owen-Smith was a bit more cautious. 'Allan Lamb made a swashbuckling 36 in 52 minutes with five fours and a six. But he was dropped twice and although he has all the shots in the book, as well as the composure of a first-class cricketer, he will have to learn to control his exuberance and be more selective in going for the hook early in his innings.'

As I was to find out in my next big game at Kingsmead against Natal. But before that, I made my debut for Claremont and joined my elder brother Mike. We played Western Province CC and it was a top club match. They had Hylton Ackerman, Fred Goldstein, John Nel (son of Jack), Gavin Pfuhl, and the quick bowler Sibley McAdam while we had the two Lambs, Burt, Ian Payne and Chevalier. We won by one wicket and I took three catches. Exactly three more than my runs – I bagged a pair against McAdam to make a nonsense of my pre-match publicity, some of which I must admit had been 'created' by my brother.

Fortunately, that didn't affect my award of the Western Cape's Junior Sportsman of the Year. Quite a week for me then – a pair and a trophy – and just four days before my first-ever game at Kingsmead.

My second first-class cricket match was one of my most memorable. Eddie Barlow had a magnificent all-round game with ten wickets and a top score of 64 in our only innings. We beat Natal on a green mamba of a pitch by an innings, and I collected seven stitches and another appearance before the management on a disciplinary charge.

On the first day, Eddie took seven for 24 as we bowled Natal out in 30 overs for 76. The top scorer was Dave Orchard, who stood as umpire in the Cape Town Test against England in January 1996, and was the man in the middle of several controversies, including the run-out of Graham Thorpe. (Having initially decided to give Thorpe not out and not refer to the third umpire, under pressure from the South African captain Hansie Cronje he was persuaded to consult the official, whereupon Thorpe had to go.)

I batted at no. 3 and joined Eddie Barlow very early, with all the warnings about hooking fresh in my mind. I'm reminded of how Ian

Chappell was in a similar situation before the Lord's Test in 1972, after he'd twice got out hooking in the first Test at Old Trafford. He told me that he'd even had a letter from his grandmother, saying that she didn't know what a hook was, but everyone said that he had to stop doing it!

Apparently Chappell bailed out from the first short one he received from John Snow and was hit. He then told himself that it hurt, so he was going to inflict some pain of his own and hooked his way to 56. It was the same with me nearly.

Vintcent van der Bijl, who played for Middlesex in 1980 and 1981, tried me with a short ball as soon as I went in and, with Eddie at the other end, I ducked and watched it go by at shoulder height at what I thought was a nice, gentle pace. As far as I was concerned it was four runs missed and I was furious with myself for listening to other people.

The next one I decided was going to go, and I waited for Vintcent to try me again. It didn't take long. I saw the ball whacked in short and picked my spot at mid-wicket. Off the mark with a six, or so I thought – except I was about halfway through the shot when the ball struck the middle of my forehead and there was blood everywhere. At the other end my partner Eddie only made two movements: one with his arm to wave on Hylton Ackerman to replace me, and one from his mouth from which I heard, 'Silly little prick. Get him off quick. I don't want blood on a good length!'

Of all the great names in South African cricket, Eddie Barlow is tops with me. People reckon that I bristle with aggression and always go in head first – but I'm only halfway up the Barlow ladder in that department. He was magnificent. Never mind the opposition or the state of the game, Eddie always fancied himself for a hundred or some wickets. He was one of the great inspirational cricketers and I've lost count of the times that I've seen him pull things off with sheer arrogance.

When Eddie ran the Western Province team, he would insist on full attendance at the nets, but there were several players who objected to him bossing them around. So his reign wasn't always smooth, but then he went to World Series Cricket and Hylton Ackerman took over, only for one season as it turned out because we were told that Eddie was coming back. Several players went to the Western Province chairman, Fritz Bing, and said they wouldn't play under Eddie again, as a result of which Peter Kirsten took over.

Eddie's main problem was that he didn't realise how badly he treated those under him, which is why he did not handle the senior players successfully.

Although I didn't know it then, that innings of mine against Natal signalled the end of my Currie Cup batting for two years. I came back at the end of the innings with seven stitches and 'I told you so' from both Eddie and Hylton Ackerman. When we got back to our hotel, the Elangeni on the sea front in Durban which was only a few hundred yards from Kingsmead, I had a headache and decided to go straight to bed.

If that was my first mistake, the second was to tell my mates. An hour or so later, they knocked on the door and told me I was going to a party with them. I refused, but they then started to kick the door down.

My room was on the fifteenth floor and the Elangeni is designed so that every room looks out over the Marine Parade and towards the beach and the sea and, oh yes, over the swimming-pool on the second floor as well. That was the first target for a couple of mattresses my mates threw out of the window, and I was told I'd follow them if I went back to bed.

Whatever my reply was, it was enough literally to turn my world upside down, as I found myself hanging out of the window by my ankles and being asked to reconsider. I wasn't bad at high diving, but not from thirteen floors up, so I gave in to their demands and stayed for the rest of the party.

There was more trouble in store for me, following various complaints from other guests about our behaviour. I was identified to the management as one of the culprits by my stitches and black eye. My defence – that a couple of mattresses were neither here nor there and that my mates would never have dropped me – didn't get me off the hook. The hotel manager pointed out that he wanted the mattresses 'here' in the bedroom and not 'there' in the pool.

I got a real ticking-off from Gerald Innes who pointed out that not many eighteen-year-olds are charged with misconduct in their first two first-class matches. The senior players thought it a huge joke that the cocky kid from Langebaanweg, full of stitches because he wouldn't listen, had twice got himself in front of the manager.

The game was over in two days, and so was my Currie Cup career for two years. I moved to Abbotts College in Rosebank to cram for exams, so the only cricket I played in for the rest of that summer was for Claremont. I got a few runs and we won the First Division. I also played the first few games of the 1973/74 season for them, but then left to do my National Service.

I wanted to do my National Service in one hit, so instead of doing eighteen months and then a series of camps in the next couple of years, I settled to do the full two years, starting in Pretoria.

3
National Service and Return to Top Class Cricket

I remained in Pretoria for three months before I managed to work my passage to George in the Eastern Cape. It was only a small town then, in the middle of a farming community about 250 miles from Cape Town. I helped to build the runway which led to a bigger airport. At that time George was famous, or notorious, as the first military base to have a women's army camp.

I played a few games of club cricket before I was posted. That was where I first met Trevor Quirk, who now commentates for the South African Broadcasting Corporation. He was captain, and not above any sort of gamesmanship which might help to win a game. For instance we were well on top in one league game, but two batsmen got stuck in and it looked as though they might save the match.

'Quirky' got four of us together and told us his plan. It takes a lot to faze me, but I couldn't believe what he wanted us to do. He insisted that it was just his way of putting some extra 'zip' into our cricket. And so the famous plan was put into operation. Two of us went in close in front of the bat on the off side and the other two at forward short leg. As Quirky set the rest of the field, the quartet chosen to break the concentration of the batsman drew a deep breath … and unzipped our trousers!

About to take guard, the poor batsman's eyes opened wide and then wider as out came everything, to make public something which was very private. He studiously blocked the first ball and then appealed to the umpire that 'his concentration was being mentally obstructed'. By this time, though, we had withdrawn the evidence from public view.

'Get on with it' was the instruction from the umpire, so we repeated the tactic, one by one, during the rest of the over. Each time the batsman turned to the umpire, we re-zipped our trousers and gave it the innocent look. Our plan worked, although not quite as Quirky had intended, because we dismissed the batsman at the other end who hadn't noticed anything! Ever since then, I've realised that a captain must be prepared to try anything, but I never used such a cock-and-bull plan in my seven years of captaining Northamptonshire!

After we'd won the match, we asked Quirky what made him think of the idea. 'Call it a flash of inspiration. No, *four* flashes of inspiration.'

I never felt settled in Pretoria, so I worked a move to George where I spent the rest of my service as a plant operator, which meant having to drive heavy vehicles about. I was in charge of a motor scraping earth mover and, as I've said, helped to build a new airport. Whenever I landed at George airport in the next few years, I thought they should have put up a plaque, saying 'Lamby nearly wrote off an earth mover here on his first day'.

Although I was much nearer home than when in Pretoria, it was still eight hours drive away, so it meant no first-class cricket for me in the next eighteen months. Dad helped out every so often by flying a few of us back to Cape Town for weekends. We could always tell he was arriving by the way he buzzed and dive-bombed us.

As with most conscripts, national service seemed a waste of time, but I can look back now and enjoy some of the memories. Like living in tents in the bush. That came after my first go behind the wheel on my first day, and my inexperience landed me in trouble and the vehicle down a 15-foot drop into a dam.

I was told to get on this monster machine by a sergeant who wouldn't have made a great driving instructor. He showed me a few levers and told me to get on with it. My first mistake was to rev a bit too hard, which meant that I mistimed my braking effort because of the pneumatic compact roller pressures.

Now there was a real problem. I was heading straight for the dam, slowly maybe, but much too quickly for a driver who hadn't the faintest idea what to do. I pressed every button and pulled every lever, to no avail. The sergeant yelled at me, but I couldn't even straighten the wheel. It was decision time – should I go down with the ship? Instinct and fright took over, because I reckoned that a posthumous medal for gallantry was not much good to me. So I bailed out.

That saved me, but it left 7000 rand worth of vehicle all set for an unscheduled all-over wash. Everything seemed to happen in slow motion, unlike the speed with which I was hauled up on a charge and grounded with the maintenance unit to handle every dirty job they could give me.

That was my second military punishment. The first one was thanks to Quirky following an incident that took place late one evening back in Pretoria. He took a few of us out for a few beers. Then a few more and then a lot more. Quirky has an astonishing constitution; even now, over twenty years later, he never stops. So it was way past lights-out when he took us back to camp. Had I been stone cold sober, I might have sneaked back into barracks safely, but I got nailed easily once the Quirky brain started to tick over.

We couldn't drive through the main gate for obvious reasons, so we parked the car on the perimeter and found an unlit area about one hundred yards down the road from where we could scale the barbed wire fence. A dozen or so Castle beers did not help my attempted conquest, and sure enough I found myself entangled in the barbed wire, with Quirky trying desperately to push me over. (If he was attempting to repeat the exposure tactics which gained that batsman's wicket that day, then I was close to having nothing much to offer!)

I snagged myself on the wretched wire and yelled out in agony. Suddenly it was like a scene out of Colditz … lights everywhere, guards rushing around, complete mayhem. I was eventually rescued from my predicament and locked up.

Extra punishment drill the next day was a formality. I remember it was unbearably hot and we were marched up and down with full packs of clay on our backs. It was a killer, but we had to keep going in precision fashion. Unfortunately, someone stepped out of line, so the monster with the stripes on his sleeve ordered us to run up and down a big, long slope. I spotted a telephone box halfway up and nipped in and rejoined the line when they came down.

I didn't fool Eagle-Eye, of course, even though I was too far away to be identified. He lined us up and asked who the clever sod was, but I kept my head down and said nothing. He must have seen

The Bridge on the River Kwai too many times, because he screamed at us and said he would make us go up and down that hill until he got a confession. Off we went, with those who knew it was me telling me to cough up and end the torture.

I didn't know who I was more frightened of, Eagle-Eye or my mates, but I kept quiet, even though some of the innocents started to drop with the heat. Finally Eagle-Eye declared, and back to the barracks we staggered. Not surprisingly, the others wanted to throttle me but I apologised and thought that was the end of it.

So it was, until our next kit inspection. These were a nightmare, because if there was a crease in the blankets on the bed, never mind anything wrong with your kit or the rifle, you were 'for it'. The rifle had to sparkle, and each one would be opened for inspection so that the officer could look down the barrel. I'd given mine plenty of polish, so I wasn't too bothered ... until he threw it back to me and asked me to have a look. The bastards had wedged the barrel with cotton wool! The result was more extra drill, which I couldn't complain about. All because of a telephone box from which I got the wrong sort of reverse charge.

In my time at George, we all met this guy who worked with the Firestone tyre company, and he knew his way around everywhere. After a few weeks, we came to an arrangement whereby, if we were able to keep up a good demand in tyres, he would ensure that we were rewarded. We discovered that if you turned too sharply in an earthscraper, especially when carrying a heavy load, the tyre would burst. In this way we discovered how to redistribute a small part of the army's wealth in our direction. We even managed five tyres in one month, and were put up for a few days in a hotel by way of thanks!

I managed plenty of cricket during this time, playing regularly for George as well as the odd representative match for the Southern Cape XI. Our captain at George was Cliffy Thomas, a South African Breweries rep. I remember being 'legless' in one game against Mossel Bay, when I tripped over the picket fence when going in to bat! I got a couple of hundreds and the Western Provinces considered me for training and practice at the end of 1974, when they were on their way towards winning the Currie Cup for the first time.

It didn't happen, so I concentrated on playing as much sport as I could. I put my name down for everything that would get me out of work and duty, and I even played hockey. The instructors were always after me, but I was good enough at all the sports to keep out of their way. That didn't stop them leaning on me at 4 am reveille and they insisted we all shaved, even if there was no hair to come off.

I also played a lot of rugby and got as far as the squad for South West Districts who played France in 1975. I didn't make the final side, but was quite happy to sit on the bench while they beat us 65–15. I was picked the game after for Western Province Association but I didn't fancy it, so I settled for guard duty instead. What a good judge I was. France 'sneaked' home 110–0! I was quite nippy in the backs, although one of my clearest memories about rugby concerns a girlfriend. Before I was called up, I was picked for Villages Under-20s against Stellenbosch Under-20s. It was a big game. I was going out then with Jennifer Millard, daughter of Terence, and I went to pick her up before the game at Milnerton. I was driving the Morris 1000 and mistimed the journey because I had to drive upwind into a strong south-easter, and we didn't arrive until 1.50 pm as the players were running out. Or rather, 29 out of 30 did, with me being rushed into my kit with the help of several pairs of hands. By the time I ran on to the pitch, our team had kicked off and I was still doing up my shorts as I took my place in the backs for the resulting scrummage. No sooner had I joined the fray than out came the ball from the back of the scrum via the no. 9 ... and I proceeded to drop a goal!

I said to our captain as I ran back to the halfway line, 'Sorry I was late, Skip. Will three points help?'

Until I left the army before the start of the 1975/76 season, my first-class cricket career was on hold. Now I was ready to see how far I could go in the game which had been my passion in life. Those first two games with Western Province had given me the taste, and I wanted more, and quickly.

I did enough in pre-season nets to get into the side for the first showpiece game of the season. As Currie Cup champions, Western Province would play the Rest of South Africa in Benoni. Barry Richards was not yet back from England, but the selectors picked a strong side, including Procter, Irvine, van der Bijl, Pollock and Trimborn. It was a 50-overs game and I only got in at the death. We scored 189 for four and they won easily by four wickets with eight overs left.

A month later we broke new ground, thanks to Eddie Barlow and a few senior players, who arranged a mixed match between the Western Province Cricket Union and the Western Province Cricket Board, which represented black and coloured provincial cricket. We mixed the sides up, and I remember Omar Henry and Frank Brache, Basil D'Oliveira's brother-in-law, playing for the other side. Looking in the scrapbook, I read these two comments.

'"The players wanted the match and it was arranged among themselves," said an official who wished to remain anonymous.'

'As one player remarked, "This is only the first step. Leave it to us and there will be no problem about multi-racial cricket".'

The next step was a 'B' team match in which I was one of six who had played in the 'A' side. Garth Le Roux was now in the side, and a photograph of us leaving Cape Town shows me standing next to him and I'm a good head shorter. To think that five years earlier he was a tiny bloke, bowled off-spinners and we even called him 'Jim' after Jim Laker. Nowadays, he'd probably get tested for steroids, because he looked like man mountain to me, and I didn't waste my breath talking about my bowling to him. He was now definitely quick.

The season featured several one-day games, and I did enough to get into the first defence of the Currie Cup, a three-day game against Eastern Province. I got a duck so wasn't sure of playing in the next match against Rhodesia. Not only did I stay, but I was promoted to open the innings with Eddie Barlow. And Mike Procter could see how happy was the hooker.

I made 37 and we won by an innings, but failed twice in the next match at Kingsmead where we lost to Natal by ten wickets. But I didn't need any stitches. I was learning. Another couple of indifferent matches against Transvaal and Eastern Province meant I was on the edge again, but the selectors stuck with me, and kept me for the game in Rhodesia.

We squeezed a draw in Salisbury, and I managed 31 in the second innings, after providing Kent's John Shepherd with his first wicket for Rhodesia in the first innings. That wasn't the only bit of joy I provided for a bowler either.

I've said how we used to lean on Big Garth as a kid when he wasn't so big, and a few years earlier I enlisted the help of a few classmates to grab him, strip him down to the way he started in life and then handcuff him to the railings of a girls' school in Wynberg. He must have told the story to the Western Province players in Salisbury, which only goes to prove that fast bowlers never forget. Nor will I forget the remarks I got from passers-by when I was also handcuffed naked to the railings outside the ground.

I would have liked to be able to draw a veil over my embarrassment, and will do so over the rest of my season in the 'A' side. I soon dropped down the order, and only got one decent score in the last match against Natal when I top-scored with 83. Bob Woolmer, who is now the coach of the South African side, played in that game which we won thanks to two great performances. Leg-spinner Denys Hobson returned his career-best figures of seven for 52 and seven more for 61 in the second, but captain Eddie Barlow's three wickets were just as important. Two of them were Barry Richards, bowled for 43 and caught behind for eight.

I was now twenty-two and starting to get itchy feet. I was playing with and against cricketers who had played in England, and I wanted to have a crack at full-time cricket. Playing every week meant that the healthy rivalry I'd always had with Peter Kirsten was taking on an extra dimension. Remember, he had played at Nuffield Week before me, but in Rhodesia he was twelfth man. Then when I joined the army, he made his first-class debut, and was now scoring masses of runs. He did his National Service after university.

He came to England in 1975 and 1976 and played a few games for Sussex. The 1976/77 Currie Cup summer brought him a new record of five centuries, four in succession, and a record aggregate of 967 runs. He also became the first batsman to score ten hundreds for Western Province and that great season earned him a scholarship with Big Garth to broaden their experience in the English summer of 1977.

I only got one hundred, against Rhodesia, but I had what was easily my best season. I finished with over 600 runs at an average of 51 and two of my best innings, 52 and 69 not out against Natal, all but brought us the Currie Cup. I had settled at no. 5 or no. 6, and knew that I had made considerable progress. The publicity I got also unsettled me, great though it was to read such nice things said about me by our manager, Tony Whitfield, and team-mates Eddie Barlow and Hylton Ackerman.

Tony Whitfield said this in an interview: 'The player to excite Transvaal officials at the Wanderers was Allan Lamb. His 66 and 52 was considered the best batting of the match and impressed former Springboks Alan Melville and Eric Rowan. They were full of praise for Lamb and thought he was one of the best prospects in South Africa'. He then added: 'Lamb has matured out of all recognition'.

Eddie Barlow's weekly article picked out Kirsy, me and Big Garth as the three stars for the future. He made the point that I was overshadowed by 'Kirsy's marvellous season'. He called me 'this non-stop bundle of activity on or off the field (find a pair of handcuffs and some railings and I'm anybody's) and I wonder how long it will be before he tires of being second fiddle and joins the race for honours'.

Ackerman said: 'What I like about Lambkin is that he's super-confident in himself. He bubbles with self-confidence and he sparkles with talent. He's also a cheeky, often naughty little schoolboy, and so popular.'

Cheeky … naughty… It's funny how mates can get completely the wrong idea about someone!

Mike Procter went further, and his were the remarks that really made me think about my future and where it lay. 'Allan Lamb, I would say, has the most ability of Western Province's impressive young batsmen. Peter Kirsten has the best big match temperament, and Kepler Wessels, full of promise though he is, is still only nineteen.'

Kepler was now at Stellenbosch University and in his first season with Western Province he topped 500 runs at an average of 36. We used to take the mickey out of him because he didn't drink or smoke; in fact, he didn't seem interested in the sort of good time that we used to love. Although we made fun of him, it had to be in a fairly gentle way because he was keen on boxing and handy with the gloves. He came from an Afrikaans background and was educated at Grey College in Bloemfontein. He was, and still is, an intense man, not especially gifted as a cricketer, but what a grafter and a brave one!

At the end of the season I was interviewed by A C Parker, the sort of kindly journalist you don't see too often in England. He asked me why I thought I had made such a breakthrough. I replied: 'Suddenly, the loose ends have come together. The big thing is confidence, and a big partnership with Hylton Ackerman and my first provincial hundred in Bulawayo made a big difference in my outlook.'

By this time, I was desperate to go overseas, but I could not afford it. All my family knew what I wanted to do, and my uncle Peter came up with the cash for my air ticket. He is dead now, but then he lived in Johannesburg and I didn't know him that well; but what a gesture to help a kid who wanted to have a go.

Eddie Barlow had given Kirsy and Garth a list of contacts in England, so I decided to join them. That trip was to change my entire life.

4
Into the Unknown

Peter Kirsten, Garth Le Roux and I flew into London on the same plane in April 1977, and were met by Eddie Barlow at Heathrow. It was my first time in England and I wanted to see everything. We drove up the M1 to Derby, and to someone used to hours of driving over hundreds of miles, the 150 miles or so seemed a little hop.

Eddie, as captain of Derbyshire, had arranged everything for us. We were put in a terraced house near Chesterfield, and got as much cricket as possible. Derbyshire fixed us up in the local leagues, with Garth playing for Lascelles Hall, Kirsy turning out for Worksop in the Bassetlaw League in Nottinghamshire, and myself allocated to Holmfirth in the Huddersfield League.

Our pitches weren't great, but it was all part of an education which was priceless. They were generally softer and with more grass than in the Cape. That meant you couldn't always trust the bounce and so could not hit through the line as you could on the pitches I was brought up on. Overseas cricketers need time to adapt to the pitches in England, and that is why so many don't do well on their first tour, or in their first season in county cricket. In South Africa, the pitches are mostly harder and bouncier, and they don't have the same variety of surfaces as in England. I was twenty-three, and had played top cricket through all the age grades for nearly ten years, and mostly on good batting tracks and in hot weather.

The one difference I did like was that anyone who made a fifty or a century would get a collection and I kept nipping in for a few quid. They averaged around £15 a time and as I was nearly broke for most of the time, it gave me an added incentive not to throw my wicket away. Garth struggled on the slow pitches, and I had the better of things when we played against each other. It was his debut at home for Lascelles and I whacked 95, including 90 in boundaries. I hit seven sixes and 12 fours, but only succeeded in slowing down our run rate.

One end of the ground was at the top of a steep hill which ran down a long way into the village, and when I hit five sixes and a four in one over off their off-spinner, all of the sixes finished up rolling down into the village. They had to send a guy on a bike with a little basket on the front to go and bring the balls back.

I caused a bigger problem at home in Holmfirth, because there was a river at one end. After I'd dumped a few balls in there in my first couple of innings, they placed a guy at that end, armed with a long pole with a fishing net on the end.

The three of us played some 2nd XI cricket for Derbyshire and Northamptonshire, and we also played for Derrick Robins in a few of his games at Eastbourne. Peter Parfitt was the manager, and when I scored 121 against Cambridge University he said to me, 'Lamby, you batted as though you've got a million pounds in the bank.' In the same match, a young Aussie called Allan Border, a year my junior, hit 159 not out.

There's no doubt about the service England has done other youngsters, with the West Indians in particular benefiting. Just think of a few who've come into county cricket with raw talent that has been polished nicely after a couple of years: Viv Richards, Joel Garner, Malcolm Marshall, Courtney Walsh, Wayne Daniel, Sylvester Clarke, Alvin Kallicharran, Clive Lloyd, and many others.

Overseas cricketers could then play in any 2nd XI games for any county, because the present restrictions were not in force then. For instance, people tend to forget that Barry Richards played for Gloucestershire 2nd XI as did Allan Border. Also, you could play for more than one county 2nd XI in the same season, which is why I played for Derbyshire and then Northants. I played half a dozen 2nd XI games for Derbyshire and got a few runs without a big score. My highest score of the summer was for Holmfirth against Elland, when I hit 149 out of 228 – with not too many ones and twos. The small ground was just right and I hit 122 in boundaries including 11 sixes. That was in early August and the next week I got 134, opening the innings both times. The game was at home and I hit my first ball for six, plus seven more to keep the local angling club's representative busy.

I also had the odd game for Northamptonshire 2nd XI, but my main hope of a contract was with Derbyshire. The secretary of Northants, Ken Turner, told me bluntly that he thought I was more of a one-day belter and the club were more interested in Kirsy. Percy Davis, their coach who spent all his winters coaching in South Africa, tried to talk Kirsy into signing for Northants, but in the end he received a better offer from Derbyshire.

They also made me an offer, but I wasn't interested, because it meant me spending four years qualifying, unless they were prepared to take me on as one of their overseas players. The difference between Kirsy and me was that he was an overseas player, born in South Africa, and with no family connections that could help him through the English registration rules.

Because Mom and Dad were born in England, my case was different. It meant I could become English after four years residential qualification, and play both county cricket and for England as a home player. I hadn't thought that far ahead, but all I knew was that I wasn't going to hang around in 2nd XI cricket until I was twenty-seven to qualify that way.

If I could play those four years in county cricket as an overseas player, fine. But Derbyshire already had the New Zealander John Wright on their books, and their preference of Peter Kirsten over me as the other overseas player (the counties at that time were allowed *two* overseas players), meant that with them I would have to do it the hard way.

It was disappointing in a way, but I'd had a great first summer in England and enjoyed every minute of it. At the end of the season, though, it was back to Cape Town and my job with a timber company. I had worked there after my National Service, and enjoyed the work as a rep. They employed a few sportsmen, but you still had to deliver or the job didn't last. I tried to do it properly, and spent my early days with the company learning all I could about the business.

I wasn't a bad salesman, although to start with I was given a lot of dodgy accounts. We had a guy back at base called Leon Price – a real wheeler-dealer who would promise a customer delivery yesterday, even if he hadn't got the wood. On one occasion I thought I had done a good deal with one buyer, but on condition he got the wood next day.

I told Leon, who gave me that famous phrase 'No problem', which is supposed to be reassuring but usually means the opposite. Leon's other great phrase was the one I used to the customer when he asked where his wood was: 'It's on the truck'. If Leon was an undertaker and he turned up for a funeral without the coffin, he'd say 'It's on the truck'.

This time I had to follow through with the complaint, otherwise I would lose the sale, so I went back to the yard. Again Leon told me, 'It's on the truck'. It was, but the truck was not leaving the yard, nor looked like doing so, until I found a driver and saved the day.

The boss was 'Butch' Watson-Smith and he was a good friend to all of us who played a lot of sport. I went straight to him when, to my great surprise, I got an offer from Northamptonshire in December 1977. Not only an offer, but delivered personally by committee man Roy Barker, who was on the board of the well-known shoe company.

The offer was a good one on two counts. Firstly, I would be taken on as an overseas cricketer, because Northants were going to end their agreements with Bishen Bedi and Mushtaq Mohammad who had gone to Packer's World Series. That would mean I'd play regular first-class county cricket. The money was not quite a non-consideration, but I was well satisfied anyway because it amounted to around £3000, plus an air fare and help with accommodation.

And who would the other overseas player be, if I accepted the offer? A Pakistani guy called Sarfraz Nawaz, that's who. I asked for time to think it over and went straight to Butch. He took one look at the contract and said I'd be mad to refuse the offer and then added that I could come back and work for him during the English close season.

Mom and Dad have never tried to talk me into or out of anything – maybe my clothes if they'd known about my Newlands swimming-pool streak – but they knew that my mind was almost made up. Sister Brenda insisted that I had to go for it, especially because it could give me the chance of Test cricket if I clicked. I hadn't thought too much about that, but Lindsay made the same point. The offer included the chance to do my four years residential qualification while playing, and then I could play for Northants as a home qualified player.

I needed to reside in England for a minimum of thirty weeks each year, but that was no problem, so it didn't take me long to sign my first English contract.

We had a different sort of celebration, thanks to Leon Price. A few of us went to the Hard Rock Cafe in Rondebosch, where we would always end with a round of Irish coffees which cost one rand a throw (worth then about 60p). Leon spoofed someone at the bar for the cost of the round – the game with each player hiding or showing matches as everyone guesses at the aggregate not shown – and won … and won, and won.

Leon was utterly fearless and kept going until, suddenly, he'd won 100 rand. Not quite a fortune, but enough to spring us a few drinks. It would have, except what did Leon do as his party trick? He ordered 100 Irish coffees and got them lined up to make a sight I've never seen before or since. There were six of us, but he invited the other customers to dip in, and not one of the coffees went cold. Certainly not my eight anyway.

The 1977/78 South African season was much different to 1976/77 in many ways. Eddie had gone to World Series and Hylton Ackerman was captain of Western Province, as well as captain of Alma-Marist where he and I had moved from Claremont the previous season for extra sponsorship and cash.

The Currie Cup season got off to an odd start with a match against Rhodesia in Salisbury. We drew the game and I didn't get many runs, but I remember the trip for two reasons. Big Garth and Kirsy only agreed to play if they could write their second-year physical education exams during the game, so the Deputy Registrar of Stellenbosch University flew up with us to supervise a 6 am written exam.

Garth was so keen to get his degree that he had already refused a contract from Sussex for 1978, which is why he wasn't too pleased when he and I were stuck for half an hour in a lift at the hotel the night before. I knew he was big, but by the time we were rescued, he filled the whole lift!

I couldn't get a run in December – that was the month I accepted the two-year contract with Northants – but the New Year changed things. I got a hundred against Natal, and it impressed two people. Dudley Nourse, then seventy, told Ackermann that he had seen most of the best knocks at Kingsmead in the previous fifty years and 'you arrive here with this little whippet of a lad who hits it as good as all of them, including Barry Richards'.

I was having a beer with the captain that night – the Elangeni manager had forgiven me – when a guy walked up and congratulated me on the hundred. I thanked him and told him I'd thrown it away. When he left I asked 'Ackers' who it was as he seemed familiar. 'That was the great Roy Drourgh, the Springbok rugby player,' Ackers replied. 'We used to watch him when we were kids, and now he's come to watch you'.

We were in the running for the Currie Cup and Garth clinched it for us with a series of great performances. He was genuinely quick and no opposing batsmen played him in comfort including Graeme Pollock and Kenny McEwan. He finished with 53 wickets in eight matches, and my 428 runs were higher than any other Western Province player except for Kirsy's 477. Our experience in England was paying dividends.

We finished the season with a Champions v Rest of South Africa game of 40 eight-ball overs at Newlands. I was 54 not out in our 222 for seven, but they won by six wickets with three overs to spare. Not a bad batting order, with Rice, Pollock, Davison, Wilkins and Fotheringham.

We were given a mayoral reception to finish things off, and I received a lot of good wishes for my first season in county cricket. From the Southern African cricketers who were playing in England in 1978, Ackers picked this side: Barry Richards, Eddie Barlow, Peter Kirsten, Kenny McEwan, Allan Lamb, Clive Rice, Brian Davison, Mike Procter, Peter Swart, Norman Featherstone and Garth Le Roux, who would be playing on an occasional basis. No places for Tony Greig, Rodney Ontong, or Basil D'Oliveira.

Mention of Rodney Ontong reminds me that he was the partner of my Pretoria club captain, Trevor Quirk, when he got into *Wisden* for the wrong reason. I never let him forget it. Only seventeen men (one twice) have been given out in the history of first-class cricket for 'obstructing the field', and Quirky can claim he is the only South African.

Quirky's defence is one which only a left-handed, wicket-keeping joker could think up. He says that he was the non-striker, when the young Ontong hit a ball straight to mid-on and ran without calling. Quirky was ball-watching and next thing he knew was Ontong telling him to swap ends. He reckons his first mistake was to accept the call. His second was when he was running straight down the pitch and the ball was about to pass him on the way to the wicket-keeper to run him out. The ball then struck his upraised hand, and there are two versions of the facts.

As told by the Border fielders, 'He panicked and swatted the ball away to stop himself being run out'. Quirky, as you might imagine, tells it differently. 'It was a self-protective gesture as I had the feeling that the ball was going to hit me on the back of he head.' Think about it. As he'd turned his head to see where the ball was, could it have hit him on the back of the head?

A straightforward case of obstruction then, but they nearly had to carry him off. First he challenged one umpire, saying that he wasn't looking, then the other one because he said that he couldn't give him out. I knew he'd get his comeuppance for landing me with that extra guard duty two years earlier!

I'd been playing cricket non-stop now for eighteen months; even so, I couldn't wait to get to England and start a full-time career.

5
County Cricket

What a first year I had as a full-time county professional. I topped the Northamptonshire batting and bowling averages, thanks to my first hundred and first wicket in the county championship. The 1978 county averages in *Wisden* show me among the 'also bowled', but I don't mind that my one and only wicket was not enough to get me into the averages proper.

Everybody remembers his first wicket in first-class cricket, and as I only ever got seven more, believe me, it's pretty memorable! Yet how could anything be sweeter than for me to get Peter Kirsten out? Laugh? I never stopped and he never started. It came at the end of a dead game against Derbyshire on their ground. I had a decent match with 42 and 63 not out, and Kirsy made 87 in their first innings.

We left Derbyshire to get 240 in about 50 overs, but they didn't go for them, so in the final few minutes we all had a bowl. The last over was down to me, and Kirsy had already mentally written the red ink star, signifying not out, into the score book.

I'm convinced that I frightened him out. By that, I mean when a batsman is faced with a joke bowler, he is so afraid of getting out in a foolish way, that he does something quite out of character. What didn't help was the remark from Eddie Barlow, who was batting at the other end. As soon as he saw me coming on, he went down to Kirsy and said, 'For f***'s sake, don't dare get out, otherwise we'll both have aggro back home next summer.'

I had a full go at Kirsy before I bowled at him, telling him to remember what a deadly swing bowler I was when we were both at school, and that I knew his batting inside out. I gave him one of my

Fred Trueman impressions: 'I'll give you one of these, one of those and then goodnight'. I made a big thing of setting my field, but it was all great banter, because I knew I only had one over before the game ended.

As I ran in, I heard Eddie mutter 'don't you dare', but all I wanted was some ammunition for when the three of us got back to Newlands. A little outswinger, and what a beauty! Kirsten caught Yardley at slip, bowled Lamb. He didn't want to go, and there was no point in appealing because the catch was waist high. I politely pointed out that we were playing cricket, not a game of statues where he'd be fined if he moved, and off he went finally. I don't know who was the more disgusted, Kirsy or Eddie, but I know who had the last laugh.

When I first went to Northampton, Alan Hodgson took me under his wing. I got on well with him, which is why he was one of the first to offer to bat for me in the court case against Sarfraz fifteen years later. A straight bloke, and good fun to be with. As was Richard Williams, who I shared my first digs with. 'Chippy' was a good cricketer, always a great team man. Jim Yardley, who previously played for Worcestershire, was another guy I got to know well. David Steele was an interesting character. His nickname was 'Crime'. Why? Think about it, deep pockets, short arms. It took me one night at the bar to work it out. Right. Crime doesn't pay. He always seemed to be trying to scrounge a cigarette. Which is why Chippy and a few of us set him up by priming a few fags with firecrackers and leaving the packet on show in Chippy's bag. In came David after batting. 'I've got to have a drag,' he said, so he picked one out of Chippy's packet. The cigarette exploded and half of it disintegrated, but he still kept puffing away as though nothing had happened and said calmly, 'My bloody lighter nearly blew up.'

My first net practice of the season at Northampton in mid-April had given me my first ever sight of snow. I was batting when we got a blizzard and I remember feeling the flakes blow against my face like grass cuttings. Within seconds I was on my own in the nets. Everyone else ran for cover, but I wasn't going to miss a sight like that, so I got the most enjoyable soaking of my life ... and with pads on.

The club put me up in the Weststone Hotel until I moved into the flat with Richard Williams and Ian Richards. Lindsay also came to

England, but she was touring and doing odd jobs, so I only saw her occasionally, mostly when we were in London. She had intended to come in 1977 but her dad, Sam, had died of a heart attack at fifty-one, so she stayed at home.

I was picked to bat at no. 4 in the first game against Gloucestershire at Bristol, but it rained for three days and we were only a two-man team anyway. Alan Hodgson and I travelled early the day before the game and booked into our hotel. We went out for the evening and when we got back, we were told that the first day had already been called off and none of the other players had bothered to come down.

'Hodgy' said we should book out, but I said no so we stayed overnight. The second day was cancelled and the rest of the team stayed in Northampton. 'Hodgy' said that Ken Turner would kill us if we stayed another night, so we booked out and slept on the floor at the house of Andy Brassington, the Gloucestershire wicket-keeper.

Not only was my debut delayed for a week, but I got a duck as well. It was against Pakistan and I was caught by Sarfraz off Sikander Bakht. Too bad for Sarfraz that he didn't catch me fifteen years later in the High Court!

Northants played twenty championship matches that year, but only three in May, so the season got off to a stuttering start. My first runs were 82 not out against Clive Rice and Nottinghamshire, but my first trip to Lord's ended prematurely. Like any overseas player, Lord's was Mecca to me and I wanted to make a big score, but all I got was a broken finger and three weeks out of the game.

Wayne Daniel bowled one to me from the Nursery end that went through the top and hit me flush on the right index finger. It hurt, but I didn't take the glove off until Mike Smith said we should have a look at it. What a mess, even the bone was showing through. That was my lot until nearly the end of June, but it says a lot for the confidence the club had in me that I was then picked straightaway after recovering from the injury, and I hardly ever failed for the rest of the season. I got my first hundred at home against Essex, and then another at Cardiff against Glamorgan, with another Western Province player, Peter Swart, in the opposition. My 883 runs at an average of 49 was a good start on pitches which varied much more than in South Africa, and against high-quality bowling, even if most of it was from overseas players.

Ken Turner now explained to me the terms on which I could play for Western Province. As I had started my four years qualifying to play as an Englishman, I must not play for any South African national side, and I must buy a house in England in 1979 to establish residence. That, together with 210 days in the country, would do the trick.

I was happy to do anything to qualify, for by now there was more involved than just a wish to play regular county cricket. My first year told me that I was good enough to play with and against the best, and I decided then that I would concentrate more on my life in England. South Africa had been my home for over twenty years, and there is no better place than the Cape in which to be brought up and to live. But I've always been one to commit myself once my mind is made up, and I now knew that if I wanted a career in England, then I'd use my four years qualifying to make a bid for Test cricket in 1982.

The registration rules then were a bigger puzzle than nowadays. For instance, Mike Procter was accepted as an English qualified cricketer after ten years, simply so that Gloucestershire could then sign another overseas player. Technically, therefore, Procky could play for England, but he told the authorities he never would. On the other hand, Tony Greig started playing for Sussex in the 1960s, and at one stage had played Test cricket for England while he was listed as one of Sussex's ration of overseas cricketers. Greig's parents, like mine, were British, so he also had to wait for only four years. Graeme Hick did seven, and even that was reduced from ten years, which shows what a maze the rules have been.

When I returned to Cape Town at the end of September, Lindsay stayed in London and I didn't see her until I went back to England the following April. My season 1978/79 in South Africa got off to a rotten start, thanks to Garth Le Roux. There's always plenty of rivalry among players from the same area, such as the Cape where Peter Kirsten, Peter Swart, Big Garth, Hylton Ackerman and Eddie Barlow all played. I had the best of it in England and, although I hadn't come up against Garth in county cricket, we were always after each other once he'd turned into a genuinely fast bowler.

All the top players took part in the South African Broadcasting Corporation double-wicket championship in Johannesburg in the middle of October, and then straight after the final we Cape players were flying to play in another double-wicket thrash in Cape Town.

Except that Garth put me out of both by breaking my nose and giving me a closed, black eye when I missed a hook off him.

As soon as I got back to Cape Town, I had my nose straightened and a plaster cast put on it. The photographs make me look like something out of a horror film, but I played against Orange Free State the same week, plaster cast and all. By this time, following the Packer revolution, professional cricket was starting in South Africa. I moved clubs to Greenpoint as player-coach, and it was the same with the other players who had played in England. Greenpoint was the first club to go multi-racial, and when I joined them, we set about enrolling coloured and black members. Cape Town has always been a bit more liberal in thinking than many other areas in South Africa, perhaps because of an influence which was more English than Dutch-Afrikaans.

The South African Cricket Union has always led the way in pushing back the barriers, and I wish critics of the country had taken more notice then. At that time, a dozen years before the removal of apartheid from the statute book, we could only chip away at it, which we did, and there were changes in the Liquor Act so that all races could eat and drink in sports clubs. Also, local leagues were organised on a multi-racial basis as were primary leagues for school children. Oddly enough the South African Board, which represented the non-white community, refused to co-operate and even objected to black players such as Omar Henry who wanted to make his way in cricket.

I first saw Omar Henry at Greenpoint in 1975. He lived in a township called Scotish Kloof, near Stellenbosch. Omar was always a great mimic of accents, especially the Afrikaans dialect and slang. It was no surprise to me when the SABC used him during and after the 1992 World Cup in Australia to do Afrikaans summarising. He was a very funny man who loved a joke, and could take it as well as give it. I remember on a tour to Windhoek in South West Africa when, in a drunken state, I sprayed Omar with a fire extinguisher. We told him it was the whitest he'd ever been and he laughed! Omar Henry was a good cricketer who deserved to play full Test cricket, and I was thrilled for him when he won his three caps against India in 1992 at the age of forty.

The hard-line overseas lobby now claims that their boycotts against apartheid worked, but what I want to make clear is that everyone played their part, including the game of cricket from the mid-1970s onwards.

I didn't have a great season in 1978/79, averaging 33 for Western Province who finished second to Transvaal in the Currie Cup, a result the locals considered a failure. I got a century against Rhodesia, but that was about it. That 107 was in fact my first first-class hundred at Newlands, and that was six years after my debut, which says something about a rash streak in my batting which I have since kept under better control.

Tom Reddick noticed my anxiety to get after the bowling before I'd played myself in and wrote: 'We all make mistakes, but Lamb has done it too often this season. Surely someone has told him that even Bradman, the greatest, played "pawky" for at least twenty minutes at the start of an innings. There was never a question of committing himself to cross-bat or full-blooded drives. Good cricket is disciplined cricket. Without it all the talent in the world is unproductive'. Fair comment, especially as I only scored 100 runs in my next six innings after the century against Rhodesia.

I went back to England in 1979 looking forward to my second season and also anxious to link up again with Lindsay. We had first met in 1974 but had never gone out together on a regular basis, but now, at twenty-five, I felt ready to settle down. Before that, though, I had to make sure that my first season in county cricket was not a one-off, as it could have been for two reasons. Firstly, I had revelled in such a lot of regular cricket for the first time in my life, but I'd heard county professionals say what a grind it could be. Secondly, a lot of cricketers have a good first season before anyone has had a look at them. Second time around, it is much harder and I didn't want to be a one-season wonder.

I had set myself quite an act to follow and knew that anything under 50 as an average would be considered inadequate. As in 1978, I started the new season with a duck against Yorkshire, caught behind by David Bairstow at Middlesbrough. As in the previous year, snow stopped play and the game was drawn.

We were hammered next match at Taunton, although I did hit 'Beefy' Botham for a couple of sixes before Vic Marks had me lbw playing no stroke. I topped 50 against Warwickshire and then won my first Benson & Hedges Gold Award against Sussex with 70 from 79 balls.

I remember our three-day game at Worcester for a temporary loss of memory by Norman Gifford that gave us all a laugh. We had lost the first day to rain, so Gifford tried to open things up by declaring on the third day as soon as Worcestershire reduced the deficit to 148. Safe from the follow-on you see … except that he'd forgotten it was now a two-day game with the follow-on only 100 runs. Our captain, Jim Watts, put them back in. Glenn Turner, their New Zealand opener and later captain, made sure of the draw, and even our secret weapon didn't succeed as my two overs were wicketless.

I needed a hundred, but the nearest I got to that in the first six weeks was 92 against Yorkshire and 94 against Nottinghamshire. Of all things, I was stumped by Bairstow for the 92, and bowled by Eddie Hemmings having a heave. It was my birthday as well, and I was furious. How much longer would I wait?

Only a couple of days as it happened, because I finally got there with 118 not out in the second innings against Notts and I enjoyed a few beers that night. I was pleased to see myself sixth in the national averages, and improved things even more with 89 against Gloucestershire which helped to save the match. Everything clicked in what was to be one of the best batting runs I've ever had.

We played India next and I got another hundred – exactly – at a run-a-minute to give me 493 runs in five innings, with two not-outs. With Kenny McEwan hitting a double-hundred for Essex followed by the season's fastest hundred, and Mike Procter bowling Hampshire out twice, the *Cape Times* headlines were all ours, even in the middle of their rugby season.

I was now leading the race to be first to 1000 runs for the season and would have done it at home against Lancashire but for David Lloyd. Kepler Wessels, who was playing for Sussex, and Kenny McEwan were bang in the running until they got out before I had my second innings on the third day against Lancashire. I needed 44 and was 20 when 'Bumble' got me, caught by Frank Hayes. Richard Lumb of Yorkshire beat me to it, and as we had no match for a week, Kepler nipped in front of me as well.

Northants had a poor season because Sarfraz Nawaz was injured for a few weeks and we couldn't bowl anybody out. But our strong batting gave us a good run in the Gillette Cup, and we made the Final at Lord's. My season brought me a couple of offers to play grade cricket in Australia, but an offer from Western Province was good enough to get me back to Newlands.

I scored a career best 140 against Derbyshire and finished my second season with over 1700 runs at an average of 67, so I was on top of the world for the last month of the summer – except for that Gillette final against Somerset. It was my third game at Lord's, including the broken finger, but we were playing catch-up cricket all the time from when Viv Richards hit a brilliant 117. That, plus two early wickets for Joel Garner, settled things, although I managed 78 before I was stumped off Viv.

My sister Barbara was over in England and I arranged for her and Brenda to get special VIP tickets with all the trimmings, except that I left them the wrong tickets and they ended up on the grass. Sorry girls! But I found out later they had brought an inflatable mascot into the ground with 'Lamb' written on the front, and maybe it wouldn't have been a great idea to wave it about in the VIP seats!

A bit of consolation for the Gillette defeat were a couple of personal awards I picked up from the *Sun* newspaper. I won £1000 for the Sun-Wilkinson Sword batting award, plus an engraved sword worth £200. The other award was the Big Hit Cup because I hit 315 boundaries in all cricket, 24 more than Younis Ahmed and 25 more than Dennis Amiss.

My top score was 178 against Leicestershire, and five hundreds and the same number of nineties in 34 innings made it a terrific season for me – and Northants offered me a new three-year contract. Of all the innings I played that year, though, I rate my best the 70 I got against Derek Underwood on a rain-affected pitch, for that convinced me that I was now a much more mature player.

Having had such a poor last season in South Africa, I was bursting to do well now for Western Province. But this summer, irrespective of cricket, was to be my best, because Lindsay and I were married.

6
The Wedding

I didn't meet Lindsay's father, Sam Bennett, until 1976. In the space of a year he had died at the early age of fifty-one, so I didn't know him for long. But what an unforgettable introduction and initiation he gave me!

He was a big Eastern Cape farmer, over 6 ft 4 in tall, and a hard man who was a mad-keen all round sportsman. I was spending some time at the Bennett farm one day and Sam and I drove out to the edge of this big lake. In the distance, right in the middle of the lake, we noticed two ducks wading happily through the water.

Sam had a 22-calibre rifle with him and I wondered what was coming next. I was soon to find out. 'Let's see just how good you are,' he chuckled and promptly gave me the gun. So here was I trying to impress a future father-in-law, and much of my fate now depended upon a straight aim.

I stood for what seemed like an eternity taking aim at these ducks, I must have resembled a golfer with the yips, but finally I forced myself to squeeze. Bloody ducks, I couldn't believe how obsessed the Bennett family were with them; first Lindsay with those six in my bathroom, and now Sam deciding that I'd better bag one or else.

Lindsay and the six ducks was a funny story. What had happened was that I should have picked Lindsay up one night, but somehow forgot, so she got into a flat I shared with Leon Price and left six ducks in the bathroom, with a note which said, 'See what you can do with these, you bastard'. We kept them for about a week, but Leon reckoned that duck farming was not part of his deal of living with Lamby, so they had to go. About 11 pm one night when we were having a few drinks I had a brainwave. 'Right,' I said. 'I know where those ducks are going'. We managed to box them after a lot of 'ducking and diving' and drove round to Tony's, a dairy farmer friend of mine. It was nearly midnight and the house was in darkness. At least it was until we banged on the door and Tony came down to answer it. I threw the ducks in and said they were his and that we were also coming in for a drink. To cut a long story short, he ended up keeping the ducks – and I finally made my peace with Lindsay.

Just occasionally in life, Lady Luck decides to smile, and on this occasion with Sam Bennett hovering behind me, she certainly did me proud. I aimed at one duck and managed somehow to miss that one but hit the other – and they were at least six feet apart! Relieved, I handed the rifle back to Sam, happy that I had done my stuff. But not according to Sam. 'We've got no dog, so you'd better swim over and bring it back.'

If that ice-cream parlour in Newlands was cold, the lake near the Bennett's farm was freezing, but off came my clothes and away I went. I remember thinking 'Lindsay, darling, I know I love you very much, but am I really expected to swim half a mile for a bunch of feathers on which I'd fluked a hit?'

When I got back to dry land, Sam was quite generous in his praise. 'At least you'd make a decent retriever.' By now I was quite proud of what I had done. My ability with the gun and the crawl had not let me down, and at least I had a trophy to show back at the ranch. Again, if only I'd known what was to come.

When we got out of the car, I casually tossed the duck to a Xhosa farmhand and asked him to pluck it and cook it for supper. 'No, boss. No boss', as he waved his arms in a distressed fashion. I asked him why not and couldn't understand his reply – until it was translated that I had only gone and shot a protected species. So much for Sam and his wretched initiative test!

The final act was the most bizarre or all. In order to hide the evidence, the duck was buried – not quite with full military honours but with plenty of ceremony. As I watched the corpse being lowered into the grave, I wondered if my effort to meet Dad was worthwhile, especially as I was due in Durban the next day for a Currie Cup match.

My short visit ended in spectacular fashion. Sam and Lindsay took me to the East London airport where there was a terrific storm. Anyone who has been to that airport knows that, even when the weather is good and calm, take-offs and landings result in your body being joined by your guts about thirty seconds later. I'm not normally a nervous flyer, but I didn't fancy it one bit – still less when we came down twice before the pilot finally got enough lift-off.

I've always been a fatalist, but I remember thinking as we went up and down, up and down and then finally up, 'if whoever is letting go the lightning has someone in his sights, firstly I hope its not me, and if it isn't, I hope he's got a better aim than I had with that duck.'

During 1979 Lindsay and I saw a good deal of each other in London. She had toured Europe and paid for it through all sorts of jobs. She wanted to back-pack her way around, and she was quite prepared to have a go at anything. We are alike in many ways – we both like a laugh and we speak our minds. There's no hiding things with Lindsay and she is one of the most straightforward people I have ever met.

I proposed to her at my sister Brenda's house in London, and when she accepted, it topped off what had been a great summer for me. We didn't travel back to South Africa together but linked up for a week at her home in early October and set the wedding date for 8 December. We decided that we would hold the reception on her Mom's farm in Post Retief near Fort Beaufort. That is about eleven hours drive between Port Elizabeth and East London, and not too far from King Williamstown. Lindsay went to school there at the King Convent, where she was taught by the Sacred Heart nuns. Her brother, Richard, also went to school in King Williamstown, where the coach was dear old Percy Davis.

Lindsay boarded at the convent and then went to teacher training college in Cape Town where we first started to going out together.

Before our wedding day, I had to concentrate on cricket, and there was plenty of that because I was now full time in Cape Town as well as in Northampton. Western Province had signed Eddie Barlow as their first cricket organiser, and part of his job was to promote cricket and the province's full-time players, Kirsy, Garth and me. We did promotional work at hypermarkets and the like, and either practised or played nearly every day.

Eddie didn't miss a trick and our photographs were in the Cape newspapers more days than not. He even got us involved in an egg-throwing day as publicity for the world championships held at Muldersvlei. The only legitimate throws were those that did not break the egg, but we were so far short of the record – an unbelievable 107 metres – that the day ended with us throwing them at each other.

I didn't get a decent score in the two WP matches before the wedding, but I managed 90 and 116 for Greenpoint before I was allowed a week off to turn Lindsay from a Bennett into a Lamb. I had my bachelor night a few days before I took off for Post Retief, but I was glad to get out of Cape Town in one piece. My mates hired an open top bus for a huge pub crawl, which sounded a good idea at the time, because it cut out the driving.

The trouble with that sort of evening is that it needs organising, otherwise it can disintegrate. We should have treated it like a long innings and played ourselves in. We started in Rondebosch and the loose plan was to work our way into town and then on to Sea Point. By the time we got near Sea Point, the noise on the bus would have stopped a crow at a range of one mile. The police were out in force anyway, because December starts the holiday month in Cape Town, and our progress had been passed on from our last couple of calls. When we were flagged down, we might have talked our way through the road block but for one thing. A yelled volley of slurred abuse is not the ideal password, and we were turned back and told to be better behaved.

That should have been the end of the evening, except for unloading each of my mates at the various dropping off points on the way back to Rondebosch. But what I didn't know was, to quote Max Boyce, 'The Incredible Plan', which my mates thought was the right ways to end my bachelor days in Cape Town, the city of my genteel upbringing and schooling.

Our terminus was outside the old cinema in Rondebosch, about ten minutes before the picturegoers walked out into the balmy, peaceful air of a December evening. The cinema is no longer there ... maybe because of the extra performance that night. I remember there was a horror film on but the customers had the biggest shock of their night out when they came out about 10.30 pm.

What they saw was me, handcuffed to the railings wearing a brown paper bag over my head, and nothing else. My one consolation was that nobody would recognise me – unless that Italian who owned the ice cream parlour in Newlands was a horror film fan. The only thing that prevented me from being locked up was that my mates were so drunk, they decided to stay and watch, so they were there when the cops arrived.

Two of them were going to take me in the cop car, but were foiled by a sudden twist to The Incredible Plan. Half a dozen of my mates surrounded the police while two more managed to unlock my handcuffs. Now the trick was to get me away without me, or anybody else getting nicked. I remember I didn't help by making sure the brown paper bag stayed put, because I had now sobered up a touch and was afraid that there might be some photographers around. I was sure that Western Province would not be ecstatic about one of their top three contracted players having a different sort of game under lights.

The bag meant I couldn't see, which handicapped the getaway, but I was bundled in to a car while the two cops were still trying to quieten down the diversionary platoon. We screeched off with the back door still open, and I was grateful when I heard it slam shut and even more grateful when I felt no pain.

My eyes still water at the thought of what might have happened, but I'm just glad that my last night in Cape Town ended as it did.

I'd been to a few weddings in Cape Town, but my own was my first experience of how they do it on a farm. The guest list was a joke, because what started as an intention to invite about 150 ended with over double that number. Even though we got married seventeen days before Christmas, a lot of people decided to travel and combine the wedding with their Christmas holiday, so distant relatives and friends came from all over. Lindsay and her Mom, Biddy, would get a call saying that so-and-so was over from Australia or Hong Kong or wherever, and could they come?

Even Percy Davis turned up, and so did Geoff Cook from Northamptonshire and his wife Judith. Geoff was playing for Eastern Province that season and it was nice to have a Northants player there. I'm still not quite sure who my best man was, because I had two groomsmen as well. Take your pick out of Peter Kirsten, Richard Morris, who also played a lot for Western Province, and my brother Mike.

The ceremony took place in the local Anglican church of St John in nearby Winterbury, and I was more nervous than ever I was when batting.

I remember thinking as I stepped forward, perhaps three of them is Lindsay's idea to make sure I don't back down. I think it was Kirsy who handed over the ring, but if my memory is unclear, blame the rest of the day … and that night and the next day. With so many people there, we decided the reception would be held in the biggest building available – and that happened to be the sheep-shearing shed.

With only thirty people in the church, all the other guests who couldn't get in were bored waiting and went to the reception. I'm not sure how many times half the guests have been drunk when the bride and groom arrived at the reception from the church, but they had done remarkably well in such a short time.

The music and drinking went on forever, and anyway Lindsay and I had decided that we couldn't go away anywhere for our first night. We couldn't drive, so we plotted for someone to pretend to drive us away, but he only took us to a cottage a few hundred yards away from the reception, and then he got rid of the jeep.

We managed to have a quiet night, and I understood why when we woke up next morning. I looked out of the cottage window and it looked like a scene from a Roman orgy film. There were bodies everywhere around the shed and the main house, most of them so motionless that an undertaker might have thought Christmas had come early.

Biddy Bennett managed to find two bodies who were moving, but wished she hadn't. She ran what was quite a big farm on her own and, wedding reception or not, she got up early that morning to start work. She opened the door of her main office, and there were a couple either celebrating or anticipating their wedding vows. Biddy coughed and cooled things down with: 'Do you mind going somewhere else?… I've got some paper work to see to.' Perhaps they were afraid of being invoiced but it did the trick.

After the wedding, my first game was eight days later against Eastern Province, when I got 75 and Geoff Cook made 23 and nine which Lindsay says proves something, although she never told me what. I followed with two fifties against Northern Transvaal and we won both games easily, so married life got off to a nice start. We lived in Lindsay's flat for a few weeks. It was in Mowbray in a block officially called Liesbeek Gardens, but she called it 'Alcatraz', and I soon bought a little cottage in Rondebosch – but not too near that old cinema.

We started off married life in style in the tiny bedroom in Alcatraz with three in a bed – in fact, nearly four. My sister Brenda was well pregnant, but had flown over for our wedding, and had nowhere to stay in Cape Town for the couple of days before she flew back home. I'm not sure how far women have to be in pregnancy before they can't fly, but I'll bet she was a border-line case. You could see her coming around the corner a full stride before you knew who it was.

She and Lindsay wanted me to sleep on the floor, but I wasn't having any. Not within a few days of getting married, so the three of us, two Lambs and a Bucknall, slept in the one bed. If Tony Bucknall had disapproved, I would have told him I was playing either second row or outside half.

We moved in to the cottage about two months before we left for England in late March, but I had a nasty shock first. Not on the field, because I had a good season, even though I thought I'd never get a hundred for Western Province again. I kept getting fifty and got into the nineties twice, including 99 against Easterns when I holed out at deep point. I topped the Currie Cup national averages for most of the season, thanks to seven fifties in 13 innings, but Graeme Pollock put me in second place with a couple of big hundreds.

7
Diamonds are Not my Best Friend

An event occurred now which affected me for several months and involved a matter which I decided to keep from Lindsay, my family, friends – in fact, from everyone I knew.

Without realising what I was doing, I got caught up in a set-up involving diamonds and the under-cover police! It started before I was married when I bought the engagement ring. The dealer offered me commission on any business I put his way, so when a solicitor mate of mine, Jules Horrak, rang me to say he'd got a deal going with some uncut diamonds, I rang my man. He wanted to see them so I took them to him, but at first he wanted nothing to do with them. He said they were land diamonds, and he only dealt in sea diamonds.

I thought that was the end of it, until he came back and said he'd got a buyer and would I meet him. What I didn't know then was that he was in trouble and saw a way out if he co-operated with the police in a set-up. I should have known better, but I agreed to meet him and I was given the bag of diamonds to keep overnight. For safety, I put them under the mattress – on Lindsay's side without telling her – and met the guy next day.

He wanted to know all about them, and could I get some more and if so, from where? The deal was worth 10,000 rand, and I would get ten per cent so I told him what I knew.

The first I knew about any set-up was when I went to DF Malan airport to fly from Cape Town to Johannesburg to play for the Rest of South Africa against the Currie Cup champions Transvaal. The match was in late March and afterwards we would fly straight to England. Lindsay had gone to Johannesburg before me, so I was with Peter Kirsten and Garth Le Roux at the airport when a guy tried to stop me as we were running to board the plane. I thought he was after an autograph, so I told him we were late and I couldn't oblige, but he pulled me to one side, showed me his badge and said, 'I think we have met before.'

We sure had. He was the undercover man, and only then did I realise I'd been set up. I missed the plane and told the other players when I joined them that I'd had a passport problem. If only… It was back to Cape Town for a statement and fingerprints, but they told me not to worry as their target was not me, but the bigger guys behind the deal. To this day, Lindsay says I was edgy all through the match at Wanderers, and that was controversial enough because several of us threatened to strike unless we got appearance money.

We had heard that the Transvaal players were getting paid, but Dr Ali Bacher settled it by assuring us that the only differential would be between the winning and losing cheques. Rain caused the match to be played on a Sunday, and we won easily, although I got 'spooked' by Hanley for two. We got 275 in 50 overs and won by 39, although Clive Rice held us up with 88 not out.

So it was back to Northampton, with Lindsay excited about setting up home there, and me worried about the diamond affair, which I had been told would be put on hold for a few months until I went back to South Africa. Even though the police told me I had nothing to worry about, I knew differently, because there would be a court case, and the publicity would be bound to affect me.

All I could do was to try to forget it and make sure I had another good season with Northamptonshire. We bought a tiny cottage in Piddington – literally one up and one down – and Lindsay spent most of the summer there, rather than follow me around England. She did a bit of promotional work for big sporting events in London such as Wimbledon, but that was it.

I knew that my form back in South Africa was on the brink of something exceptional, and my third county season was my best, both personally, and from the team's point of view. We only finished twelfth in the county championship, but we got to another Lord's final, and our Benson & Hedges Cup win against Essex made up for the disappointment of losing the Gillette final the previous year. Also I was given the Gold Award by Ken Barrington for my 71 and we won a thriller by six runs.

I topped the national averages and was made one of *Wisden's* 'Five Cricketers of the Year' so, diamonds or no diamonds, you could call it a golden year. I once read about Barry Richards that he would look down the Hampshire fixtures to see where the most challenging matches came in terms of the stronger sides and the best bowlers, and he would then make a special effort in those contests.

I didn't do anything as clinical as that, but I did get a big kick when I scored runs against the best bowlers. It isn't a matter of trying harder, but it's the extra challenge that gets the adrenalin flowing and I've always enjoyed a battle when it is one against one.

I started with 88 against Derek Underwood, but even that didn't compare with my 113 against Mike Procter at Bristol, especially as we won the match by eight wickets, having been set 308 to win in 85 overs. Richard Williams helped me in a third-wicket partnership of 216, and I was off and running. Not only that, but the press started to mention the possibility of me playing for England in 1982. I kept quiet about that, because I knew the opposition there was to playing 'foreigners' in the national side. Although I had thought about it, I wanted the move to come from other people, so I got on with my cricket.

I scored 97 to help win the next game against Derbyshire, again on a declaration, and when I had scored 437 in my first six innings, people even started talking about 1000 runs in May. As I only had another six possible innings that month, it was never a starter, but my good form continued. I hit 93 against Derbyshire and then my first hundred at Lord's – 112 against Middlesex when we were right in the cart at 97 for five. Extra pleasure again there, because Vintcent van der Bijl was in the middle of an extraordinary first season in county cricket, and when I went in to bat, he reminded me of those seven stitches eight years earlier.

I couldn't miss – 149 against Worcestershire and a stack of runs in the John Player Sunday League. With plenty of runs coming from our other batsmen and Sarfraz now in top form, we had a terrific first half of the season – fourth in the championship, third in the John Player with six wins out of eight and a Benson & Hedges final against Essex.

The press was now beating the England drum, with Peter Jackson and Pat Murphy both saying that the TCCB could hardly stop me if I fulfilled the requirements of all the registration rules.

I went into the Lord's final third in the averages behind Kirsy and Graham Gooch. I got in at 61 for two and stayed until the 52nd over on a pitch on which the ball didn't come on. So 209 was a good score. 'Goochie' was the one wicket we wanted, of course, and at 112 for one, he was 60 and with Kenny McEwan starting to motor, we looked like losing. Then Tim Lamb came on, and the scorebook reads: 'c A Lamb b T Lamb'. He middled one like a tracer to me at mid-on and it might not have gone in cleanly, but it stayed and we were on our way. Sarfraz and Peter Willey squeezed them so well that we won by six runs, even though they only had eight wickets down.

When 'Sarf' started the final over, Essex needed 11 runs to win – 10 actually because they would have won on a tie – but Sarf was masterly, bowling full and straight, and we were home and dry.

By the end of July I topped the averages with 1257 at 83 and Kirsy second with 1307 at 81. Clive Rice was fifth, and van der Bijl fourth in the bowling list, so South Africa was flying high. Another hundred against Lancashire started August well, and 152 against Leicestershire gave me a chance of reaching 2000 runs for the season.

The possibility of a place in the England Test side was now being discussed, and I knew Northants were keen because that would open the door for another overseas player if I agreed. When I heard that Procky and Brian Davison were applying to be declared English I decided I would have a go as well. Our application was heard at Lord's on 4 September. Their applications were granted, but mine was deferred while more information was sought about my family background. Procky announced he would not play for England, but I was different because of the four-year rule.

My season tailed off a bit, but I still headed the national averages with 1797 runs at 66.55, and I just pipped Kepler, who came with a late run to finish 1562 at 65. Kirsy completed the hat-trick by finishing third with 1895 at 63, and Vintcent topped the bowling averages with 85 wickets at 14.72 apiece.

I did a weekly column for the Northampton *Chronicle and Echo* throughout the season, and I signed off with this: 'All through this summer, it seems that there has been speculation about my own position as far as Test cricket is concerned, and I must stress again that the whole picture remains open. If it proves impossible for me ever to play Test cricket for South Africa, I would be delighted to play for England, always provided they wanted me.'

'I have recently bought a house near Northampton, but that is a logical move because I intend playing for Northants for some time yet, and it is always better to invest in your own property. On the cricketing front, I am keeping my options open. The definite facts are that I will be playing for Western Province this coming winter, and for Northants next summer'. Now it was back to Cape Town and those bloody diamonds.

Once I knew the court case would go ahead, I had to tell Lindsay and my folks what had happened, and like all those things which you keep bottled up, it was a relief that it was finally out in the open. The worry was that the police first told me that they couldn't nail the guy they wanted who was doing the dealing because he'd been in a boating accident and there was now a mental problem with him.

I told them that I was now close to being another mental case if I was done after all I'd told them. I attended court every day, and was not encouraged by the appearance of some of the heavy mob. Talk about Mafia – I would rather have faced Big Garth with no box on for fifteen years than cross those guys.

My so-called mate, Jules the solicitor, was bang in the middle of everything and after the case he was struck off. In the end, and much to my relief, I was not called in court, so I was in the clear. Not that cricket crowds let me forget the publicity.

My first game after the court case was at Newlands, and I was soon made aware of the terrific sense of humour of the Cape Coloureds. My first boundary was greeted with 'That's a nice sparkling shot, Lamby.' They were even more lively after lunch, and when I missed outside off-stump, I heard them say: 'I bet you can cut diamonds better than a cricket ball'. At least the case was over and I could get on with my life without worrying about prison or a hefty fine. Lindsay and my folks were very understanding about everything, including my reasons for keeping it from them for months. Another great example of the protective aspect of family life.

The high spot off the field for me that season was to be nominated as one of four contenders for the Western Province's 'Sportsman of the Year'. Morne du Plessis and Rob Louw from rugby were also nominated, as well as Alan Chist from table tennis. It was Cape Town's premier event of the season and was held at the Mount Nelson Hotel, with that great Welshman, Carwyn James, the guest of honour who presented the awards.

The voting was done by the sportswriters, and it was a great thrill to be announced as the winner, with water-skier Terry van der Merwe named as 'Sportswoman of the Year' – I could have towed her around Table Bay anytime she said. I won because of my last season in England, and I didn't know then that I would be named as one of *Wisden's* 'Cricketers of the Year'.

Life was good now I had a well-paid contract with Western Province, and the promotional and coaching work I did meant I was always in the limelight. I also had a private sponsorship worth R5 a run, R100 a catch and R50 for every 50 and R100 for a hundred; but I didn't earn much before Christmas. I didn't get a hundred, and only scored two Currie Cup fifties, but my 93 against Transvaal helped Western Province win the Protea Challenge title.

I often look though my scrapbooks and my Mom kept a cricket special that the *Cape Times* did for the Datsun Shield. It is dated 18 December 1980 and on the back page is a photograph of the Western Province Primary Schools cricket team which took part in the Perm Primary Under-13s week in East London. They catch them young in South Africa, because that particular sponsorship started in 1972 and a lot of good cricketers played in their week. Gary Kirsten is on that 1980 photograph, and so is Joel Stransky, one of South Africa's World Cup rugby heroes.

When the Perm company celebrated its twenty-first year of sponsorship in 1993, a banquet was held in Bloemfontein on the eve of the one-day international between South Africa and India. It was done for the kids, and the lay-out was tables of 12 with one Test cricketer on each table. Also the 200-odd kids were given a miniature cricket bat for autographs, and they had a whale of a time. When the Managing Director spoke he asked anyone in the room who had played in a Perm Under-13 week to stand up and eight of the South African team stood.

India were South Africa's first touring side after re-admission, and Kirsy told me a good story. He had been run out by Kapil Dev in Port Elizabeth – backing up with no warning. Kapil ran into bowl, held on to the ball and took the bails off. He claimed that Kirsy had been warned the previous match, but there was quite a scene, with Kepler's bat apparently becoming tangled with Kapil's shins later in the over.

At the banquet, one little kid asked Kirsy for his autograph and proudly announced; 'I saw you out on television. It's easy isn't it? I've done it twice this week already'. Kirsy said he didn't know whether to laugh or cry.

I owed Western Province a big innings, and it came at Newlands against Transvaal in early February. I scored 130 and batted for over four hours and we managed to hang on for a draw. The local paper reported two things – the first that Transvaal thought I was out in single figures for a bat-pat catch, and that I earned R750 from my sponsorship. That innings made me the first batsman to pass 500 runs and that put me in the first of two sets of headlines in a week.

Immediately after the Transvaal game, Ken Turner rang from Northampton with news that was to change my whole life. 'The TCCB Registration sub-committee have granted your application to play county and Test cricket as a qualified English player with effect from April 1982. You must retain a home in England during the next fouteen months, and then the selectors will be free to pick you'.

I could hardly believe it. I had thought about the possibility from my first year in county cricket onwards but kept very low-key about it when the press started to speculate during my third season in 1980. I knew there would be opposition in both countries: South Africa, because if I got into the England side then I would tour, so that was the end of my time with Western Province. My three-year contract ran out in March 1982, so there was no problem there, but I wondered what the reaction of the public would be. They might see it as me jumping ship.

As for reaction in England, I knew there would be plenty from people who thought there was a big danger of the England side being filled with so-called foreigners. Tony Greig hadn't done me or players like me any favours. I don't blame him for joining World Series, after all he was only doing what I was now proposing to do – make the best of any opportunity that came along to further my career. But there was still a lot of ill-feeling about the way he had signed up players on the quiet.

The press in both countries had a blast when Lord's announced their decision on 17 February 1981. In England, they made a lot of the point that Northants could now get another overseas player, as could Gloucestershire, Hampshire and Leicestershire because of the granting of English qualification to Mike Procter, Christopher 'Kippie' Smith and Brian Davison. Also, Kippie's very promising brother Robin was on the way, and with several West Indians coming through because they had schooled in England, I could understand the views of people who wanted to keep England for the English.

The TCCB Secretary, Donald Carr, made a good point on my behalf. 'Lamb is qualified by right. In fact, our registration rules are stricter than those laid down by International Cricket Conference rules.' That was proved by Graeme Hick, whose seven-year qualification was more than ICC wanted, and that was reduced from the original ten-year period he was told he would have to do.

Matthew Engel wrote: 'Lamb is clearly more English than most, but wider issues may be involved, particularly if other South Africans join the trend. Black cricketing countries may well be unhappy if the England team began to look like a side door round the apartheid boycott. English-born cricketers and supporters may also resent it'.

I was knocked over by a press rush for quotes, and made these two points. 'It is the ambition of every cricketer to play Test cricket. There does not seem to be much prospect of South Africa playing Test cricket in the near future, and I must take advantage of the opportunity to play for England.'

That was fact. As was my follow-up; 'If I'm ever lucky enough to play against South Africa in a Test, watch out. Once you've made up your mind who you are with, then you must stick by your team.'

Ted Partridge of the *Cape Sunday Times* did a big interview with me the following week, and again I was honest about my motives and the fact that I would stick with the consequences through thick and thin.

'From now on, my life will be geared to winning an England cap, but what chance have the others got? It eats my heart out that guys like Peter Kirsten, Clive Rice, Mike Procter and the others, although world-class, just cannot get into Test cricket because of the politics in sport'.

Ted asked me if I had any regrets about not playing for the country of my birth. 'Of course I have. When I was at Wynberg school I wanted Springbok colours more than I wanted a sunny tomorrow. But I must say that when it became obvious that I would play cricket for a living and that I would play more of that cricket in England, I changed my boat in midstream.

'I now have a house in Northampton and I am totally orientated towards the British way of life. From the day I first played for Northants and realised I could hold my own, I just wanted to play Test cricket, and because I had the luck to have parents who were born British, it meant that I had an outside chance of qualifying to play for England, so of course England was the team I wanted to play for.

'And now, if I make the team I can tell you it will be a dream come true. You have no idea what it's like sitting at home in England watching a Test on TV, knowing that you may be there one day. It spurs you on to practise and sweat it out in the nets like nothing else. And that's what happened to me once I made the decision to apply for registration as an English player.

'When I had the call from England to tell me I had been granted a registration, I just couldn't sleep. I know I haven't been selected yet, but by the time the truth hit home, I'd already smashed the West Indies for two "tons" for England at Lord's. For me, this is the biggest break of my life. I've never had the chance to play really big cricket, and you can bet your typewriter to a tickey, I'll take every chance that comes my way.

'Now people ask me if England is a "second chance" after South Africa, and I have to say no. England was the country I knew could give me the chance to play Test cricket, so I always dreamed of playing for the England team'.

Ted Partridge's final question was about how I would feel if the miracle happened, and I played for England against South Africa in an official Test. I meant every word of my reply, made over fifteen years ago, as I think I have proved since over and over again.

'There is no question about it. I would be with my team-mates. It doesn't matter what team you play for or against, you want to win. I would kill myself to make sure of victory for England. And by the same token, if my best mate, Kirsy, was in the Bok side, he would bust a gut to get me out. That's what sport is all about. As far as I am concerned, I am now an Englishman, and that is how I will play all my cricket. Its always been all or nothing with me, and that's the way it is now.'

A lot of playing colleagues and opponents in South Africa supported me. Mike Procter said that nobody should point the finger at me. 'Allan has his own future to think of, and he can't be expected to sit around for ever.' Eddie Barlow said that 'money can't buy a Test cap' and other cricketers made the point that I was a professional cricketer with my first loyalty to my family and my career.

Ken Turner helped me with the press in England. 'He has it all going for him. Apart from the obvious talent, he has the necessary technique, the will and the concentration to succeed at the very top. Too many batsmen in England rely on sheer talent – and it invariably fails them when the pressure is on. Allan is not one of them.'

The 1980/81 season finished in a blur. Western Province had its worst season since my debut in 1972, with injuries to Kirsy and Garth mainly responsible for the decline. I finished with 578 runs at an average of 44, and my Makro sponsorship was worth R4,025.

The coming twelve months would be my last as a cricketer who was not qualified to play Test cricket, and I wanted my next seasons in England and South Africa to be special.

8
The Road to My First Cap

We returned to England in April 1981 and my first headline was celebrating me as one of *Wisden's* 'Five Cricketers of the Year'. The five represented an almost clean sweep for overseas cricketers, although Robin Jackman had played most of his cricket for Surrey. The other three were Vintcent van der Bijl, Clive Rice and Kim Hughes.

I wanted to score consistently as well as maintain the standard of my first three county seasons, I clicked right away with 133 against Lancashire, who now had Michael Holding playing for them. I hit 96 in boundaries, and that started a press bandwagon rolling for me, twelve months prematurely. The political debate, following the Jackman affair in Guyana, was now red-hot. 'Jackers' had been found to be politically unacceptable because he had played cricket during English winters in Rhodesia and South Africa, and his wife Yvonne was a Rhodesian. Nobody in the West Indies had said anything until England got to Guyana for the second Test. Within a few days their Minister for Sport, the former Test left-hander Roy Fredericks, delivered a message from his government that either Jackers was removed from the tour, or England had to leave the territory.

A C Smith, the England tour manager, handled things brilliantly. He took the party to Barbados and, after a few days of hard negotiating, the tour continued with Jackers making his Engalnd debut in Barbados, and it became a four-match series.

The SANROC (South African Non-Racial Olympics Committee) black list got longer and longer, although neither Jackers nor I was on it. There seemed no logic behind the names that were on it – or rather those not on it. In short, it appeared to be an arbitrary list of 'disapproved sportsmen' drawn up by an anti-apartheid movement. The view of the TCCB and the Cricketers' Association was that their members should be free to pursue their trade all the year round, including playing and coaching in South Africa.

I would have done most things to avoid prejudicing my chances of playing for England, but that did not include breaking my Western Province contract because of a black list. The SANROC President, Sam Ramsamy, started to threaten me. 'He [Lamb] must declare that he will not play again in South Africa,' he said. 'If he plays for England, we don't hound him in that respect, but he has definitely to give up his South African ties ... If he returns there, we will be hot on his heels to make everyone aware of this and make sure he gets banned everywhere else.'

My answer came in my weekly newspaper article. 'I am prepared to resist strongly any attempt to bar me from cricket in South Africa. The TCCB have agreed that cricketers can go anywhere to play cricket to follow their profession. With that decision as my guide, I have no intention of being told where I can work by an organisation such as SANROC ...

'Although I am qualifying this summer with the target of playing for England in Test cricket, the foundations of my career are firmly in South Africa. It would be harder for me than for most players to make a break, and I do not intend to do so. So, I intend to carry on playing cricket where I wish in whatever country I choose.'

The more runs I scored – and I reached 500 in my eleventh innings – the more the arguments raged. I did a feature with a horoscope magazine, and they prophesied this for me in late June 1981: 'Gemini with Scorpio rising. You are more dual-natured than ever, with contrasting constructive-destructive impulses. Income means could improve, but losses may outweigh gains unless extravagance is curbed.'

The runs kept coming – 127 against Worcestershire and best of all, 162 against Procky and Gloucestershire. And I passed 1000 runs for the season in eighteen innings, which inevitably stirred up the political angle even more. The TCCB had caught wind of a possible England 'rebel' tour of South Africa, and every county player got a letter warning us that we might be banned if we played in any 'international matches' in South Africa.

What pleased me more than any other players was the comment from Peter Lush. 'Restraint of trade does not apply in this case because players are free to continue furthering their careers by coaching in South Africa and playing in Currie Cup matches as they have done over the years.'

I scored five hundreds in all and topped 2000 runs for the first time, but the season had a dreadful finish when we lost the NatWest Trophy off the last ball to a Derbyshire leg-bye. As I was run out for nine in our innings, it was the most disappointing of my three Lord's finals, and I felt especially sorry for Geoff Cook whose 111 so nearly won the match, but it did earn him the 'Man of the Match' award from Viv Richards – unusual for a member of the losing side.

My merry-go-round continued. Back to South Africa and what looked like my last season with Western Province. I played in the Mutual double-wicket tournament, and this remark from my three year old niece, Tamryn, was reported in the *Cape Argus* after I got out second ball. 'Asked for her impression of the cricket, Tamryn said, "Uncle Allan put on some white clothes and walked a long way to some people also in white. He didn't know what to do so he left."' That's how to describe a dismissal, never mind, 'I got a leg-cutter' or 'I didn't see it after a few beers'. 'I didn't know what to do' is much better. In fact, perfect.

The 1981/82 season was one of the most dramatic I ever played in. Western Province won the Currie Cup for the twelfth time – fourteenth if you count two tied titles – and the announcement in February of the England 'rebel' tour sent shock waves all round the world. Everyone was caught up in it, not just the Gooch party, but anyone in South Africa whose playing future was in danger.

That included me because I was named in the Western Province side to play them in March, but Ken Turner sent me a frantic telegram telling me to withdraw, for fear of queering my new English registration. On and off the field, one dramatic event seemed to follow another, but none more so than when I went down with meningitis in the New Year.

It happened on the final day of the Currie Cup match against Transvaal and I was shivering although it was a stinking hot day. I hit a catch to Lee Barnard off Neal Radford and walked off feeling sick and dizzy. Lindsay was sitting in the main enclosure, and I went straight to her and asked her to drive me home. The game was a certain draw, so it didn't matter if I left early, and I felt so rotten I thought I was going to pass out.

As soon as we got home, Lindsay called the doctor and he took one look and had me in hospital inside an hour. I hadn't fielded on the last day because of how I felt, but now I was very worried at falling ill for the first time in my life – and the new English season only three months away. All I had dreamed of. All I had done in my three years in county cricket. Surely it wasn't all going to disappear?

I was examined in the Groote Schuur Hospital by Dr Sundgren, and he diagnosed viral meningitis, which affects the spinal cord and is not as serious as the more virulent bacterial sort, which affects the brain.

It was a jinx season for Western Province because Garth had a muscle injury which kept him at half throttle, Stephen Jefferies broke a right wrist and Denys Hobson went down with chicken pox. I had the full treatment, including the lumbar puncture to drain the cerebral fluid, and then I had to spend a week in a dark room because I couldn't see.

I made a rotten patient, but the doctors told me that I had only suffered a mild attack and I should recover within three weeks. I made it a bit earlier than that, and probably played before I was fully fit, but I wanted to help the side to nail down at least one trophy. Not only were we going for the Currie Cup, but we reached the final of the Datsun Trophy against Natal at Wanderers. That was to be the worst-tempered match I have ever played in because of two run-outs which upset everybody.

The Datsun final equalled the closest ever finish in the history of the competition – we won by two runs, but the headlines were all about two run-out incidents. The first one involved Vintcent van der Bijl and me, and the second one Kirsy, Big Vince again and Paddy Clift. The game was a real nail-biter between two strong teams captained by Kirsy and Procky. We had our strongest side, Lawrence Seef, Roy Pienaar, Peter Kirsten, Kenny McEwan, myself, Adrian Kuiper, Stephen Bruce, Omar Henry, Garth Le Roux, Stephen Jefferies and John During, and Natal had Robin Smith as their twelfth man.

Their side included Barry Richards, Rob Bentley, Chris Wilkins, Paddy Clift, Tich Smith, Leicestershire's Les Taylor and Big Vince, so both attacks were strong. The bare bones are that we made 178 for eight and kept them to 176 for eight, but the game goes into history for the wrong reasons.

The two sides hardly spoke a word after the game and here, first, are the two captains' comments:

Kirsy: 'You live by the sword. You die by the sword'.

Procky: 'I'd rather lose a match than win it the way Province did'.

It started when I was batting with Adrian Kuiper, and he was on strike to Vince. He played the ball back and Vince fielded it. Neither of us thought about a run, in fact 'Kuips' immediately stepped to one side of the stumps and signalled to the dressing-room for a change of bat. Vince picked the ball up, saw me a yard or so down the pitch and pretended to throw the stumps down.

I laughed – all good clean fun between two cricketers who'd played against each other a lot in the ten years since he caused me to have seven stitches in the forehead. But well after the ball was played, and with a new bat being called for, he threw my stumps down, appealed and got the verdict. I couldn't believe it on two counts. Firstly, that he had done it, and secondly that Umpire Perry Hurwitz did not rule that the ball was dead. I gave Vince the biggest mouthful I've ever done on a cricket field, and he would not have won any award for silence. If I could have reached his chin, I'd have hit him, but I stumped off. That made us 109 for five, and from then it was a matter of batting out our overs.

The dressing-room was in uproar, but Vince wouldn't admit he did anything wrong. 'Heavens, I'm thirty-three and not going to change the way I play the game. The man was out of his ground and I threw his wickets down. It's as simple as that. If Allan, who is one of my close friends, believes that I was joking with him just before running him out, then I am very, very sorry. My action was totally spontaneous and I was overjoyed at trapping him because I believed I had outwitted him in a legitimate manner. It was a quirk of cricket – like getting a good batsman caught at third man while hooking.'

Now for chapter two which we entitled 'The Equaliser'. Natal were 172 for seven in the 54th over – seven wanted off nine balls with Vince on strike and Paddy Clift at the other end. Jefferies had bowled magnificently and he finished with four for 17 from his 11 overs. The second lot of trouble started off the fourth ball of his final over because we all thought he'd taken a fifth wicket.

Vince nicked it – or so we thought – but he stood his ground and insisted that the ball had hit the stumps instead. Our wicket-keeper, Stephen Bruce, threw the ball in disgust to slip and it was tossed back to Kirsy in the covers. Vince got his second volley of the match and things were red hot when Paddy Clift walked down the pitch to try to calm things down.

That was all Kirsy needed. He ran straight to the bowlers' stumps, took the bails off and appealed. Same sort of incident, same umpire, and same decision. The difference this time was that the ball had gone through three pairs of hands, so there was every justification for claiming that the ball was dead. The crucial wording of the law is that whether a ball is 'dead' or not is purely in the opinion of the umpire. Perry Hurwitz ruled it was not dead and the lid blew off.

I wasn't happy about either decision, but Kirsy insisted that Vince had started it and therefore got what he deserved. Natal were just as livid as we were, with the added salt in the wound that they lost the match after needing 18 runs from five overs with five wickets in hand.

Kirsy issued this statement: 'I have a strong competitive temperament and nothing will kill that spirit in my game. But by the same token, I admit that what I did to Paddy Clift went against my grain. I have never run a man out like that before in my life, and I will never do it again.

'I still consider Vince started the whole thing,' Kirsy went on, 'and my action was totally related to his. I know he doesn't play cricket that way, but what got to us was the absolute jubilation of the man and his team-mates at having done it. We were stunned, though I admit we never planned any unfair revenge. What I did was completely spontaneous, and I admit it was not sporting and in the true spirit of cricket. I feel a captain must be strong, I will not be bullied and I feel I must lead my men with the strength they deserve and expect. That is why I threw down Paddy's wicket when the opportunity presented itself.'

It was another couple of months before Kirsy and Vince apologised to each other and to the rest of us. More of that later.

All I know is that both dismissals were wrong, even if they were correct within the letter of the law, which I doubt. I have stood for dozens of nicks when I've known I was out, but I never show out when I get a roughie the other way. It is the way I was brought up, and I have never been a fan of walking – mainly because some of those who do walk pick their times. When it doesn't matter they go, but in a tight situation, it's eyes down for a full house.

The national newspapers were full of it all for a week. Views were sought from everybody who had ever played the game, and there was a smashing cartoon which showed a batsman halfway off to the pavilion when the stumps were broken and the umpire is shown giving him run-out, with the fielders leaping around in triumph. The caption has this comment from the batsman: 'For heaven's sake, Mr Umpire, you said it was the tea interval'.

Television and radio made a meal of it, and it needed something sensational to happen to knock it off the sports pages. We got it on Saturday 27 February 1982, when the 'rebel' England tour was announced. I was nominated in the press as a certain selection for South Africa, but that Ken Turner telegram convinced me that I should ask not to be considered, and that was that.

What does interest me is that the South African Colts XI picked for the first match of the 'rebel' tour included Neal Radford and Robin Smith, both of whom were trying to register in England as a home qualified cricketer. Adrian Kuiper was captain, and the wicket-keeper was Dave Richardson.

And what about the full team for a four-day match? Mike Procter as captain, Barry Richards, Jimmy Cook, Peter Kirsten, Graeme Pollock, Clive Rice, Alan Kourie, Ray Jennings, Garth Le Roux, Vintcent van der Bijl and Stephen Jefferies. I was originally named in the XII, but I dare not think who would have made way for me if I'd played. What a class line-up.

I had contacted the TCCB after I heard from Ken Turner, and the advice was so strong against me playing that I never gave it a second thought, because I was now only a few weeks away from being available for official international cricket. I was so determined to stay in the clear that I even pulled out of the Western Province game against the Gooch team. I had a talk with the convenor of selectors, Ken Funston, and he agreed that I should step down.

I could have also missed the final Currie Cup match of the season at St George's against Eastern Province, once it was put back to early April because of the 'rebel' tour, and I was due to report back to Northants on 1 April. But Ken Turner gave me permission to see out the season, and so I played in my last Currie Cup match for Western Province for over ten years. My last first-class innings was a hundred and nailed down a precious seventh batting point. I finished with a blaze which brought me 21 runs in the last over before lunch on the second day. We won by ten wickets, with Big Garth and Jefferies taking 17 wickets in the match and finishing the season with 43 and 41 wickets respectively.

It was good to finish a wonderful chapter in my cricket career with two trophies, even though that Datsun medal came after so much bad feeling, and we might have made the treble, but for a marvellous 120 from Graeme Pollock in the semi-final of the Benson & Hedges on 5 April at Wanderers.

I signed off with 67 which helped us to 368 for eight from 50 for four, and we fancied our chances after we got rid of Jimmy Cook and Alvin Kallicharran for 32. Then came 'Geeps' and we were gone by four wickets with three overs to spare.

The next day I flew with Lindsay to England, hardly able to think of what might come my way if I started the season well. It's funny the tricks your mind can play. On the plane over I thought of the great three seasons I'd had for Northants, and how I had started each season with a bang. Now, there was extra pressure on me, because I had been written up in the British press as an England certainty from the time of the announcement of my qualification in mid-February.

I have always been confident of my ability to score runs against any side under any conditions, but now I had negative thoughts – like what would happen if my first few innings all ended with a run-out, or a brilliant catch or a crap decision? The law of averages ensures that every cricketer gets their share of bad luck, and I prayed that mine would be put on hold.

The England batting line-up was in the melting pot because of the 'rebel' tour, so there were several places up for grabs. Both openers, Gooch and Boycott, were ruled out and I reckoned the selectors might open with Chris Tavaré which would open up one middle order place.

The TCCB banned the 'rebels' for three years, which shook everybody rigid. Gooch and his players thought they might get a year, but they were shocked when the board hit them so hard. They thought of taking legal action, but decided to wait until after the annual meeting of the Cricketers' Association at Edgbaston a week after I got to England.

I was in a funny position, having just been declared English, but I sat in a corner while a meeting with well over two hundred professionals argued whether the banned players should be supported in an appeal to reduce the three-year sentence. It didn't take long to work out the mood of the meeting with not much sympathy for the fifteen players concerned. The day could have been a mess, but for the Association's President, John Arlott, who chaired the meeting brilliantly. His views on South Africa were well known, yet he ran things utterly fairly, favouring nobody.

We heard all the arguments about freedom of choice, and being professionals who had the right to ply their trade anywhere. If the 'rebels' had prepared a better defence, or rather got somebody other than Geoff Boycott to be their main spokesman, I think they might have gained more support. Bob Woolmer spoke well and I knew what he was talking about when he told of all the coaching he'd done with Avendale in Cape Town. Also, he said correctly that there was no apartheid in cricket, which was mostly true. By that he meant that blacks and coloured now played freely with the whites, but I now see that that was only part of the argument, because the non-whites went straight back to apartheid once the game was over and they left the ground. But having done well, Bob repeated the 'freedom of right to work where they wanted' and was mown down by the counter-argument that the majority of people in South Africa didn't have the right to work and live where they wanted.

What carried the day was the argument that most of the county pros in the room would never play for England, but their future depended upon tours to England by the other countries, India, Pakistan and West Indies, who might break off relations if there were more 'rebel' tours.

I listened to all the arguments, but I never got rid of the feeling that most of the guys in the room felt a mixture of sympathy and envy. Envy, because they would have also taken the money if they were good enough to get an offer. The proposal to support the TCCB ban was carried 190 to 35, but I still say that if the 'rebels' had done better for themselves, the result might have been the same but the margin would have been narrower. In a way, I supported the rebels, and I also couldn't forget that Peter Willey and 'Ned' Larkins had played for England and were now banned, while I was close to a first cap. They were bitter, and I felt awkward in the same dressing-room as them.

The week after the meeting, the MCC side to play the Champion County was announced and I wasn't in it. Everyone told me that it meant nothing, but it did to me, especially as Ian Greig, Tony's brother who was Sussex's wicket-keeper, was picked – another new Englishman. The batting order looked a likely England line-up, and Paul Parker had been given a chance ahead of me. He had spent a few years in South Africa playing and coaching, although he went to Australia in the 1981/82 winter.

My first game was an easy one at The Parks against Oxford University, and I helped myself to 140. I know the Universities used to provide reasonable opposition, but that is no longer the case and I can't see any reason nowadays to classify their matches as first-class. The farcical situation of who would play with and against whom of the rebels was perfectly illustrated by the Northants dressing-room.

The TCCB had agreed that rebel players would not play against the tourists in that split-tour 1982 summer, India and Pakistan. So Willey and Larkins dropped out against India, who played Kapil (he came to play with us after the tour). Also, Sarfraz played the first half of the season with Peter and 'Ned', but they couldn't play against him when he was playing for Pakistan. And there was I, born in South Africa and quite free to play with and against everyone.

What was still bothering me was that India, the first tourists of the summer, might object to playing against me, but when they flew into London on 30 April their manager, Raj Singh, said they would not have any objections, and now I was raring to go in our first championship match against Yorkshire. I got 34 in the second innings, but apart from 93 in a Benson & Hedges game against Nottinghamshire, I couldn't get going.

Surely I wasn't going to fall at the first hurdle? I tried to relax, but kept finding ways of getting out. In the middle of May, just over two weeks before the first one-day international at Headingley, we played at Lord's, but I was caught behind off Mike Selvey for 55 and, when we followed on, I was lbw to John Emburey for 18.

Another MCC side was named to play India, and again another middle-order batsman was picked and I wasn't. Derek Randall was in the runs and I was not, but it made me more down than at any time in my previous three years in county cricket.

The Chairman of Selectors, Peter May, helped by saying that I wasn't considered because the selectors did not want to take too many players away from one side and they had decided to give Geoff Cook a chance as opener to replace Gooch and Boycott. The same newspaper report then spoiled it a bit by saying that the selectors would watch me play for Northants against India on 5 June just before the first Test.

To hell with that. What about the two one-day internationals first? I wanted to play at Headingley so badly it hurt even to think about it. All through my career, I had breezed from one level of cricket to another. It was not that it had all come too easily, because I reckon I earned everything that came my way from Nuffield cricket onwards. This was different, because I had gambled my lot on playing for England, and I was now too impatient for my own good. I have been under a lot of so-called pressure in my life, but I can honestly say that I felt my world would fall apart if I missed out. All those headlines and articles. All those prophecies from other people about what I would do. All those runs in England over the previous three years, and now, just one big hundred against Oxford. Why didn't I get nought there and a big score against Yorkshire?

The selectors met on Friday 28 May, and would announce the squad on Sunday. Lindsay was just as worked up as I was. She told reporter Alan Robinson, 'One half of me dreads this weekend. The other half can't wait for it to come. I tell you, I'm just a bundle of nerves. He says he is shutting it out of his mind, but how he can do that I don't know. It's eating me up. He keeps telling me not to get stewed up. Honestly, you'd think it was me waiting for selection'.

How would I know the team? Would they ring me and tell me? The BBC have a radio programme called 'Friday night is music night'. As far as we were concerned, Friday night was sleepless night. So was Saturday night. Would I make it or not?

9
Finally Picked

I didn't know what to do with myself on the Sunday morning. Would the Chairman of Selectors ring me to tell me that I had made the England squad for the one-day internationals against India? And if he didn't, would that mean I wasn't in? Should I listen in to the radio, or just get away from everyone and everything and wait for the news to come to me later? Lindsay said we should not stay at home, so we went to a farm owned by a good friend, the late Jed Pocklington. His place was in Horton and our cottage was in Piddington, so it didn't take long to drive there.

As soon as we got out of the car and Jed ran out to meet us, I knew I had made it. He broke the news that I would be playing in my first one-day international at Headingley! Never before or since have I known such mixed feelings. I was so happy I nearly cried. All that work, all the help given to me from Mom and Dad, my uncle Peter, the coaches and teachers at school, my mates in the Western Province side and everyone at Northampton, particularly Ken Turner. And most of all by Lindsay who'd done everything possible to encourage me, put up with the difficulties of being married to a travelling cricketer, and also with my many moods, particularly in the first months of that 1982 season when my mind was in turmoil.

I would convince myself that I would be picked, and then I'd build an even stronger case why I wouldn't. I've always tried to follow the *que sera sera* approach to life, and I've batted the same way, but that first big selection was different. Waiting for it was the greatest test of my self-belief I have known, before or since.

I'm not over-dramatising it, but there was so much at stake – not just for me, but for cricket in general. Packer's World Series had split the game from top to bottom and Gooch's 'rebel' tour of South Africa had done the same. Not just in England, but worldwide with the SANROC black list, and cricket was probably at its most politically sensitive at that time. I know most players say that they don't take any notice of the press, in fact some even say they don't read what is said about them.

That's rubbish, because I've been in too many dressing-rooms and there isn't a player I can think of who has not known about things written about him. As for me, Mom and Lindsay have made sure I never forget my publicity, because of their scrapbooks.

Every Test cricketer remembers his first selection, but there can't be many who have had such a build-up over two or three years. I wasn't a kid anymore – a few days short of twenty-eight – for at least two of my four years qualification, the press had banged on and on.

That Sunday was like VE-Day and New Year's Eve combined. I got messages from everywhere, and I had a very emotional call back to Cape Town to Mom and Dad. Jed cracked open a bottle of champagne – and another, and at least another couple. Northants had the Sunday off in the middle of our three-day game at Leicester where I'd played well for 102 the day before. When I got to three figures, I remember thinking it might have come too late, because the squad was picked the night before, and I had not had a great May.

By Monday morning, I was back to earth and nervous about how I would be greeted in the dressing-room. And also there was the biggest occasion of all – when I reported to Leeds and met the other England players as a colleague for the first time.

I couldn't have wished for a better side to be playing against than Leicestershire, because David Gower was a big help to me on the Monday morning. He went out of his way to congratulate me and explained all that he could about the procedure of reporting for the match, the pre-match get-together and so on. I had an exciting telephone call from Lord's in which I was asked for my various measurements for cap and sweater, etc – I nearly referred them to that Italian ice-cream parlour owner in Newlands.

All the players at Leicester swamped me with congratulations – and it meant a lot to get a handshake from Peter Willey and 'Ned' Larkins, who, I'm sure, felt in some way that I should not be playing.

I was bombarded with advice, but I will always remember what Brian Davison said to me. 'Lamby, don't change a thing. Go out there and bat as only Allan Lamb can. That is all you need to do.'

I have only ever played one way, and have always been prepared to back myself, so it was nice to hear that from 'Davo', who I knew was also mad keen to be registered as English. It is difficult even now to explain to anyone from outside South Africa what playing international cricket meant to a couple of generations of cricketers in that country who never had a chance of doing so. I'm not pleading their case, but when you start out in top cricket and you realise that no matter how good you are, you've no chance of playing official Test cricket, it is bound to have an effect.

I found it frustrating before I upped my roots and switched to England at the age of twenty-four, but then I found out something else about myself. I had such a good first couple of seasons in county cricket that the odds were, had I been English, that I would have been given an England chance then. But I always knew that couldn't happen for four years, which is why I'm better placed than most to understand what Graeme Hick went through in the seven years he had to wait. He was helped a bit by starting at eighteen, so he was three years younger than I was when he made his England debut, but we both came into international cricket with a batting handicap that young English batsmen wouldn't have.

Players like Kenny Barrington, Graham Gooch, Dennis Amiss and Keith Fletcher were picked for the first time in their early twenties. They were found out and went back to county cricket to work on their faults. With 'Hicky' and me, we were past that formative stage when the call came, so we had to live or die with what we'd got. By that I don't mean we were unable to work on different aspects of batting but our basic method and the habits that go with it were too deeply ingrained to make a radical change in a few months.

As it happened, I got off to a good start, but Hicky didn't and it took at least three years before he was able to sift the mass of advice he got and establish himself.

My last innings before my first for England was not my best. Nick Cook was bowling for Leicestershire then and I'd only got a single when I had a dart at the next delivery. Six. So I had another dart next ball. Six. I thought that five home runs in a row would make a nice headline, so I went for it. I fell short by about 50 yards caught at mid-off by Nigel Briers, and 'Cooky' has often reminded me that I fell for the three-card trick and that superior intellect won the day.

Now the waiting and the fretting was over, and I couldn't get to Leeds quickly enough. I took Lindsay with me, although she insisted that she would stay somewhere different to give me the best possible chance of getting over my early nerves in the England set-up. She has always been a step ahead of me in things like that – and in a few other areas as well! – and what she did then is just one example of the terrific help she has always been to me in my career.

I was booked in to the Dragonara Hilton by the station in Leeds, and we didn't arrive there until around 10 pm, with Lindsay having nowhere to go. She has often reminded me of what happened next. She offered to find her own bed and breakfast somewhere, and I agreed. So that was the start, me disappearing off into my five-star hotel, while Lindsay roamed the streets looking for a pillow to kip on. And that was the time of the Yorkshire Ripper as she keeps reminding me.

Not only that, but because the players were all driving straight to London next day for the second game at The Oval, she had to organise a lift home, and then find her own way to London. She tells me that I even moaned when, just before she went searching for accommodation, she reminded me that I would have to leave her a ticket on the gate next morning.

What a demanding wife! What more did she want? I took her up the road to the bus station to help her find a bed, and then she wanted a ticket as well!

I met the captain, Bob Willis, and the rest of the guys and they did everything to welcome me. I didn't want to get off to the sort of start I had with Western Province at Newlands when I helped the bar profits of the old Newlands *Sun* and was carpeted next day. So I just had a couple of drinks and an early night.

Not a very peaceful one, because my 'roomy' was Derek Randall, and even when he was asleep, his arms and legs never stayed still. You never knew what he'd do when he was awake, because he was the most restless man I've ever known. Not that first night, but somewhere on tour a year or so later, I remember I got back late into the room and he was already asleep. At least I thought he was because his eyes were closed, but those arms and legs were semaphoring all over the place.

I sneaked into bed so as not to wake St Vitus, and was soon asleep. Not for long, because I was woken up with 'Lamby, do you want a cup of tea?' I thought I'd overslept, but there was 'Rags' with nothing on except his pads and holding a bat as he practised his shots in front of the mirror. I then peered at my watch and it was 5 am. I immediately had a sense-of-humour failure, but settled for asking him to get me a glass of water, whereupon I locked him in the bathroom. For a while.

Next morning was a blur of breakfast and the short drive to Headingley. The first time I knew it wasn't all a dream was when I walked into the home dressing-room, and there in a neat pile was all my kit, shirts, long- and short-sleeved jersey and the England one-day cap. This differs from the full Test cap in that it has only one rampant lion on it – what was then the Prudential lion in gold wire – whereas the full cap has three lions.

When I walked on to the field for fielding practice, it was nice when Kapil and a few other Indian players came over to congratulate me, including Dilip Doshi, a good bowler and a great guy whom I'd got to know well when he played for Warwickshire. Dilip was mad keen on music and later we would often bump into one another at Rolling Stones' concerts. One thing's for sure, they never had a greater fan.

It was a very hot day – around 85 degrees – and with a lot of rain having fallen overnight, Bob Willis was always going to field first if he won the toss. He did and I was glad to get into the match fielding first. Vic Marks was left out of the XII, and my first appearance for England was in this batting line-up. Wood, Tavaré, Lamb, Gower, Randall, Botham, Miller, Taylor, Allott, Dilley and Willis.

I was told I would bat at no. 3, because even way back then it was a problem spot and Gower preferred to bat at four. I didn't mind, I would have batted anywhere for England. We had them going at 68 for five, but Kapil whacked 60 off 36 balls and they gave themselves a squeak with 193. I padded up and waited with mixed feelings as Barry Wood and Tavaré nearly killed the game off with an opening partnership of 133. I'm a good 'waiter' but the occasion, the crowd of 14,000 and so many firsts in the previous few hours all combined to put me on edge. Also, cricketers never like watching from the side and the Headingley dressing-rooms were then at backward square-leg in the building which now houses the offices and some hospitality boxes.

The other worry for me was that the clouds built up for certain rain, and I just prayed I'd get in before that happened. Then 'Tav' did the decent thing and got out lbw to Madan Lal, and I was in. And nearly out first ball, because I got a nick to where first or second slip would have been in a Test match and it went for four. 'Woody' came down and said 'at least you can tell your grandchildren you smashed your first ball for England for four'.

I blocked one, took two to fine-leg, played another couple and then play was held up because of a political demonstration. When the four 'demo' people came on with a banner, I thought it was about me and my heart sank, with the television cameras there, and I knew it would flash round the world in no time. It was a huge relief when the police grabbed the banner and marched them off, and I realised it had nothing at all to do with me – it was a local protest against the detention of twelve Indians in Bradford.

I hit the next ball for four but got bogged down as the thunder got closer. Woody helped me through it and I was going well when the rain started and we were still 13 runs short. I took the 50th over of the 55-overs match, bowled by Yashpal Sharma and hit him for four and two to tie the scores. I would have loved to have hit the winning run on debut, but Sharma stuffed that up with a no ball so I finished with 35 not out and Woody 78.

I've never been slow to have a beer after a match, and I enjoyed everything after the match before we set off for London. I got a lot of congratulations, but the one I prized most was when the Indian manager, Raj Singh, picked me out in the hospitality tent to shake my hand and welcome me to international cricket. I drove to London more relieved than anything else. I hadn't batted anywhere near my best, but at least I'd got a few runs and I was determined I would be more relaxed at The Oval.

Again, David Gower went out of his way on the eve of the game to integrate me into things, and Ian Botham and Bob Willis also made sure I was not left out of anything. I have to say it was the first time in my life I ever felt shy in cricket company, but I was terrified of saying or doing the wrong thing because, as only the third South African to play for England in fifteen years after Basil D'Oliveira and Tony Greig, I didn't want to give anyone a chance to criticise my selection.

This time I had a few drinks and didn't go to bed so early, and I felt fine next day when we batted first and I got in earlier when Woody was out for 17. As soon as I took guard, I knew it would be different. At Headingley, everything seemed to happen so quickly, but now the bigger spaces of The Oval – the biggest playing area in England by some way and one of the biggest in the world – seemed to bring everything back to normal.

I got to 50 off 71 balls, and the fact that I only hit two fours showed that I worked it around nicely. Gower was a big help as he creamed it everywhere and we put on 159 before David had a slog and holed out. I went through the nineties slowly – or most of them because I was on 99 when Sunil Gavaskar brought everyone in to make me work for that one extra run.

I wasn't going to pussyfoot about, so I went for the big one – and was caught and bowled by Madan Lal. I faced 110 balls and the way I got out did me no harm at all with the media. Richie Benaud on television said that 'Lamb is a new great power for English batting. His glorious and powerful stroke play brought a new talent to the Test arena and I am just as impressed by his willingness to sacrifice his wicket for his side.'

The Indians were good enough to join in what was quite an ovation from the big crowd, and I walked off as proud as at any time in the nine years since my first-class debut. We got 276 for nine and won easily despite another great 47 from Kapil.

The one sad thing among all the joy and excitement was that when I got back to Northampton I heard that Tom Reddick had died. He did a lot for me and I can do no more than print what I wrote for my *Sunday Times* column in Cape Town, dated 6 June 1982.

'I can't help thinking that South African cricket has lost one of its great coaches. He was an old friend and I count him as my mentor. Players like Peter Kirsten, Garth Le Roux, myself and all the others of us who learned our cricket under his strict but knowledgeable eye in the Western Province have lost a great and true friend.'

I didn't have to wait long for the next lot of great news. The selectors picked the side for the first Test at Lord's that night and announced it next day, and I had made it. The real thing. A full-blown proper five-day Test – and at Lord's as well. Also in was Geoff Cook, back for Woody, and Derek Pringle was picked for his debut.

It was also Bob Willis' debut as a full Test captain, making him the fourth player to lead England in twelve months after Botham, Mike

Brearley and Keith Fletcher. It was a reminder to me, if I needed one, of what a fickle game cricket can be. Everyone was talking about me playing Test cricket for the next ten years, but all I wanted to do was to score enough runs to keep my place, and take it match by match. The old football cliché, but it makes so much sense. Cricket – in fact any sport – is about the here and now. You can plan all you like, but sheer luck can play a cruel part. Anyway, there is always the opposition who have planned as well and we can't all be winners.

I love the story of the old Scottish soccer international Alec Jackson who was transferred to Arsenal before the war. The manager, Tom Whittaker, pioneered the pre-match team talks using a board with miniature footballers on it.

He was just in the middle of explaining a planned move from the kick-off, when Alec, sitting in the front row, gently slid his foot under the board and kicked all the players into the air.

'What did you do that for?'

'The opposition have just made their first tackle'.

Before my Lord's Test debut we had a game against India in which the fall-out of the 'rebel' tour meant that 'Willy' and 'Ned' Larkins had to drop out, but I was free to play. I remember talking to Kapil (who played for Northants in the second part of the summer) about bowling on the flat pitches at Northampton, and he quite happily told me, 'I've come here for my batting, not my bowling'. It was a good job Ken Turner and the committee weren't listening, although he's such a pleasant bloke, it's almost impossible to get shirty with him.

Sarfraz, who was already playing for us before he joined the Pakistan team, is a different sort of guy, although just as likeable, but in a different way. I remember in my second or third year at Northampton, they had brought Jim Watts back as captain, and he was keen on everyone doing pre-season training. The only trouble was that 'Sarf' turned up a couple of weeks after the rest of us!

Jim had worked himself up into a real lather, so you can imagine the situation when he was giving us all a team talk in the dressing-room one day when Sarf walked in with a big box. Not a word about turning up late. It had not even crossed his mind. He put the box down and said, 'Hi guys. Hope you're OK. Here are some presents for you.'

But when 'Watty' said he'd be fined for reporting in so late, Sarf got a big laugh with his reply, 'Fine away.' When Jim let him have both barrels, he promptly replied, 'My father said I must always play cricket for the love of the game'.

Now I had the taste of the big stuff, I could hardly wait to get to Lord's. This time, the pre-match get-together was a formal one. There is always a dinner at which various tactics are discussed, and the new boys sit next to the chairman – in this case Peter May. I found him to be a lovely man. Shy and difficult to talk to, but I respected him for all he'd done at little more than my age. The other players thought the same, and although the press said that he was finally ousted because of the players, I don't think that was true.

I only played under one other chairman, and have to say that Ted Dexter was just about the most laid-back man I have ever met. They said that as a captain, he was a moonman, and I can understand what they meant. The Sussex players used to say that when he led them on to the field, they followed him as much out of curiosity as anything else. Attention to detail was not his great strength – a bit like that great Aussie, Keith Miller who once led New South Wales on to the field, grabbed the ball and gave the great field placing order, 'Scatter'.

Dexter was a great theorist, but I don't think he was always able to follow through but, like May, he must have been a great batsman to watch.

Once the dinner started, I kept my eye on Ian Botham, because I already felt after a couple of games in the same dressing-room that 'Both' and I had the same sort of attitude to life and cricket. We believe in enjoyment, which is not to say that we don't take things seriously, but I reckon it is possible to do that and still have a laugh.

I stayed quiet, even when Both dismissed the idea of any Indian being able to play at all. Gavaskar, Kapil, Vengsarkar, Viswanath, Shastri, it didn't matter which name came up, Both would say 'no problem' and have another drink.

I made sure I didn't overdo it and had a reasonably early night, which didn't do me much good. We won the toss and I was in and out inside the first hour – lbw to Kapil for nine runs with no movement of my feet. My technique has often been criticised, and I admit it is one all of my own. I always put the bat in front of my pad when playing forward, and I haven't got the biggest forward stride ever seen. That is because of the trueness of the pitches in the Cape on which I learned my cricket, but I've always gone with what I've got, and I wasn't going to change just because some of the purists reckon I wasn't the most elegant player they'd ever seen.

Randall's 126 pulled us right off the floor. Together with 60s from Both and Edmonds he helped us from 96 for four and 166 for six to 433 and, after making them follow on, we won by seven wickets and I finished with 37 not out. As at Headingley, rain threatened us on the final morning, but I hit the winning boundary off Kapil.

My second Test at Old Trafford was only memorable for one thing, and it wasn't a big score from me. I got nine out of 425 with Both getting 128 and Geoff Miller 98. It was only a one-innings match because of rain, but that downpour brought me an unexpected treat. David Gower gave me a lift in his Range Rover, but we didn't get far before it pissed down so hard we broke down.

It meant a long wait for the AA so 'Lubo', as we called him, had a brainwave. He had got a Stilton cheese and wine award in the back of the car so he said we may as well have a go at it while we waited. I played 77 more Tests after that one, but never again did I get through a cheese and bottle of port so early in the evening. It brought a new meaning to the phrase 'any port in a storm', as long as it was vintage! Incidentally, Gower got that nickname from 'Lubo', a Greek grillroom-cum-wine-bar in Adelaide because he patronised it so regularly.

England kept the same XII for the three-match series, but I felt I was now under pressure after two ordinary matches. The third was at The Oval so I was hopeful that I would be just as successful as I'd been in the one-day international. The critics had started, saying that I was a bit too impetuous, and that after three innings with one not out. I know we've got to live with them, but they make things difficult at times.

I was still batting at no. 3 and Cook and Tavaré started us off nicely on a belter of a pitch with 96 for the first wicket. Then they both got out and Lubo and I put on 89 before he was out and in came Both to play his biggest innings for England, and one of his best.

He murdered them with orthodox hitting, almost literally because the first time he middled one he broke Sunil Gavaskar's leg, fielding at silly mid-off. I got cracking properly for the first time for England and thought I might even reach 100 before the close, but I had to sweat overnight on 96. I was dropped by Sandeep Patil when I got to 50, but that apart, I felt good.

I slept well enough and soon got the four runs I wanted. It was such a good pitch that I hoped to make it a big hundred, but Both ran me out on 107, no trouble at all. As I walked past him, he apologised and said, 'Sorry mate, but don't worry, I'll make it up to you out here.' He delivered all right, with 208 at nearly a run a ball – it was the fastest double ever scored for England based on balls faced. I received a pile of letters and telegrams from friends and family in England and South Africa, and one of those I prized most was from the tennis champion, Frew McMillan.

Lindsay kept every telegram sent to me and, looking back through the many I received before my first cap, I treasure every one. Especially those from South African officials at that time, such as Fritz Bing of Western Province and Charles Fortune, who, as well as being well-known as a broadcaster, was Secretary-Treasurer of the South African Cricket Union from 1972 to 1984, and also from journalists like Rodney Hartman and Michael Owen-Smith. I must have had 30 from South Africa, and not all from Cape Town. I often used to think that Mom and Lindsay were mad to spend so much time on doing the scrapbooks, but I now have a great library of everything I have ever done.

Life was good. My third Test and my first hundred, plus that 99 in the one-day international, and when I followed up straight away with 118 in the first one-dayer against Pakistan, I thought I was in for a golden run. I should have known better, because cricket will leap up and bite you whenever you think you've got it licked.

In the three Tests against Pakistan I made 6, 5, 33, 0, 0 and 4, so after the high road against India, I was back in the crowd sweating on being picked for the Ashes tour of Australia. The killer was my duck in the Lord's Test. Not just me, but Lubo and Robin Jackman as well. Lubo was a last-minute replacement as captain for Bob Willis, who'd got such a stiff neck after batting against Imran and Sikander Bakht in a helmet for such a long time in the first Test that he couldn't turn his head an inch.

The three of us went out to dinner after the third day's play, and we decided to eat at the nice French restaurant in St John's Wood High Street, called 'Au Bois St Jean'. We were on the wrong end of the game, with Pakistan having scored 428 with a double-hundred from Mohsin Khan, and overnight we were 227 for nine, needing just two runs to save the follow-on.

Right Home on the range in Langebaanweg. My first dropped catch at two months.

Right Fishing – one of my first loves, aged four in Saldanha.

Left Five years old in Veldrift. Frankie Dettori and Walter Swinburn were lucky I never took riding seriously!

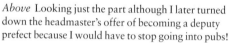

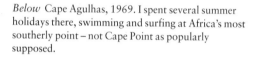

Above Looking just the part although I later turned down the headmaster's offer of becoming a deputy prefect because I would have to stop going into pubs!

Below Cape Agulhas, 1969. I spent several summer holidays there, swimming and surfing at Africa's most southerly point – not Cape Point as popularly supposed.

Above What a poser! I played as much rugby as cricket in my teens and was considered quite nippy at outside half.

Below Taken during my innings of 129 for Wynberg v South African Cricket Schools in 1972. A strong bottom hand is already much in evidence!

Right National Service days in George, where I helped to build the present airport.

Left The best day of my life. It took me six years to convince Lindsay she was doing the right and proper thing.

Left Nearly 'helmet hit wicket' against Pakistan at Lord's in 1982. Mansoor Akhtar is at slip waiting to catch one thing or the other off an Imran Khan bouncer.

Below Driving John Bracewell during the fourth Test v New Zealand at Trent Bridge, 1983. Warren Lees is the wicket-keeper.

Above A typical David Gower team talk. It's 1986 and we are in the middle of a second successive 'Blackwash'. 'Goochie' is almost smiling.

Right World Cup semi-final against India in Bombay, 1987. I have just caught Chetan Sharma off Eddie Hemmings amongst the fire crackers.

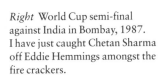

Left The evening after the night before. I have just hit 18 off Bruce Reid's final over to win a day-night match in Sydney in 1987. Twenty-four hours earlier we had been to a party given by Lindsay's friend Lizzie Cattell, who got the party going by 'spiking' the food!

Above Now where's that cab? Robin Smith's England debut v West Indies at Headingley, 1988. We put on 103 for the fifth wicket before I tore a calf muscle going for a quick single. Physio Laurie Brown confirms the damage and I had to retire.

Left Guyana, 1990. The only exercise we had because the Test match was uniquely abandoned after three days without a ball being bowled and two one-day internationals were played instead.

Right Captain and vice-captain discussing tactics before the fateful Trinidad Test when 'Goochie' broke his hand and I took over for the fourth and fifth Tests in Barbados and Antigua.

Above On my way to 109 in the second innings of the second Test v India at Old Trafford, 1990.

Below Umpires John Hampshire and Barry Dudleston inspecting the ball during the second Test at Lord's against Pakistan, 1992. Taking keen interest are (from left to right) Mushtaq Ahmed, Wasim Akram, Javed Miandad and Aamir Sohail.

Not too orthodox but that's how I have always played. Too chest on with feet pointing towards mid-off and hands apart, not together, on the handle. The lesson is to stick with what works for you.

'Gatt' was 32 not out and Robin Jackman was not off the mark, so naturally some of the dinner conversation centred on those two runs. Jackers was typically unconcerned and as the odd bottle of wine disappeared, he was even talking of how we could win the game.

Sometimes I think that someone up there listens in to conversations like that and decides when the time is right to take action. Like that night in the High Street, because within 45 minutes on Sunday morning, we had not only followed on after Jackers was lbw to Imran for a duck, but we were nine for three with Mudassar getting all three, including Derek Randall for nine and Lubo and me for ducks.

The dressing-room was pretty quiet with 'Both' now out in the middle with Chris Tavaré, but Jackers suddenly started to have hysterics. When he was finally able to speak, he pointed at the captain and me and said 'Not a single f****** run between us this morning and what did we all have to eat last night? Duck, that's what, bloody duck'. As Lubo said, 'Thank God the rest of the team didn't eat there'.

We lost easily by ten wickets, despite Tav scoring the second slowest 50 ever in first-class cricket – ten minutes short of six hours – and he also became the first batsman to fail to score a run for over an hour twice in one innings.

The game was one long niggle from start to finish, and I felt sorry for the umpires, David Constant and 'Dickie' Bird. 'Connie' had already been pulled out of the series against India because of their objection, and the Pakistan players seemed to go out of their way to make things as difficult for him as possible. Abdul Qadir went berserk when an lbw appeal against Both was turned down, and both Connie and Dickie had to speak to Imran Khan about it. Connie also had a go at Haroon Rashid for appealing for lbw against me from short-leg, with nobody else joining in. Javed Miandad, who had been warned in the first Test for claiming a catch against Gower on the bounce and then drop-kicking the ball away, had to apologise to Both when he hit him on the arm with a throw from short range after the Qadir appeal, so it was all systems go for the umpires.

I've never had problems with any Pakistan player as an individual, but it is as a team that they become difficult. Imran has made it clear over the years that they believe they see racism and nationalism behind a lot of the incidents in which they have become involved. They seem to think there is an anti-Pakistan bias throughout cricket, but I have to say that they get into more incidents than any other Test side.

Sledging is one thing, and I have never minded that. In fact, in the right way, I welcome it as part of the game I've always known since I was at school in Cape Town. South Africa and Australia are dab hands at it, and it often stirs me up to play even better, and I have never let it upset me, not even when I copped a mouthful from Rod Marsh the first time I played against Australia at Perth later in 1982. As I took guard he asked me if I'd got any family. I said yes, and he said he hoped I survived to see them again.

That is all part of the game to me, but some games involving Pakistan have an altogether different atmosphere. As with India, you don't really understand what they are saying. With the West Indies, you've done well if you stick around long enough to get a few verbals.

From Lord's to Headingley and another Test I wanted to forget, with a second successive duck and four. That was the game when Bob Willis showed what a stickler he was for behaviour and discipline. Robin Jackman had a frustrating time with several close appeals going against him, so when he bowled Wasim Bari, he charged down the pitch pointing him off to the dressing-room.

Willis grabbed him, took him back towards mid-on all on their own, and finger-wagged a public bollocking. I admired Willis for that, although I have never seen much wrong with a bit of spirit from bowlers when they get a wicket. At least it shows they care passionately enough to get wound up, although I accept if the authorities decide something like that is over the top, they are entitled to want to stamp it out. Times have changed in the fourteen years since then, because the increased television coverage, particularly on satellite, has brought a new dimension to the game.

The television people now want to spice everything up, and it is always a matter of how far they are allowed to push the barriers back. Certainly, argument and controversy is just what they want. Anyway Jackers got bounced, but accepted it like the great pro he always was. I was down to no. 4 in that final Test because Gatt had batted at no. 3 for Middlesex and the captain sorted the order out he thought we were all happier with.

So ended my first home summer playing for England. I wasn't satisfied, far from it, despite my hundred against India, because I hadn't put another decent score in the book. It is only on runs scored that a batsman can be properly judged at Test level. In county cricket, it is a bit different, with match situations often calling for a sacrifice in a chase for quick runs.

That doesn't happen too many times in Test matches, because the drawn match is such an important part of top cricket, especially in a three-match series where, if you lose one game, you're struggling to win the other two. Unless one side is miles better than the other one, most Tests are sparring matches for the first couple of days. Usually then, the pattern of the game means that only one side can win, so the other one looks to get out of it with a draw. So, whatever is in the book over a long period for a batsman is what he's worth. A total return of 255 in ten innings – one not out – wasn't good enough, particularly with 107 in one innings. I suppose it showed that I could play at top level, but the last thing I wanted was to be labelled a hit-or-miss batter. My style of play and approach have always carried an element of gambling, but I knew I had to be more consistent if I was to stay in the side.

10
My First Tours

I never thought I would miss out on the Australian tour, but it was still a relief to hear my name when the party was announced. What a place to start, playing to keep the Ashes which Botham won for us in 1981. The top brass of a touring party is always important, and I was pleased that Bob Willis was captain and that the manager would be Doug Insole. I didn't know much about Doug, but he had been a power in English cricket ever since he finished playing for Essex. He had been Chairman of the Selectors and I was told he was a fair man who knew the game inside out.

I still was bugged about how the other players felt about me, South African born, now in the side instead of an English-born batsman, so I decided to put it to two or three of them early in the tour. We were playing in Newcastle and I went out one night with Willis, Gower and Botham. I put it to them straight that, ever since my debut six months earlier, I had this thing that I was regarded as a bit of an outsider. It was the best thing I could have done, because it cleared the air and set me right for the tour. They told me that as far as the dressing-room was concerned, once I was in it, I was the same as everyone else. I was welcome and I should forget any thought that I was different.

By the time we got to Perth for the first Test, I knew that Australian cricket suited me well – there were so many things the same as in South Africa. Not just the climate and the pitches, but the attitude of players. They played it hard – much harder than county cricket in England – and that is because there are fewer sides and so each game takes on more importance that in county cricket. In England it is all too easy to forget a poor performance because there's another match the next day.

The big difference this made to us on tour was that we soon learned there was no point in 'walking', because none of the Australians did, and we were handicapping ourselves unnecessarily. I have no great hang-up one way or the other about staying until I'm given out, even for an obvious decision. The only point I always made when I was captain was to tell the guys that if they stood, I didn't want them showing out when they got a rough one.

We had a team meeting and decided that we would all stand our ground, but I knew that would be difficult for some, such as Geoff Cook, Chris Tavaré and Geoff Miller, who had been brought up to respect what was always a great tradition in county cricket. I agreed with the policy, but when it came to talking about the bowlers, I didn't.

The management was keen to avoid any bother, but by telling the bowlers to curb unnecessary appealing, I reckon it robbed them of a bit of aggression. They were told about sledging as well but as I've already said, that is a part of the game to me.

Everyone was told that we would be fined if we stepped out of line, so I reckon we started the series at Perth in the wrong way. Not quite with one hand tied behind our backs, but it was not going to help us in what looked like being a close series. I reckon that Insole laid down such strict principles because of the ground he thought the authorities had lost to Kerry Packer and the WSC four years earlier.

I nearly didn't play in Perth, because Both pinned me in the nets with a bouncer, but the chin strap of my helmet saved me. My seventh game for England was a dramatic one in many ways, although it was drawn. It was the game in which Terry Alderman ruined his shoulder in making a citizen's arrest on the field during a pitch invasion which brought twenty-six arrests and made Greg Chappell take his side off for fifteen minutes while order was restored.

It all happened on the second afternoon, and Tav's performance can hardly have helped. He batted all the first day for 66 out of our 242 for four. This time he went for 90 minutes without scoring on that score of 66, and the crowd decided to make their own entertainment.

Both was playing in his 55th Test and, as the first cricketer to score

3000 runs and take 250 wickets, he was then just about at his peak. I soon put to the test our decision not to 'walk', when I got a thick nick to a ball from Dennis Lillee. It was such an obvious one that Lillee didn't stop to give me a coaching lesson as he whooped his way down towards the slips. Their greatest danger was being injured by one of the splinters off my bat, but I stood there and hoped for the best. I wandered down the pitch and tapped the divot, not looking at the umpire. Finally I had to look up and there it was. No finger.

The Aussies went 'ape', and I then got the most abuse I've ever heard, before or since. What pleased me was that I didn't let it get to me, working on the basis that the more upset I made them, the more it was in my favour. When I did get out for 46, caught by Marsh off a bat-pad which ballooned off one from Bruce Yardley, I went without appeal because they could have heard the bat contact the other side of the River Swan.

I was about twenty yards off when suddenly I felt my arm being grabbed by 'Marshy' who kept hold until I was close to the pavilion gate.

'What are you doing?'

'Making sure you go this time and don't change your mind, you South African bastard.'

Well, I could take that and laugh, because it was a straightforward gesture, made out of frustration maybe, but with a bit of humour to it. That is the difference between playing against Australia and Pakistan, and it's got nothing at all to do with racism. I always played my cricket hard and to the limit, but I never allowed things to carry on once we were off the field. The only previous exception was after that Datsun final when Vintcent van der Bijl and Peter Kirsten got involved in those two controversial run-outs.

What happened at the end of that day in Perth underlines my point. We went into the Aussie dressing-room and they had masses of prawns and beer. I looked at Dennis, and he looked at me, and nothing was said for a few seconds that seemed like forever. Then he broke the ice: ' Have a beer and a prawn, you little shit'. I laughed and we were away.

Dennis' favourite drink was Bunderberg rum and dry ginger, and if he'd had a big night he would run it out next day. As soon as he started sweating after he came on to bowl, he would flick his finger across his forehead and say, 'Neat Bunderberg and dry ginger'.

Dennis has a great sense of humour. When he spent his time as a coach in Northampton, he used to fool people in the pubs who didn't know him and tell them he was a crocodile farmer, and he always carried his samples with him. Whenever he and I used to go into a pub, he would look around and say, 'Lamby, they haven't sprayed this pub for Funnel-Web Spider', which is a lethal insect with a poisonous bite. It was only then that I realised that not all Aussies refer to women as 'Sheilas'.

That regular getting-together of the two teams after a day's play always used to happen when I started playing Test cricket, but it died a death a few years later. I think the game is the poorer for it, because there's nothing better to keep the proper spirit of the game going than to talk it out at the end of a hard day on the field. It stopped in 1990, and it was Allan Border who was responsible for that. Graham Gooch went round to see him after play, having played for Essex with him and knowing him well, but 'AB' said no, he had taken over the captaincy at a low point as far as results were concerned, and had spent a great deal of time and effort in building a new side with the sort of hard approach to the game he wanted. He was also pushed by Bob Simpson to get tougher and cut out some of the chat.

Even so, I didn't agree with what he did and I reckon he lost a lot of friends as a result. Stopping those close-of-play get-togethers has done the game a lot of harm, and I'm sorry for the modern young Test player that he is missing out on what was one of the most enjoyable things about playing Test cricket. Of course it's a hard game, and so it should be. But it's not war.

I got 56 in the second innings and was now actually starting to look forward to Tests, believing, instead of hoping, that I would be picked.

The second Test was at Brisbane, and we were smashed by seven wickets thanks mainly to two Aussies. Well, one and a bit, if Kepler Wessels will forgive me. He scored 162 and 46 on his debut for Australia, and with Geoff Lawson taking 11 wickets and Marshy snaffling nine catches, we lost, although with only an hour to spare. Marshy took his 300th catch, a world record, and the other personal landmark was Lubo passing 3000 Test runs.

The crowd enjoyed themselves as well, and not just because of the result. Someone smuggled a pig into the ground with 'Ian Botham' painted on one side and 'Eddie Hemmings' on the other. When they let this pig loose we were in the field and ten out of our eleven pissed ourselves, including Both, but for some reason Eddie didn't think it so funny. The Aussie behind the joke apparently sedated the pig and carried it into the ground in a great big 'eskie' with an apple in its mouth, telling the gateman that it contained his food for the day. He then bided his time until the pig woke up before he let it loose on the field.

We didn't let Eddie forget it in a hurry either. After the game we had sponsored cars to get the players back to the hotel. Eddie was the driver of one and Fowler, Willis and I were passengers. Eddie was driving very slowly. All of a sudden, 'Foxy' pipes up and says, 'Any chance of putting your trotter down?' The car came to an abrupt halt and poor Foxy had to get out and walk. The Aussies lost two players through injury on the last two days – Carl Rackemann and John Dyson, who ducked into a delivery from Willis and got whacked on the shoulder.

He was lucky to be there. On the rest day in the Perth Test a couple of weeks earlier, we had a great day. Both teams were invited to Rotness Island, about forty-five minutes across the water from Perth, and there was plenty of food and wine on offer. Perhaps because the match looked a certain draw, we had a full go, and there weren't too many stone-cold sober players out of the two teams. A few of the more drunken climbed on a powerboat, and with Hookes and Both on board, it was no surprise when the odd player 'fell' overboard, like John Dyson who was the luckiest man alive – which he mightn't have been if someone hadn't had the sense to put the engine in neutral, as John went straight under the boat but fortunately came up the other side uninjured.

Whether it was because we were one down when we went to Adelaide, or whether it was because we simply got the pitch wrong I don't know, but we lost the toss, chose to field first and only drew the game after we followed-on, thanks to 114 from Gower in the second innings.

We all had a look at Les Burdett's pitch on the morning of the day before the match, and as it looked damp and well grassed, there was then a case for us fielding first. But Les kept the covers off in the afternoon when a blistering sun dried it out, and the final cut he gave it was a close one, so it was much different next morning. I know that

Willis had changed his mind, but when he asked around the dressing-room a few batsmen, including me, thought we might as well have a bowl first. I know Both was in favour, but it was definitely not the right thing to have done. In his book later, Willis blamed himself for listening to the batsmen, some of whom he reckoned were in favour of fielding first for the wrong reasons – namely that we were afraid of what Lawson, Hogg and Thomson might do.

That wasn't my view, but if the captain says he got it wrong, who is to argue? I was having a good series, what with the 46 and 56 at Perth, 72 and 12 at Brisbane and 82 and eight in the third Test. Those old-timers who don't agree with my stance on 'walking' were probably glad when I was given out on appeal at Adelaide to something down the leg side off Lawson which I never got close to. All part of the game to me, although I desperately wanted an Ashes hundred. The worst part about it was that at 181 for three and Both going nicely, we looked certain to get the 239 we needed to save the follow-on, but our last seven wickets went down for 35.

From Adelaide we went to Hobart where we played on an impossible pitch. Derek Randall was hit in the mouth by Michael Holding, and had 'Mikey' not done the decent thing and pitched the ball up until he was taken off, someone might have got killed.

We had a lively few days there, where we stayed at the Casino Hotel. Late one night, one drink had followed another, and Lubo and Both decided I needed a swim. In I went, not into the sea or a river or even a swimming pool, but straight into the fish pond outside the hotel. When I climbed out, fully clothed of course, there was water and goldfish everywhere.

I didn't hang around, but marched – or rather waded – through the hotel soaking wet and went to my room to dry off. Only when I took my trousers off and dropped them on the floor did I realise I had a visitor. The right pocket moved, and then moved again. I thought I was seeing things, but one of the goldfish had gone for my small change when I joined them in their pond!

From there it was back to dry land and Melbourne where we played the fourth Test, and it turned out to be the closest and the best of all my 79 Tests. It was a game that made all sorts of history, with Both getting Thomson caught by Miller off a rebound at slip by Tavaré, and our winning margin of three runs equalled the narrowest in Test history – when Australia beat England at Old Trafford in 1902.

There can't have been a game in which the scores of the four innings were so close. We batted first and third, the Aussies second and fourth and the four totals went 284, 287, 294, and 288, and there were eight scores of over 50 including 83 from me, which was my most valuable innings for England so far.

Batsmen could score runs on the pitch, but the fact that 13 of the 40 wickets to fall were bowled or lbw shows that there was always something in it for the bowlers. Even the close-of-play scores were neatly parcelled out, with the first three innings all finishing at close-of-play one day, and all four innings starting with the first ball of each of the first four days.

We went in with a change of game plan regarding the off-spinner, Bruce Yardley. In the first three Tests he had bowled 200 overs for 451 runs and 13 wickets, so we reckoned if we could tap him about, it would upset Greg Chappell's bowling strategy of giving his three quicks short spells.

Cooky came back for the injured Randall which meant that Tavaré dropped to no. 3 and me to no. 5, and when I went in, we were in the cart at 56 for three and Tav was bedding down. As far as I was concerned, it was drop-anchor time, but Tav wasn't having any. He remembered the team talk and, as the decision was to whack Yardley, that was what he intended to do. As soon as Yardley came on, he plonked him over the top and did it several times. We put on 161 before we both got out within a few minutes and the Aussies must have been pleased to bowl us out for 284, with our last seven going for 67.

We also had a game plan for Chappell himself and Norman Cowans pulled it off a treat. We had bounced him out a couple of times already, so when he came in I dropped out to the squarer of two long-legs. Melbourne is such a huge playing area that there is no point in going right on the fence so I was told to stay about ten yards in.

'Flash' bounced it, Chappell went for gold, and I caught him without hardly moving. On any other ground it would have been six. David Hookes and Marshy held us up with 53 apiece, but 'Dusty' Miller cleaned up the Aussie tail and after they were 261 for five, it was our turn to be pleased when they were all out for 287.

Day three was a reprise of the first two. We were 45 for three, but 65 from Fowler, together with solid efforts from Both (46), 'Pring' (42) and Bob Taylor with 37 got us to 294 and left them 292 to get in two days.

Neither side could ever say they had the edge at the end of three of the most exciting, gripping days of cricket I'd ever experienced, but the fourth day swung both ways in what seemed to be a decisive fashion twice. At 171 for three with Border and Hookes having already put on 100, we looked gone. Cowans had already nailed Chappell cheaply again – this time for two when he hammered one straight to Gunner Gould, on as a substitute in the covers.

Now Flash was inspired. He got Hookes, Marsh, Yardley and Hogg, and caught Lawson – all inside an hour to make Australia 218 for nine and apparently give us the game.

They needed 74 when Jeff Thomson joined Allan Border, who was out of nick and had had a poor series. He came in to bat in the second innings standing at 83 for five times out, and we fancied ourselves to get back to 2–1 in the series with little trouble.

Well, there wasn't any 'little trouble', there was a whole stack of it. Willis rightly decided to bowl to 'Thommo' as much as he could, so he gave AB a single every over, and he took it. That fourth evening, they put on exactly half of the 74 they needed to leave the game still in our favour, but not by very much.

It could have taken one ball to finish the match the next morning, but 18,000 Aussies turned up to watch, many of them with their 'eskies' as though they were there for the day. We stayed with the same tactics, but we couldn't shift Thommo and now they must have been favourites with only six runs wanted as Willis started an over to AB.

It was a magnificent over, with two runs coming from the first three balls, but then three spot-on block-hole balls meant we could start an over against Thommo. What was extra special about the last Willis yorker was that he'd mis-counted. Having wound up his concentration for what he thought was the last ball of the over, he then turned to decide who would bowl and to what field, only to realise that he'd got another ball to bowl.

I feared the worst, but to his eternal credit, he did it again and now the real drama started. Who else to bowl other than golden-arm Both, so Willis called him up and gave him two slips. Four to win, and Thommo decided that the time had come to win the game. He aimed a square cut, the ball flew to Tavaré at first slip who couldn't hold it. He knocked it up and behind him, but 'Dusty' Miller nipped round the blind side and took the catch.

All hell broke loose, both on the field and in the television commentary booth, where Channel Nine had gone away for the break between overs and missed the wicket. Not only that, but so had our video operators in the dressing-room. Bernie Thomas had filmed all the play, but went for a leak and left 'Piggy' Hemmings in charge. The trouble was that he'd got cigarettes going in both hands and forgot all about the JVC camcorder.

As for Tav, some of us were nearly off the field when Bob Taylor turned round, and saw him, still standing at slip as white as a ghost, thinking of what so nearly was. What a morning, what a finish, what a day and what a night that was. As Both kept telling us, he had to get the wicket, because he had given AB the Duncan Fearnley bat with which he so nearly won the match.

We could hardly believe it at first. After never being in the series, if we now won the New Year Test in Sydney we could retain the Ashes. Just one more hit from Thommo and we would have been buried. Now we knew how down they must have felt. The game ended an hour before lunch, but the celebrations went on and on.

In mid-afternoon, Eddie Hemmings was returning to our hotel, about six hundred yards from the MCG, accompanied by Gladstone Small, who was out there coaching and playing. Eddie was suddenly approached by an expatriate Brummie who wanted to talk about home as well as the win.

After congratulating Eddie – not knowing that he had forgotten to film the final ball of the match – that fan said: 'Nice to see a Warwickshire man, Bob Willis, as captain, and didn't he bowl well? Tell me Eddie, I've been reading about another Warwickshire bowler who nearly got picked to come out here – someone called Gladstone Small. Will he make it?' Eddie pointed at 'Glad', striding along with them, coat-hanger shoulders and all, and said, 'Ask him. This is Gladstone'.

A look of sheer disbelief, a shake of the head and, as the ex-Brummie peeled off in another direction, he muttered, 'Bloody funny that, Eddie. Mine was a serious question, so don't take the piss', and was gone.

There were three days between the last two Tests, and the Aussies were unchanged. We brought back Randall for Fowler, who had a broken bone in his foot, inflicted by Thommo in Melbourne, and Eddie for Pring. The captain gave us a terrific team talk in which he laid it down that one big effort could save the whole tour.

He lost his fourth toss out of five, but got the early wicket he wanted in his first over. The only problem was that, having run out Dyson by at least a couple of feet, Willis could not believe what he was seeing and hearing from Umpire Mel Johnson when he said 'not out'.

What happened was this. Kepler Wessels played a ball straight back to Bob and had a mental blackout when he called Dyson for what was not even half a run. The *Queen Mary* passenger liner could probably turn around quicker than Willis, but he had so much time that when he darted the stumps down, Dyson was not even in the frame. Channel Nine's freeze frame, which was used in the afternoon paper, showed the ball hitting the stumps with nobody or nothing else in the picture – except the tip of Dyson's bat held about shin high because the batsman was not close enough to run it in along the ground.

Occasionally, an umpire can be distracted by fielders or the wicket-keeper, but not this time. Bob Taylor had not got to the stumps, and Cooky at forward short leg had chased after the ball when it was played back to Willis. It was the easiest decision of all to give. Give Bob Willis credit. He swallowed his disbelief and disappointment and got on with the game, but as Dyson went on to score 79, God only knows what effect that decision had on the end result.

At the tea interval, Johnson announced he would hold a press conference at the close of play, and for a couple of minutes he played a blinder. 'I don't have the benefit of a television replay, so I have to call them as I see them', etc. Had he stopped there, that would have been that, but then he added: 'In my view, it was either six inches *in* or six inches *out,* and that's too close to call'.

One of the Aussie agency men decided he'd try that one on our manager, Doug Insole, so he asked him what he thought of the principle that 'six inches either way is too close to give'. Doug rather spoiled things by asking if he meant lbw but the pick of the bunch was the cartoon on the front page of the *Sydney Morning Herald*. It showed Johnson with the dark glasses, white stick and guide dog. The bowler and non-striker were looking at him, and the bubble caption said, 'Now, remember. It's one woof for out, and two for not out'. After that, don't let anyone ever say that the Aussies can't take the mickey out of themselves.

AB did as much as anybody to stop us winning with 89 and 83, so although we won at Melbourne, we had played him back into nick. Hemmings got 95 as nightwatchman and Randall came back well with 70 and 44. Dear old 'Arkle', as we call him, he's always been a bit of a walking disaster, and is a sucker for a bit of mickey-taking. I had told Both about that morning when I woke up at 5 am and there was Arkle having a nude net in front of the mirror. Both had also had a rough night because of Eddie Hemmings, who Both claimed could 'bloody well snore for England'.

Both and I were ripe for a bit of mischief and, unfortunately for Arkle, we picked on him at Brisbane. We knew that when a wicket fell and it was his turn to bat, he would grab his gloves but he never put them on until he was almost ready to take guard. So we got hold of a few packets of condoms and wedged one in each finger and thumb of his gloves.

It worked a treat. He jumped the gate at the Gabba and sprinted in, doing all those loosening exercises that threatened to separate his arms and legs from the main fuselage, and we watched to see how he would cope.

It was better than a music-hall act. It took him a few seconds to work out what the offending items in his gloves were, and then he spent the next minute or so while everyone was waiting for him to take guard trying to wedge one French letter after another into this pocket while he looked around innocently as though he didn't know what everyone was looking at. As Both put it, 'a waste of ten good pokes, but it was worth it'.

We then played in the 'World Series', and I got 100 against New Zealand and 95 against the Aussies in front of what was then a world record crowd at the MCG of 84,513. It showed me the way the cricket world was going. That game was a day game, but the New Zealand game at Sydney was under lights, and I could see that, with the exception of England, floodlit cricket would be the norm around the world within ten years or so.

The players might moan about the pressure of playing so much cricket, and what a killer it is to get to bed after midnight and then be up early for a plane flight to the next venue, but as soon as a new game starts, they are caught up in the excitement and swept along with the crowds who love it.

Sydney was the scene of a car accident involving Gower, who won a new Datsun car in the tour, and put the cash value into the general players' pool. What the sponsors didn't know was that their prize-winner was behind the wheel in a car at the Double Bay traffic lights when he crashed into a brand new Datsun. Whose fault? I'm not saying, except that most left-handers are fully paid-up members of the awkward squad.

Lindsay had come on most of the tour, and based herself in Sydney with a great friend from England, Liz Cattell. We have to pay for wives, so she contributed by helping Liz in her catering business. Personally, I believe it essential that wives come out for a few weeks. I know the arguments that the guys feel they have to look after them and that team spirit is fragmented, but the overall effect on the marriage if they don't come at all is surely more important. Besides, the average player is more settled with his wife around, and is bound to be more relaxed and therefore play better.

Plenty of give and take is required between the players and the authorities to decide the best way to handle this. I know that South Africa and Australia don't allow any family to stay with the team at all. They argue that a tour is a tour and if the players are paid well, they must toe the line. England, I think, is different because players spend much more time on the road during a home season than the cricketers of other countries.

During my time, in one year, we have toured the West Indies from January to April, then played a complete home season until September, and gone to Australia for three or four months in the middle of October. That makes around twelve months in which Test players are at home for a total of around eight weeks, which is certainly not a good situation. Much more thought needs to be given to these arrangements by the cricket authorities everywhere.

Back home in England from Australia I decided that although I had a good tour, I hadn't made it count as much as I should have done considering I got in seven times in ten knocks. An aggregate of 412 runs is okay, but I knew it would have been much better if I'd gone for that on a couple of occasions.

That said, I now felt completely at home in the England set-up. I was close to being a regular, and although the press wouldn't let go of my South African background, the dressing-room was different. I was accepted as an equal in every respect, so the rest was up to me.

Something I couldn't live down for a long time was my tactical intervention before the Brisbane Test. Bob Willis asked me about Kepler, and I said that he was a candidate for a catch in the gully, so they put me there. Sod's Law wasn't it? I dropped him before he was 50 and he went on to that 162. I even taught Both a few sledging words in Afrikaans, but it only made Kepler concentrate even harder.

When Kepler moved from Sussex to Queensland, it was because he was involved in the Packer circus, and he married Sally, an Aussie girl. Nor was I bothered when he made his debut for Australia against England at Brisbane. This was an oddity really, and the bookies in Cape Town ten years earlier would have bet long odds against two South Africans playing against each other in official Test cricket, but neither of us for the country where we were born.

When Kepler became linked with the Aussie 'rebel' tour of South Africa, however, I warned him off. I told him what the consequences would be, but he wasn't long for Australian cricket anyway. He fell out with their Board when they introduced a graded system of contracts and put him on about the third level. It didn't surprise me much when he decided to move back to South Africa permanently.

The main difference between Kepler and myself is that he was prepared to uproot himself and his family a second time. With me, my commitment to England was complete, and never once have I thought of going back to live in South Africa. I feel so strongly about it that I believe Kepler should not have been allowed to captain South Africa after playing for Australia. As far as I am concerned, once you play for one country, that is your lot.

The 1983 season was my first World Cup before we played four Tests against New Zealand, and I had one of my best years. I averaged over 50 for Northants, and started off the World Cup with 102 against New Zealand and 53 against Sri Lanka. I hardly missed, and when we beat Pakistan twice I thought we were bound to reach the Final. But India squeezed us well in the semi-final at Old

Trafford, and pulled off an impossible-looking win at Lord's against the West Indies.

When Kapil left Northampton in early June, Ken Turner said 'We'll see you on 25th June'.

'No, you won't, Secretary. That is World Cup Final day and India will be there.' Laughs all round, except that Kapil was spot on.

Now I wanted above all else to start scoring Test hundreds. I was 30 and had come on to the scene so late that I could only count on five or six more years, even if everything went well, so it was important to start well on one of my favourite batting pitches at The Oval. I did, with 102 not out in the second innings and we won easily. The next game at Headingley brought one of the best unrewarded pieces of bowling I've ever seen from Richard Hadlee. New Zealand bowled us out for 325 and 252 and won by five wickets, with Lance Cairns taking ten wickets, Ewen Chatfield six and Hadlee, who must have beaten the bat 50 times in his 47 overs for 89 runs, not getting one single wicket. He bowled so many unplayable fast leg-breaks that it was almost a joke that he couldn't get anyone out, but he still finished with 21 wickets in the four-match series. I rate him as the best bowler I know at moving the ball at pace, which is why I was pleased with my unbeaten 137 against him in the last match on his home pitch at Trent Bridge which sealed the series for us. But I had no doubt he would continue to be a force when we visited New Zealand in early 1984.

11
Huntin', Shootin' and Fishin'

I've always loved sport, and not just team games. When I was still at school, we used to have wonderful holidays in Cape Aguillas – the most southerly point of Africa, not Cape Point as the tourists are told. That was where I learned to fish and surf. We would fish off the rocks and ever since then fishing has been a great love of mine.

I learned to shoot at the same young age, twelve to fourteen in the winter holidays either in the Karoo, or in Zimbabwe with an uncle of mine, Paul Donnelly. He would take me round checking farms and we would spend a lot of time in the bush. We would sleep on camp stretchers, and I remember waking up one night to see elephants close by. I crawled under the jeep – that was one trunk call I was not keen on – working on the ostrich theory that if I couldn't see them, they couldn't see me.

Uncle Paul was a terrific snorer – one night he was so loud he even woke the monkeys and you've never heard such a row. Monkey screeching and him snoring – it was like listening to a drunken wake stopping to watch a couple of pneumatic drills at work.

I also spent some time with a friend in Northern Transvaal, and I learned to shoot kudu and antelopes with a rifle. What I enjoyed most was the walking we had to do to track the game. As a kid, I found it exciting to watch the tracker look for spoor of genuine wild buck, before we tracked them.

My gun debut in England was slightly different. Peter Huggins of Hartwells Motors, who sponsored my car, took me shooting at Blenheim Palace, and I hadn't got a clue what to expect. I turned up in jersey, jeans and boots, and was about as out of place as a stripper

114

in a monastery. Plus-fours and pukka smart hats were the order of the day, and they looked at me as though I'd landed from Mars.

I had to borrow wellies, so there I was on my first shoot, looking like a refugee from Oxfam when we lined up. Now remember, I believed I was the last of the Great White Hunters and I had never heard or seen driven birds before. The first pheasant broke over me and I let go twice and never touched a feather. I could have died, especially when everyone started making fun of the Great White Hunter. Since that first shoot, Lynn Wilson has taken a lot of trouble to show me the right etiquette and I have improved a lot. I wouldn't say I'm bull's-eye class, but at least I am dressed properly when I miss.

Another first with the gun I shan't forget in a hurry was my introduction to stag shooting in Scotland through Ian Botham.

We brought along our families and stayed in a good hotel. We just happened to call into a pub in Callander and we met a stalker, who told us they were starting to cull out the stags. This was October 1983, and we asked if we could go along next day. He told us how to get to an old farmhouse which was the starting point. We set off in cars that could drive over any terrain, and there were eight of us, including Both's father-in-law, Gerry. He succeeded in going to sleep and snoring his head off, despite all the jolting as we went across country.

By this time we were halfway up a mountain, and Both said he was tempted to shoot Gerry and to hell with the stags. When the action started, Both didn't nail his stag but I got mine first time. Both went looking for a second chance, and suddenly there were so many gun-shots it sounded like a re-make of the gunfight at the OK Corral.

What neither of us knew was that we were supposed to be limited to one stag each, so when Both not only got the equaliser but went 2–1 into the lead, I nailed another one before the stalkers could stop us. Both was now shooting like he batted – letting fly at anything that moved, and that's why, instead of two stags, we ended up with four, plus a fox and a grouse.

The locals weren't too impressed when we got back to the pub, but a few rounds of Scotch settled things down. What I didn't know was that I had to be blooded for my first stag. Both had already been done a few years ago, so he enjoyed the ceremony more than anyone. A dab of blood, another Scotch, a dab of blood and so on until my face was covered. More Scotch and I forgot what I looked like as we went back to the hotel.

When we got there, the place was heaving with a coachload of American tourists who had called in for tea and scones. They took one look at the bloodstained hooligan from Langebaanweg and went on their way.

Lynn Wilson also introduced me to grouse and partridge shooting, but my debuts were no more successful than the pheasant shoot. The grouse shoot was in Northumberland and I was given a loader who stood with me in the butt while we waited for first sight of the birds. He warned me that as soon as I saw them, they'd be about 200 yards away and to line up and shoot straightaway. Know-all Lamby decided to wait a bit longer to make sure of a hit, but the birds had come and gone in what seemed like a second and I didn't have time to pull the trigger once. A bit like being bowled out playing no stroke.

The partridge shoot was at Highclere Castle and the rules there were that you could only shoot at birds flying over your own individual channel. I had Charlie Spencer on one side and Lynn on the other, and for a few minutes they were banging away while I never had a bird fly overhead. I got bored, so had a pop at the next few birds I saw, and was immediately accused of poaching into their territory.

I remember September 1983 was the first time I went salmon fishing and, guess who with? Botham. He had organised a couple of log cabins near the River Teith and we took the families. We went for a couple of weeks, but it did nothing but rain for the first week, so we didn't fish a lot. Gerry was with us, but his business partner died suddenly and he and Both went to the funeral at the start of the second week, so I was on my own.

I had a gilly who took me to a part of the river where everyone was catching fish – except me. I couldn't get a bite, and I was getting desperate because I knew what Both would say that evening. I told the gilly that we would have to buy some, and we paid good money for two 14-pounders. When Both came into the pub, he asked me how I'd got on, and was quite pleased with life when I told him I'd had a blank day. He told me not to worry as it had taken him five years to land his first salmon, so it knocked him back when I casually produced the two salmon.

He got his own back next morning. He insisted we made a 5 am start and promised me a good stretch of the river. He went upstream and I only found out later that he'd given me the worst part of the water – my gilly said that the last salmon caught there was about twenty years ago. Sod's Law came my way for once, because I hooked a big one, and Both waded down to help me land a 28-pounder.

Now I was 3–0 up and that's how it stayed for the rest of the week. He's the same with everything in life. He can't stand being second to anybody in anything, and I have always been the same, too. That competitive urge is one of the reasons why we've been such good mates for nearly fifteen years – plus the way he made me welcome into the England dressing-room in 1982. We both love country sports for the same reason. We find peace and relaxation, as well as meeting the most pleasant people you could wish for.

12
Controversy in New Zealand and Pakistan

I had enjoyed a good break before we left for the most controversial tour of my time – to New Zealand which started early in January 1984. On the way we stopped over in Fiji and my wearing of their traditional grass skirt and garlands went down well, but we were only five days into the tour proper when we were given a taste of what was to come.

An English tourist called Ian Brooks accused us of being drunk in the hotel he was staying in, and that sort of mischief was the start of a bandwagon that never stopped. He sounded off about all the England cricketers being pissed, and named me as being in a bunch of them. As it happens, I was with a few travelling supporters who were rowdy, but they weren't players.

As far as I am concerned, the behaviour of the players on that tour was little different from any of the other eight tours I have been on. I've always enjoyed a drink, but it has never affected my approach to my cricket. Different preparations are the norm for any team or touring party. What suits one won't suit another. Early quiet nights are not for me. Wasn't it the famous golfer Walter Hagen who was told on the eve of a big match-play final, that his opponent was already in bed, whereas here he was, Walter, going nicely in the bar at 10 pm? 'Yes, he might be in bed, but is he sleeping?'

I won't have any part of curfews for that reason, even if occasionally we go a bit too far. My approach was always to play it hard off as well as on the field. Like I say, cricket is a game, not life and death, and I'm glad I played most of my Test career with people like 'Both' and Gower, for I've generally managed to walk the thin line between what some people would regard as acceptable activities off the field and what they wouldn't. But there have been a couple of times when I suppose I got carried away – the first time almost literally. It was on my second tour of Australia in 1986/87 under Mike Gatting and we were playing Western Australia in Perth where the Americas Cup was being held. We had a big dinner at the White Horse offices of Harold Cudmore. The evening went on, and so did the early hours, with Both, who is the one guy who never ceases to amaze me with his consumption of booze, now taking on a crew member with a broken arm in a Scotch-drinking competition.

We finished at 5 am and John Emburey made himself responsible for getting Both back to base. He didn't dare go through the main entrance of the hotel, so he had a crack at the tradesman's entrance. Somehow, 'Embers' got him up a flight of very narrow stairs. He said: 'I couldn't carry him, so it was push, pull and drag. I didn't get the full use of my right arm back for two days.'

The start of our innings a few hours later was not a pretty sight. Lamb and Gower repeated our ducks of St John's Wood High Street, and when Both was pushed out to bat, he got halfway to the middle before he realised that he'd given himself an extra handicap ... he didn't have a bat.

I could only guess at how he felt, but he saved us and the day with a savage 70 in which he smashed the ball all over the ground. That didn't make the papers, but my casino trip with Kerry Packer on the next tour in 1990/91 did. I was captain because 'Goochy' was injured and at the end of the second day was not out in our second innings together with Jack Russell. We were 56 for three having got a small first-innings lead in a match which was to be over inside three days.

We were back at the hotel when Tony Greig rang and said that Packer wanted to meet us and have a drink, so Gower and I went. He asked us to join him for a meal in the casino at the Hotel Conrad, and so far, so good. The girls were with us, but Packer wouldn't have them playing at our table, so he gave them money to play with and said he would finance us. That removed one worry from my mind. because I knew he was a big gambler, and I didn't fancy playing with my own cash at the table.

Packer told us that he would make all the decisions and then we would spilt the profit. When we were ahead about $A10,000 each,

I told him I was keen to go and that I would play again another time. I thought that the profit would pay for Lindsay's trip, but he said he wanted to play for one more hour before he went to his room to watch the Aussies playing rugby league in England on television. I still wasn't keen, both because of the time and the chance that the profit would disappear, but the other guys wanted to stay so I stayed as well.

As I feared, we got cleaned out, so I wasn't too happy when we finally got back to our hotel about 1 am. There was some consolation from the fact that I hadn't lost a penny, we'd had an exciting night, and I was stone cold sober because Packer is a teetotaller.

There was never much chance of the story not breaking, but the first time I was tackled about it I was told that we'd been seen still up at 5.30 am. That was untrue but I didn't deny it, because I didn't think I'd got anything to defend myself about. I did say to the Aussie journalist, 'What's it got to do with you?' I told the same true version to the manager, Peter Lush, when he asked me about my late night, and there the matter ended. Except that we were rattled out next morning and lost by ten wickets, so the press decided that they had a nice big stick to beat me with.

I suppose as England captain it would have been better had we vacated the casino when we intended to – about 10.30 pm, and then nobody could have invented anything.

As for that 1983/84 tour of New Zealand, I admit that I dabbled here and there with pot, but only socially. I say that not as an excuse, but to nail the lie that the team indulged in the habit in our dressing-rooms. We never did, and I'm not proud that I did so at all, but at the odd pop concert and at dinner-parties it was so much the normal and accepted thing there, that I did get mildly involved. I'm not making a great moral issue of it, but I'm glad that my only involvements, first as a kid and then on that tour, were only fringe ones, and I have no hesitation in saying that I would never let anyone I know get involved now. Part of growing up, I suppose, but it's not clever.

The stories on that tour became wilder and wilder – with the pot, we were supposed to have done it in our bedrooms and put towels down under the door to hide the smell. The worst story of all concerned Both and me and a couple of girls in our room – the one in which a window got smashed when we broke into our room because the front door was locked. It was our last night there before we moved to Wellington, and it was only when we arrived there that the trouble started. The manager had reported the broken window to the police and they questioned us about it. Also, A C Smith wanted to know the facts and we agreed to pay $400 for the damage.

The story of that night was a big part of the pending court case between the *Mail on Sunday* and Both, but the girl who made the accusations finally withdrew them. As I pointed out at the time, if I'd got a girl in my room for a bit of the naughties, I wasn't likely to leave the door open for anyone to walk in as she admitted she'd been able to do.

Yes, we'd had a few and yes, we had a bit of a party, but that was it. The hotel manager called the police and then our manager, A C Smith, saw us and asked for our explanation, which he accepted.

He was probably the best of the managers I toured under. I found him fair and a players' man through and through. Doug Insole, my first manager, was the same. I believe he wrote in his report that I was easily led, but some people would say that that is the story of my life. It would be truer to say that I have enjoyed being led, if that is what has happened, and I've done a bit of leading myself.

Norman Gifford was the assistant manager in New Zealand and Pakistan, and he was brilliant. He had played and toured himself, so he knew what was acceptable and what wasn't, and he didn't mind helping us after a heavy night by making sure we woke up at the right time, particularly Both and me. When we were sleeping off a heavy night and he couldn't get us up, he would puff away at his pipe and smoke us out.

That 1983/84 tour of New Zealand and Pakistan was my worst as a batsman. In the six Tests I scored 160 in nine innings, despite getting into double figures six times. We lost both series 1–0, although we did very well in Pakistan to draw the last two Tests after losing Both and Willis (Gower took over the captaincy), and having illness to put up with in the Faisalabad game.

By now I had played in 21 Tests and scored around 1200 runs at an average of 34. 'Adequate, but should do better' would have figured on a school report, so the 1984 home series against the West Indies which was to follow was important to me. This series, and the next one away in India, had plenty of dramas which I saw from very close quarters.

13
Lindsay Lamb

My relationship with Allan, or 'Lamby' as I call him, has been one in which we have never tried to keep a stranglehold on each other. Since we first met in 1974 when I was training to be a teacher in Cape Town, we hit it off straightaway. What with his cricket and my studies, things were bound to be hit and miss, but we generally made it work well. Then he had his first trip to England and I was intending to go with him, but Dad died from a heart attack. He was only fifty-one. He and Mom were so close that I wanted to stay with her, otherwise I'd have made the trip with Lamby. I'm the eldest of three and when Dad passed away, I was twenty-one, Jane was eighteen and Richard sixteen.

I did everything to earn money in those years, including selling wines in the morning and working in a steak-house at night. I was also a rep for Reckitt & Colman, so I've never been one to sit back and let the grass grow.

We had a family farm and Mom wasn't going to let it go after Dad died, so she ran it for nearly ten years before Richard took it over, and he still runs it to this day. If I'm half as good at being a parent as both Mom and Dad were to me, I'll die happy, because they struck exactly the right balance between letting me run free and still exercising a bit of control. Taking the horse-riding analogy, they let me roam on a loose rein, and I hope Mom agrees that it worked well.

When Lamby decided to have a real go at county cricket in England in 1978 I also went over with an old friend, Sue Crank, and we based ourselves in London while he lived in Northampton. During that time I lived anywhere and everywhere, including touring and tent camping in Europe, while Lamby was in some grotty digs with some of the other Northants players. Richard Williams was one of them, and I loved Lamby's story of 'little' Richard, who is only about five foot six, and who used to ride a motorbike. One day, when he'd got his head down into the wind and rain and wasn't paying attention to what was ahead of him, he drove straight up the ramp of a parked furniture van and tangled with a table and chairs before he had a chance to look up to turn right.

I would see Allan whenever he came to London, and he proposed to me at his sister Brenda's house. She was married to the England rugby player Tony Bucknall, and they have always been very close to me, especially when all the trouble broke out after the 1983/84 tour of New Zealand.

We'd been married then for five years and with most of that time spent waiting for Lamby to become qualified to play for England, life was full and exciting.

I enjoyed my first trip to Australia. Other than South Africa it is my favourite country to visit. It took just that one tour to convince me that the wives were better off joining part of the tour rather than staying at home – and not just to shorten the time of separation. I'm not stupid, I know that cricketers are no different from other young men on the loose, which they mostly are on tour, being forever in the spotlight. I also know how on-coming the Aussie girls are. I have seen enough of life as a student and then living and travelling in England to know the score, but I made a big effort to make everything work between Lamby and me. I've always known that he would never pass over an audition for *The Virgin Soldier*, but as long as it's not front-page headlines, I can cope. I've always loved him, although it would be dishonest to say that things didn't change after that tour of New Zealand. I was there only for the early part of it because the side was going on to Pakistan next … and touring works out very costly as expenses for wives are met by the players.

I was shattered when all sorts of rumours started to come out as soon as the players got to Lahore. Never mind the drugs, because I knew Allan had dabbled as a kid, and he told me that he was amazed to find what a socially acceptable thing it was in New Zealand. I admit that I wasn't happy about it, but an occasional evening smoking pot wasn't going to be the end of the world as far as I was concerned.

It was the sex stories that tore me apart. In my view, there's no smoke without fire. Again, I want to make it clear that I was not so much bothered whether it was true or not, I just couldn't take it being all over the front pages. In any case, I'd rather not know at all even it was true. You see, I love Allan and always have, and that kept me with him when it would have been so easy to walk away.

A lot of marriages go bust at the first sign of trouble, but I didn't want that. From March 1984 onwards, I found out a lot about myself, particularly in the first few weeks. He telephoned me from Pakistan to say that Both was coming home early and would bring a letter with him which would explain everything. He told me that there had been a set-up with a couple of girls, and not to believe what I read. I had that proved to me in Barbados on the England tour of 1985/86, and Ally Downton and I were also unwittingly involved in Antigua on the same tour. The players had gone off to Jamaica while we stayed on in Antigua, and the day they were due back, we moved from our flat into the team hotel. As we were booking in, a journalist heard the two of us asking when the players would be coming and told us that we would be all right, as they were all keen to meet new girls.

Guilty or not, I suppose that getting Both to bring me this letter was all Lamby could do, but I was in such a state that I didn't know what to make of things. We were then living in Hardingstone, and the arrangement was that Both would pass by on his way home and give me the letter. I made a lasagne for lunch and waited ... and waited and waited. The afternoon came and went, and by now I could have slit Lamby's throat if I could have got to him. It was all too much, and to make things worse I was having to cope with it on my own.

It seems that Both forgot about his promise to Lamby and drove straight home; I suppose he had troubles of his own, so it was understandable. The difference between the situation at the Lamb and Botham households was that Kath Botham now had her husband with her, along with her family and friends, to provide support. And me? I was on my own and at the lowest ebb of my life.

The old saying maintains that life was never meant to be fair, but this was ridiculous. The press were now camped outside my door, and I felt like a prisoner. I couldn't face them, but how could I escape? It was quite craftily done in the end. Brenda was a pillar of strength and she telephoned to tell me to get down to her place as soon as possible. As Lamby's sister, she knew him better than anyone, so she understood he wasn't perfect – but she wouldn't have had him any other way. I felt the same, but somehow we had to let the press storm blow itself out and then see how much we were affected by the fall-out.

I escaped from home with the help of my neighbours who smuggled me over a back fence and then drove me to Newport Pagnell, where my car was parked. From there I drove to stay with Brenda and Tony. The next day I wanted to lose myself, so I went by train to the Ideal Home Exhibition in London, but that was a waste of time. The next day a photo of me appeared on the front page of the *Daily Mail*, portrayed as young and innocent, and I knew that somehow or other I had to get through the two weeks before Allan came home.

By this time I'd had his letter and that didn't help me at all. It was one long denial of everything, but I not only had to suffer the pain of the stories, but also the anguish and public humiliation, despite the fact that I always knew that other women found him attractive, being a friendly and genuinely warm character, and he was never going to be a Trappist monk.

Brenda and Tony helped me to keep sane, and Mom at home was also a terrific help. When Allan came back, I knew then that there was a big change between us. It wasn't a matter of believing him or not, because those bloody newspapers had eaten into my soul. It is almost impossible to describe the effect they have. When you go shopping you think everyone is pointing at you and whispering about you. Even dinner parties with friends were a problem, because everyone was too bright for comfort and went out of their way to show that nothing had changed regarding their friendship. But nobody, not even Allan, could know how deep the scars were.

I hated him as passionately as I loved him, and I felt so strongly I just wanted to dig at him, physically if necessary, with my fingernails. I wanted to hurt him just as he had hurt me, and I came very close to attacking him as the only way to get my own back. So many times, before and after he came home, I thought of leaving him, but it was almost like the film *Fatal Attraction*. But there was a difference from the old cliché of 'can't live *with* him, and can't live *without* him'. With me, I didn't know if I could continue to live with him, but I *knew* I couldn't live without him. A small difference, and yet a big one, if you see what I mean. It took months to get back on to an even keel, and in that time I found out something else. It is rubbish to say that you can't love someone without trusting them.

I knew I loved Lamby, and still do, but I don't trust him. I'm not sure if that's a weakness or a strength, but it's the truth. I've always been an honest person, but the most difficult person to be honest with is yourself.

There is always an excuse knocking about if you want one, but I was brutal in my self-examination. Did I want to stay with Lamby if I admitted I didn't trust him? And if I did, would that affect things between us to a degree where he would decide I was giving him an open cheque to do what he wanted? Or were his feelings strong enough to want to try to earn my trust again?

The answer, over twelve years after a trauma that would have scuppered more relationships than not, is that we are still together. We have two smashing kids, and we have made it work. I can't imagine a bigger watershed than the two years of 1984 and 1985, and it took all of that period to get a working relationship going again. It was hard work, but the big thing was that I saw we were both prepared to do it and that helped a lot. Life with Lamby has always been a bundle of surprises, and I wouldn't have it any different.

What I would say now is that I would take Lamby to the cleaners if it happened again, he wouldn't know what hit him. I'm stronger and older now, and he'd end up believing that a corrugated cardboard shelter under Waterloo Bridge would be the equivalent of Buckingham Palace by the time I'd finished with him.

There are periods even now when it isn't easy, but time has healed a lot, and I reckon we both have something to be grateful for from that awful and soul-destroying tour.

Within twelve months I went to join him in India, and was immediately arrested in Bombay because I had not got a visa. I had been to South Africa and when I got back to London, I collected my second passport from Lord's and didn't check about the visa as I should have done. I assumed, wrongly, that it had been done with Lamby's and it wasn't until I got to Bombay that I knew differently. I spent six hours under arrest and missed my connecting flight to Delhi. Quite a good start to my trip. Finally, the authorities agreed to let me fly to Delhi where I spent another five hours trying to get a visa. I rang Allan, only to be told that that was my problem, so I knew where I stood again.

I felt it was like being in a time warp back to Leeds in June 1982 when he put me on a bus at 10 pm to find my own place to stay, while he walked back into the Dragonara. Now I was in Delhi, on my own again, with only Lindsay Lamb, née Bennett, to help me. She didn't let me down. I got the precious visa and decided to take a taxi to Agra while I was in the area. The driver was a Mr Singh and I insisted we didn't stop once during the five-hour journey, not for anything, just in case he shot off with my luggage!

At least I saw the Taj Mahal before I joined up with my husband, and normal service was resumed. Well, nearly normal service. I went on seven tours in all, and I would tell every other cricketer's wife to get out on those trips.

If you don't keep your husband's bed warm at night, then someone else might. That's not being cynical, just realistic. The other thing the authorities should consider is that a cricketer is more likely to have a proper night's sleep with his wife in bed beside him, rather than a temporary stand-in and all the 'parallel gymnastics' that would follow.

You've got to be strong to marry a glorified travelling salesman, but as long as you and he agree proper lines of demarcation, you should crack it. Play it that way, and never expect to be considered first unless your husband says so. It's that loose rein approach again, and, believe me, it works.

14
Gower in Charge

The 1984 home series against the West Indies was the one in which Andy Lloyd, on his home ground at Edgbaston, nearly lost the sight of his right eye when he ducked into a delivery from Malcolm Marshall, and when Winston Davis broke Paul Terry's arm at Old Trafford and was indirectly responsible for me being accused of playing for myself and not the team.

Apart from the second Test at Lord's, this was the most one-sided cricket contest I had then played in. We lost twice by an innings, and once each by 172 runs, by eight wickets and by nine wickets. We played nine specialist batsmen in the series and we were sunk without trace. Part of the trouble was that our team meetings were too negative and too many of our players developed a defeatist attitude. They were so intent on just surviving that they prevented themselves from succeeding. I knew that their four fast bowlers were world class – or rather three of them were, Garner, Marshall and Holding, but you couldn't say the same about Winston Davis or Eldine Baptiste.

The exception to the negative aspect of the team meetings was Both, who never admitted that we had the slightest problem, especially with Viv Richards. 'One out for the hook and I'll bounce him out' was like a gramophone record at every team meeting. The trouble was that we were too defensive against Viv from the start. Viv against England was like Both against Australia; he knew he'd got the eye on us and he used to impose himself right from the start of a match.

To be fair, apart from scoring 117 in the first Test and 72 at Lord's,

Viv only registered 61 runs in his other four completed innings, but he didn't need to with Gordon Greenidge, Haynes, Gomes and Dujon all getting hundreds, with Gordon's a terrific double-century at Lord's and another one at Old Trafford. I decided after the first Test that there was no point in ducking and diving, because the bullet with your name was never far away, so I decided to take them on.

That's not boasting, but common sense. Most of the time the West Indies bowlers were so much on top that everyone was round the bat, so you got full value for anything you got away, either off the middle or the deliberately played top edge.

I know I got a heap of praise for being the first England batsman to score three hundreds in a home series against the West Indies, but I still didn't get to 400 runs in the series, so I felt that I'd missed out somewhere.

The Lord's Test was different. Ian Botham bowled them out in the first innings, taking eight for 103 and, when he got 81 and I weighed in with 110, we were actually able to pick our time to declare early on the fifth day. I got some fearful stick in the press for taking the umpires' offer of the light the night before when, with 53 minutes to go, we were 328 ahead. 'Pring' had just come in, he could not see when the light was good, let alone when it was dark, and when I knew we were going to be offered the light, I looked up to our balcony, but nobody was there to advise us.

I thought we could lose the tail in no time, and as the West Indies wouldn't bat in that light, that could give them a full day for around 340 or so. That's why, after talking to Derek Pringle, I went off. It was as though I was on trial next morning. 'Lamb was booed all the way to the pavilion last night after making an amazing decision to go off for bad light', appeared in the *Sun*. Brian Scovell in the *Daily Mail* had got quotes from Gower, now captain in his own right, that the decision was mine, so the flak all came my way. What really settled it for me was when I knew that Clive Lloyd was going to bring back Marshall instead of Harper the off-spinner, who had just bowled Geoff Miller.

Only when I returned to the dressing-room did I find out why there was nobody on the balcony when I looked up for guidance. The television was on and everybody was watching Wimbledon, but not for the tennis. I got a few 'well played' comments before Both said, 'Hey, Lamby. Do you want to see some highlights of your innings? He then pushed the play button on the video and on came a blue movie. So that's why I was left to make my own decision about the light. At least I was not out overnight, which was more than could be said for the bloke in the movie! As Both put it, 'If our openers could stay in as long as him and play as many strokes, we'd never lose a Test match.'

Anyway, right or wrong, our situation was put into a different perspective next day when we batted on for twenty minutes and left them to score 342 in 81 overs. The rest is history, with Greenidge hitting an unbeaten 214, and the West Indies won with over 15 overs to spare. The way Gordon played that day, it would hardly have made any difference when we declared, because nobody could bowl to him. Both and Neil Foster went for 186 off 32 overs and that was more down to Gordon's brilliant play rather than bad bowling.

That was our last chance in the series and we blew it. I remember a couple of incidents in the game involving Both and Viv which shows one big difference between two great players and their attitude towards the game. There was always great rivalry between them and they were big mates, but Viv always set out to smash Both if he could.

He'd got to 72 in the fist innings when Both nipped one back from the Nursery end and strangled his lbw appeal because it was high and there might have been a nick as well. Barry Meyer gave Viv out and later apologised to him, but that wasn't the point. He dragged himself off at about two yards a fortnight, showing out all the way to the crowd that he wasn't out.

I didn't respect him for that because I've always believed that anybody is entitled to stand for anything, provided he goes with no fuss when he's given out. The difference between the two Somerset friends came when Both was also going well with 81 in our second innings when he was given out lbw to Big Joel Garner.

He looked disappointed briefly, but then walked off without any fuss, even though he'd hit it. In fact, the press never picked it up and it was only in a chance conversation with one of them in the next Test at Headingley that Both happened to mention he'd got a touch. He took his fair share of flak from the press in his career, but one thing they could never level at him was poor sportsmanship. He could get wound up with the best of them, but that was pure aggression, not cheating.

The best of my three hundreds was in the next Test at Headingley. I was now batting at no. 5 and went in at 53 for three and got the full treatment on a typical Headingley pitch from which the ball went up and down as well as sideways. I scored exactly 100 and helped the side to 237 for six at the end of the first day, but they cleaned us up for 270 and went on to win inside four days, with Marshall taking seven wickets with a plaster cast on his broken left wrist.

So to Old Trafford where I was in more trouble after another hundred. Again I got exactly 100, although this time I was not out under controversial circumstances. I was roasted by the media because they accused me of playing for myself and putting Paul Terry at risk when he came back after nine wickets were down to try to stick around while I got my hundred. Those critics can't have it both ways. All through my career I've been given stick for getting out to attacking shots, and I reckon I would have had a much better Test average if I had been selfish and not played for the side.

Davis had broken Terry's arm earlier, so he was in plaster and could only bat one-handed, holding the bat with his right hand. I was on strike when he came in, and faced the first five balls from Michael Holding without moving from 98. I told Paul we'd run whatever happened off the last ball, and we had an easy single to fine-leg. Paul called me back for the second run, which I took because I assumed that 'Lubo' would declare, as Paul told me when he came in that he was only there to try to help me to three figures. I started to walk off, only for the captain to wave us back, leaving Paul to make what he could of Garner. He lasted three balls before he was bowled.

Pat Pocock had come back for the last two Tests and was as full of theories as usual. He was a terrific off-spinner, but I've never heard so many theories about batting and cricket in general come from one bloke. This time he offered Paul a real lulu. 'Bat left-handed. That will protect your broken arm better'.

'No thanks. I don't fancy walking around with two broken arms.'

Pat was at it again in the final Test at The Oval. He went in as night-watchman and survived until next morning. In the Cornhill tent that night he was chirping away about what he was going to do in the morning, conveniently not mentioning that he'd bagged a pair at Old Trafford.

Joel joined the group and Pocock offered him his wicket in the morning in exchange for 20 runs. 'Big Bird' just smiled and shook his head. Pat tried again, more in hope than expectation.

'Ten runs, then?'

'No deal, man'.

'Four?'

'Not even one run'.

As the scorebook shows Garner was right. Pocock c Greenidge b Marshall 0.

I ended the summer with another hundred in the one-off Test against Sri Lanka and had this written about me by 'Blowers', the one and only Henry Blofeld: 'His whole approach as a batsman has changed. Two years ago he wanted to destroy an attack in perhaps one session. Now he is prepared to take more time to cut out the risks and consciously to build an innings in a way few contemporary batsmen are able to do. He has matured through this new self-imposed discipline into one of the most effective batsmen of his time.'

If the summer was the highpoint of my career so far, the winter of 1984-85, and the tour of India, was to start off in the worst possible way with the assassination of Mrs Gandhi, the Prime Minister. And I had a falling-out with the manager, Tony Brown.

No England tour has ever got off to a worse start. Mrs Gandhi was assassinated within hours of our arrival in Delhi, and the whole city erupted into a mass of riots and fires. We were confined to our hotel and given a massive security armed guard. A petrol station close by exploded and because things were in such chaos, the players had a meeting in which we aired our views. Gower was captain, and by this time I could count myself as one of the senior players, together with Pat Pocock, Phil Edmonds and Mike Gatting.

Cricket was the last thing on everyone's minds. It was also clear amongst the players that there was a strong view that we should call off the tour. I certainly held that view and offered to be the spokesman to the management.

We asked Gatting to call Tony Brown for a meeting. He came storming in, so I can only guess that Gatt had told him I wasn't keen on staying. I got up and started to speak, but he interrupted and said, 'You're the instigator of all this. If you feel like that you can take your passport and f*** off'.

It was the most inflammable time in my Test career and I told Lubo that under no circumstances would I play under Brown as manager. I was so wound up that if I could have got on a plane that night, I would have walked out of the tour, and therefore probably out on my England career. I was lucky that Lubo and Norman Gifford knew me so well. Since my Test debut three and a half years earlier, we had spent a lot of time together.

Had Lubo not been captain and Gifford the assistant manager, I doubt whether Brown or I would have listened, but Lubo defused the situation with some smart talking, and the matter never came up again. Of all the managers I've played under on tour, I trusted Tony Brown least, because the tour of India made me lose my faith in him. I also toured with him to the West Indies in 1985/86, but I never knew where I stood with him. I suppose the mistrust was mutual, because it was said to me that he made a remark in March 1996, when I was battling to play my last season and the TCCB were determined I would not play if this book was published before the end of the season. When he was informed that I wanted to play but that I refused to submit the draft to the Board before it went to the publishers, HarperCollins, he said: 'What does he want to be – a cricketer or an author?'

The political situation in India was so tense that, for the next week, nobody knew what would happen. We couldn't even practise for a while because of the state funeral, and it was a relief when we flew to Sri Lanka for a few days while the two cricket boards decided what would happen. While we were there we played a game against a President's XI, and an eighteen-year-old little genius scored his maiden first-class hundred despite having his innings interrupted for a visit to hospital after Neil Foster hit him in the face. It was Aravinda de Silva, and we saw enough then to recognise his huge talent.

The Indians suddenly wanted us to fulfil the original itinerary, which meant no first-class cricket between the first and second Tests. We weren't having that, but a compromise was worked out whereby one of the one-day internationals was shifted to the end of the tour and a three-day game put in against North Zone.

After a month, we had settled down a bit, only to go back to square one on the morning of Tuesday 27 November, the day before the start of the first Test in Bombay. Perce Pocock telephoned the home of the British Deputy High Commissioner, Percy Norris, to thank him for a smashing evening he and his family put on for us the previous night.

He was one of the first to be told that Percy had been shot dead by a gunman on his way to his office only fifteen minutes earlier. Perce knew him as a friend and was shattered. He immediately told the captain, the manager, Norman Gifford and Bernie Thomas, but the rest of us were kept in the dark until later that morning, just before our net practice.

They kept it from us because, with a terribly sad irony, we were lined up in the hotel gardens for the touring party photograph which would appear on the front of the official Christmas cards we would all send home. When they told us, we were numb. On the way to the ground we passed within two hundred yards of where he was killed, and it knocked the stuffing out of us, just as I'm told happened in the middle of the Barbados Test match in 1981 when Kenny Barrington died of a heart attack.

Nobody wanted to practise or play the next day, but we were told we had got to soldier on as best we could. The Taj Mahal hotel can never before have been swarming with so many armed guards. We heard that Percy was being driven by his chauffeur and neither was armed. The car was a standard model without bullet-proofing, and all we could think about was the senselessness of it all. He had been honoured in the previous New Year list and was not far off retirement.

That tragedy struck home with all of us. Peter Smith wrote this in the *Daily Mail*. 'Given a free vote, I believe every England player would wish to return home from this most bedevilled tour. They slept under armed guard last night on the eve of the Test they don't want to play. They are being asked by the Foreign Office local diplomats, the Indian Government and the TCCB to play a Test that their hearts simply aren't in.

'Tony Brown said, "We have two choices. We play the game or we go home. Some of the players are apprehensive but, with all the security, being out in the middle might be the safest place. There was some consideration about putting back the start for twenty-four hours but that would have given the players more time to sit around and think".

'I believe the decision is wrong. I don't blame Brown, who is managing his first tour. He is caught in the middle. Calling off the tour is not a decision he can make. Throughout the troubled last month, he has acted with great dignity, his calmness soothing the anxieties of David Gower and his team.

'But how much more can we ask these sportsmen to endure before Lord's realises that one Test – one Test series – is irrelevant on a tour already hit by two assassinations, rioting, looting and mass murder. I have not been with a side so stunned and shaken as this one following the shooting of Mr Norris.'

Peter Smith was one of the most trustworthy of journalists and he got the mood of the side spot on but what could we do? We were told to try to put everything else out of our minds, so we had to play.

Tony Lewis presented the other side of the debate. 'I am delighted that the England manager and captain resolved to stay and play. They must be complimented on making a courageous decision with so much gloom and doom around them.

'Their resolve not to rush for the nearest dug-out was right. Of course everyone is nervous and a little afraid, but if you run away from a cricket match because of an unpremeditated murder, terrorism will rule every corner of our lives'.

Fowler asked, 'If a cracker goes off, how are we supposed to know whether it's a bullet or not?' The tension was impossible to put out of your mind, and I could understand why the West Indies and Australia would not go to Sri Lanka for the World Cup. It was a similar situation. We played and they did not, but I would have been much happier to call off that Test and I know the other players felt the same.

It would have been a miracle if we had won, but miracles in cricket don't happen that often. We were beaten by eight wickets, but from the lowest point on tour of any side I have been with, we hauled ourselves back to become one of only two England sides to win in India in nine tours since the Second World War. Tony Greig's side was the other one, eight years earlier.

The turning point was the second Test, at Delhi. Once we got a lead of 111, thanks to 160 from Tim Robinson, Perce Pocock and Phil Edmonds strangled the Indian batsmen in the second innings by taking eight for 153 between them off 82 overs and we won by eight wickets. Despite our first sight of Azharuddin scoring three hundreds in his first three Tests, we also won at Madras and drew the other two matches at Calcutta and Kanpur.

'Foxy' Fowler and Gatt got double hundreds at Madras, and Neil Foster had his best Test with 11 wickets, including Gavaskar, Vengsarkar, and Amarnath twice. We had a bit of an incident in Hyderabad in the match before that Test. We were staying at our hotel which overlooked a big lake. A few of us decided to sail around the lake after dinner one night in a couple of gondolas. We were coming in to land when suddenly we were bombarded with a shower of oranges, thrown from a couple of the rooms on the second floor.

All good fun, except the aim was bit off and one or two guests on the patio got an unscheduled delivery of orange juice. Receiving the pith, I suppose. The management got a few complaints and insisted on an apology before the matter was closed. Who were the entrants in to the Hyderabad Orange Whanging competition of 1985? I never have been a whistle-blower, but let's just say that the captain was not tucked up in bed reading when the first orange was thrown.

In the rain-ruined third Test at Calcutta, we had bowled altogether 217 overs for only seven wickets with poor Richard Ellison and Pat Pocock getting one wicket between them for 105 overs of blood, sweat and tears. Then, a few minutes before the end of a dead game, on came Lamby with India's deputy openers, Manoj Prabhakar and Ravi Shastri, all set for a nice easy couple of not-outs. I measured out a long run and charged in with my imitation of Bob Willis. By the time I was halfway to the crease, I felt knackered and got slower and slower before I let the ball go. As it left my hand, it was almost in reverse thrust.

Manoj played three different shots before he tried a fourth as the ball hit his pad. Out. Plumb lbw. In the book. Did I give the bowlers some stick! It was my first and only wicket in a Test match. There are seven other batsmen, including five more Test players – Wasim Bari, Sadiq Mohammad, Chris Balderstone, Graeme Fowler and, of course, Peter Kirsten – who will go to their graves wondering how on earth they managed to get out to me, for they, and David Lloyd's son Graham and Ian Redpath of Essex, were my only victims in over 450 matches. No rubbish there!

From India we had to go to Australia for a so-called World Championship but we were never in shape for that after the four months in India, especially with those two tragic deaths in the first month. In the semi-final we needed to score 214 in 32 overs to nip through the back door into the final. I managed 81 off 69 balls, but we never got close, and it was a shame that such a good result in India should have been tarnished by the two weeks in Australia.

Despite this, I was pleased for David Gower because with him as captain, the dressing-room was never dull. He always seemed laid-back, of course, but I know him well enough to say that he feels as strongly about things as the rest of us. He has his highs and lows and is bitterly disappointed when he doesn't score many runs, but his way of dealing with that is to hide his feelings and present a front to the public which is often misleading. They think he doesn't care, but he does. And he's as tough a fighting competitor as someone who scowls his way off when he's out.

The next home series against Australia in the summer of 1985 was a great one for him and for England. We beat them 3–1 and he made 732 runs in the six Tests with a double at Edgbaston, 166 at Trent Bridge and 157 at The Oval to make sure we won back the Ashes. I was ordinary with 256 runs in seven completed innings, but did enough to get picked for my first tour of the West Indies. Tony Brown was manager again, and what a fiasco of a tour it turned out to be.

To start with, the Gooch 'rebels' were back, and that didn't help. Goochie himself, John Emburey and Pete Willey didn't help team spirit, because I reckon they went out there in the wrong frame of mind. There was a good chance that we might run into political trouble, and I'd hear them say things like 'the first bit of trouble and we should bail out and go home'. Which was fair enough, if there were lives in danger.

They were all on the previous tour there in 1980-81, and I know they had a bellyful after the Robin Jackman deportation from Guyana, but you can't live in the past forever. Goochie at that time was not a happy tourist and one of the reasons why Peter Willey played 15 of his 26 Tests for England was because he had a bolshie attitude to life and he refused to let anyone get on top of him. He's a toughie and I respect him for a lot, but he was one of those who made it clear that the West Indies was not one of his favourite places to tour.

It needed just one thing to put the whole party on the back foot, and it came when the Prime Minster of Antigua, Lester Bird, had a pop at Gooch in a way that got under his skin.

Goochie has always been touchy about South Africa, and the Bird song of war got to him. He said that he was so insulted by his criticism of him that he didn't want to go to Antigua for the final Test, and it took a summit meeting in Trinidad before he was persuaded to play by Tony Brown, Willis, Gower and Donald Carr, who flew in from London especially to talk to Gooch.

Before that, the first Test in Jamaica was one of the most frightening I've ever played in. We weren't too confident after Mike Gatting got pinned flush on the nose in the one-day international a few days earlier by 'Maco' Marshall, and I can't remember feeling so nervous as when I had to pass him as he was led off with his nose spreadeagled and blood all over.

It was bad enough taking guard with blood on the crease, but I felt even worse when Maco stopped halfway in his run-up to deliver my first ball. He went to the umpire, gave him the ball and said, 'I can't bowl with that. There's a piece of Gatt's nose stuck in the seam'.

The Test pitch was like a hard corrugated sheet with huge cracks. Michael Holding's first ball to Gooch went straight over his head off a good length and nearly hit the sightscreen full. I thought there was no point in hanging about so I whacked the first wide one for four, and heard Viv from slip call out, 'No more drive balls Maco. I want him to smell the leather'. Knowing that Gatt would smell very little for a few weeks, I was quite keen to keep some distance between the ball and my nostrils. Maco followed instructions and it came close enough to me for me to catch a glimpse of the label 'Duke's' as it screamed by. I've usually managed to find a bit of fun in cricket, whatever the state of the game, but not that morning in Kingston.

The next Viv remark was another confidence-builder. 'Come on Maco. Let's see a serious delivery.' I turned round and asked what he meant. He just smiled – then said, 'It's one that you eat, Lamby'.

I'm not saying I was keen to get out, but when I was given out to a dodgy appeal for a caught behind, I walked. Usually I stand for everything, but I just fancied a change of scenery because it struck me that life can, on occasions, be more important than a cricket match. Phil Edmonds was different. He was beamed twice by Patrick Patterson and the second one flattened him. It hit him under the heart and he collapsed. He fell on his wickets and was obviously out, hit wicket. But Phil wasn't going to go that easily. As he was helped to his feet by some very concerned fielders, he casually put the bails back on and nobody appealed. So he continued his innings.

His wife Frances was sitting watching, and a local journalist asked her what her first thoughts were when Phil was poleaxed. If the journalist thought he was going to get a few good human quotes about her fears, he soon knew different.

'Darling, my first thought was, "Now in which drawer at home are his insurance policies?"'

We lost easily, as we did all the other games to cop a second successive 'blackwash'. It was easily the hardest tour I've ever been on, because we were smashed sideways in every match. Patterson was a real loose cannon. Bloody quick but all over the place. We never competed, mainly because the guys seemed to accept the inevitable and just bat in a survival mode, and we weren't helped by the lack of good practice facilities on most grounds.

The exception was David Smith of Sussex, who took the bolshie attitude too far the other way. I was in with him at Port-of-Spain, and he had such a go at their bowlers that I spent all my time trying to shut him up. It started when he was hit by 'Patto'. When someone went to see if he was OK, he waved him away and said, 'That was my fault. It should have gone out of the park'. Dessie Haynes politely pointed out that 'it hasn't', whereupon Smithy told him to shove off and mind his own business ... or something like that.

They had a full sledging row, and I thought it was time to step in. I wasn't so bothered about the image of the game, but I was concerned at the effect Smithy would have on their other bowlers. The row went on with Viv now involved, and arms were being waved about.When Viv politely told him that he 'had got the equaliser' I went down the pitch.

'Look Smithy, life's tough enough against this lot when they're calm. What's the fun in winding them up? We'll end up getting six an over.'

'Bollocks. Tell Viv I'll see him after,' was the gist of a reply that wasn't the most helpful I've ever heard, and we were both given a working over. I've never prayed for a colleague to get out before but when Greenidge caught Smith on the hook off Patterson for 47, I thought that would calm things down. I heard a cheer as our next batsman came in, and I turned to have a look who it was. Only Both, swinging his arms as though he was going to murder them!

We lost just as soundly in Barbados where, as usual, there were a few thousand England supporters and they had a full go at us after the match because we didn't have net practices. I know that practice helps most times, but I've never believed in naughty boy nets like that. The management seemed to lose the plot. Tony Brown didn't get on with his assistant, Bob Willis. He didn't seem to know what his role was and spent most of his time organising the bowling machine to rocket a few shells at us. I felt sorry for Lubo, but we all had a laugh when he walked in to bat in the final Test in Antigua.

The double-decker stand to the left of the dressing-rooms was packed and several ghetto-blasters were going at full pelt all through the match. When Lubo walked in, they synchronised, with each one blasting out a new calypso which was riding high in the charts, 'Captain, your ship is sinking.'

And sink we did, with Viv hitting the fastest ever Test hundred off 56 balls. The British press were thumbing through *Wisden* to check on the fastest 50 – his came off 32 balls – when one of them said, 'Hey, he's 90 not out. What about the quickest hundred?'

Two of his sixes were astonishing shots. John Emburey was bowling and Viv shimmied his feet to try to throw 'Embers'. He guessed right and as Viv retreated leg-side to hit him inside out, he followed him and speared in an ankle-high full-toss which would have missed leg stump by a couple of feet. Ordinary batsmen would have tried to help it to round towards square leg, but Viv was never ordinary. He stayed inside the line and hit a skimmer towards Neil Foster at long off. I thought Viv would do well to reach him on the full, until 'Fossie' suddenly craned his neck backwards to watch the ball sail over his head about six rows back.

That was a carry of at least ninety yards – and from a low leg-side full toss. Both wouldn't let the ball go at the other end, because he was after the one wicket he needed to equal Dennis Lillee's 355, and thought he was bound to get one with the slog on.

He bowled a little outswinger outside off stump and short of half volley length. Viv's ears went back, he hit it on the up over extra cover, over the boundary rope, over the ledge of the first layer of the double decker stand, over the second ledge and into the 11th row of the top deck. That was a carry of around 120 yards – and over extra cover if you please.

I had a poor series with 224 runs from 10 innings and knew I would struggle to keep my place when we got home for the two series against India and New Zealand. Gower was sacked after India beat us at Lord's and Gatting took over. The switch was handled badly by Peter May. When he asked Gatt if he would take the job at the end of the match, Gatt asked for time to think about it and was told to give an immediate yes or no.

Then Gower was left on his own at the press conference, with PBH even refusing to make any comment on the switch. All the press wanted was some sort of comment on his captaincy in 25 Tests, but May would not say one word.

Yes, he'd had a bad tour of the West Indies, but he did beat Australia at home and India away, so surely that deserved a bit of praise?

15

'When you're Dropped or Injured…'

I had a poor couple of Tests against India in 1986, scoring only 65 runs in four innings, so I was glad to be picked for the one-day games against New Zealand, even if the one at Old Trafford caused a few headlines because of our visit to a wine bar in Hale the night before the match. A guy came up to me and said that I shouldn't be drinking champagne, and I told him I play better on champagne. I know we run the risk of being criticised when we have a drink, but I also don't see why that should stop me relaxing when I want to. Some cricketers cut the risk out by not being seen much in public, but I count that as giving in. We won the Old Trafford game, thanks to Bill Athey's 142 not out, and I was hopeful that I could get back into the side for the Cornhill Tests. I'd been lucky with injuries, but now I developed a knee problem that was worrying. I was told that rest would cure it, but I didn't want to miss any games for Northants unless I had to.

I wanted to know what my Test chances were, so I asked Gatt. He said that I was more or less certain to be picked, so I went to Geoff Cook before our weekend game against Glamorgan at Swansea. I told him the position and asked him to rest me so that I would definitely be fit for the Test. He agreed, but was not too pleased when he heard the England side on the Sunday morning and I wasn't in. Geoff was the man who actually told me I had missed out. He said, 'You have bullshitted me', and when I asked him why, he said that I wasn't in the XII. I couldn't believe it, not after what Gatt told me.

I know that the England captain doesn't always get his way, but I lost a bit of trust in Gatt after that. I played in the final Test against

New Zealand at The Oval and came back with a duck, bowled by Ewen Chatfield. I played in the one-day games, but now I was worried in case I missed the tour of Australia. Again Gatt told me not to worry as I was a certainty, but I couldn't help saying, 'You mean like against New Zealand?' My knee was still troubling me and I had a brace which I needed to inflate with my mouth, so I got a few jokes about do-it-yourself blow jobs.

Until 1992, my final year in Test cricket, 1986 was my worst season at home. I tried not to get depressed, but five years as an England regular had given me a good lifestyle, and I had shown that I could play against the best. It doesn't matter who you are, when you're dropped, all you think about is that it could be the end of your run. And I was thirty-three, so I couldn't afford too many games out of the side. It was a huge relief to hear that I was going to Australia, and it was good to be part of a new set-up, what with Gatt making his first trip to Australia, Peter Lush and Micky Stewart as the new management team and John Emburey also making his debut Down Under.

From a results angle, it was one of the two most successful tours I have made – India in 1984/85 was the other. We were expected to be hammered, but Both set the tone with a terrific 138 at Brisbane. He smashed the daylights out of Merv Hughes – 22 in one over – and with the rest of us getting a few, we scored 456, made them follow on and won by seven wickets. Embers bowled them out in the second innings, and we were on our way. Also it was our first win in 11 Tests, so it was the start of something special. We drew in Perth – yours truly 0 and 2, but Broad, Gower and Jack Richards all got big hundreds and we were never on the wrong end of the game. Adelaide was another draw. 'Broady' got another hundred and so did Gatt, but I couldn't get going with 14 and nine not out. Both missed the game because of a rib injury, and was nowhere near fit for the fourth Test in Melbourne which started on Boxing Day. He still insisted on playing and what a match he had. Dilley pulled out on the morning of the match and Gladstone Small came in, and between them he and Both won the match by bowling the Aussies out for 141. They each got five wickets and Both caught three for 'Glad'.

Broady did it again, with his third hundred in three Tests – only Sutcliffe and Hammond had done that before in Australia – and with most of us chipping in we got 349 and had them by the throat. We beat them in three days, and what a party we had. There were a few on that trip, because Elton John was also on tour, and we went to a lot of his concerts. Not many big concerts are planned around a Test itinerary, but Elton made sure he saw all the Tests.

David Gower and I gave a drinks party on the eve of that one-day game in Sydney, the one in which I managed 18 off the final over from Bruce Reid. Because it was an afternoon start, a late night didn't matter so much, and a lot of the players and media went to a party for which Lizzie Cattell, a big mate of Lindsay's who had quite a sense of humour, did the catering.

I'd heard of spiking drinks to get a party going, but Lizzie did something different. Quite early in the evening, I thought one or two of the guys were going nicely. I'd only had a couple of drinks and when other people start to get pissed and you're still sober, you wonder what's going on

George Michael, Richie Benaud, Tony Greig, Bill Lawry and most of the television guys were there, and it got noisier and noisier. I went into the kitchen, where Lizzie was smiling to herself. I asked her what was going on and she asked me if I'd had anything to eat. I hadn't and that explained why I was off the pace. She had only gone and spiked some of the canapes.

It reminded me of the same sort of incident in our tour of New Zealand in 1984, when some friends made a cake for the manager, A C Smith. A couple of slices and he was gone. One mouthful was enough for anyone.

There was plenty of champagne at the Sydney party, because the Bollinger agent, Rob Hurst, did a deal with Lubo and me. He offered us two cases of different champagne, depending on the result of the series. An Aussie win would get us a top of the range RD75. A drawn series would mean the vintage Grande Nanée, and if we won we would get the non-vintage Bollinger.

The tour was a great success, and it all started from the top. Lush and Stewart were brilliant, and with 10 players who had never played in Australia before, they involved Lubo, Both, Dilley and me for advice. They were feeling their way, but weren't too proud to say so and they listened to whatever we had to say. I enjoyed 'Lushy' at least as much as any other manager I played under, although towards the end of his time, I found I couldn't trust him as much. The more I reflect on managers, the more certain I am that A C was easily the best. He never let any of us down in public and was a players' man through and through.

I had a poor series personally, so I knew that I would struggle at home in the series against Pakistan, who would be playing five Tests in England and then three in Pakistan.

All I could do was to hope I would go to India and Pakistan for the World Cup, but even when I was picked, I was told that I was not certain to stay for the three Test series. Too right, because even though I was our top batsman in the World Cup, I was sent home straight after the Final in Calcutta. We played our qualifying matches in both countries, and it was in Rawalpindi that Goochie and I got into a spot of trouble with the management over a late night. We were a bit unlucky, because we went to a party at the British High Commission immediately after we booked into the hotel. We assumed our bags would be in our rooms when we got back, but the porter left them outside in the corridor. We stayed at the reception after everyone else went back to the hotel, so we had no chance of convincing the management that we had an early night, when our bags were still out in the morning.

We had a good tournament with the usual spot of fun and games in the middle. The best was in Rawalpindi, when Javed was given out lbw by Tony Crafter. That sort of dismissal was about as rare as Both and I running an evangelist meeting after a 'dry' month without a drink.

Javed walked off, and had to pass a group of us congratulating Phil DeFreitas who had beaten the system. A remark was passed which Javed heard – nothing insulting but just suggesting that his surprise at being given out didn't quite square with the merits of the decision. He stopped, came back and waded into the middle of us to gently place his palm against Gatt's cheek. That sort of set the tone for the tour, and it was no surprise to me what happened later at Lahore and Faisalabad.

I made runs in every game except against Pakistan in Karachi and felt in good nick, so it was disappointing to go home before the Tests started.

We beat India in the semi-final in Bombay, thanks to Goochie playing one of the best sweeping innings I have ever seen, and Eddie Hemmings diddling out Kapil after he had just been hit for six. Eddie had wanted a fielder at mid-wicket, but Gatt disagreed. Eddie looped one up as though to prove his point and six was signalled. Another conversation with Gatt who reluctantly went to deep mid-wicket. The trap was too obvious, so when Eddie tossed the next one up even higher, we expected the block. Not with Kapil. With no heroics needed, he went for gold, and Gatt did not have to move one step to take the catch.

We expected to play Pakistan in the final if we beat India, but Australia put them out in Lahore, so it was the final that the whole of India and Pakistan wanted least, England against Australia.

I know we lost, but I also know why. Not because they played better than us, but because we had the wrong batting order.

I had a big discussion with Gatt and Micky, because I thought I should have gone in ahead of Bill Athey. Nothing against him, but I had been in such good form and I knew we couldn't afford to get bogged down. I had gone 87 not out, 30, 76, 9, 40, and 32 not out, with most of the runs coming when we needed to up the tempo. We couldn't afford to get stuck against the Aussies; wickets in hand are all very well, but you can't afford to fall too far below the asking rate and I pleaded with them to let me go in early. They wouldn't listen and paid the price. That's why we lost by seven runs after too many of us had to have a slog in the second part of the innings.

The Calcutta crowd were brilliant considering it was England against Australia, but it was a sickener to miss out on what would have been England's first ever World Cup win.

It was in Calcutta on 'Lubo's tour' that I had a fairly unusual New Year. A few of us went to the Tollygunge golf club for New Year's Eve, and guess what? Lamby stayed on after the other players went back to the hotel, so now I'd got the problem of trying to arrange transport at well after midnight. I walked on to the main road and took a chance with the first car that stopped for the lonely Englishman just a couple of hours into 1985.

It was one of those trishaws that, flat out and downwind, can get up to about 10 miles a fortnight. It was a trip of about four miles, so after we had covered double that distance and we were nowhere near, I knew I'd picked a driver whose geography was even vaguer than mine.

It was now 3 am, and Calcutta is not the ideal place to roam around on your own, but I didn't want to extend the mystery tour much longer. I made him stop, paid up and got out and wondered what was next. I'd had plenty of Indian whiskey, but the next few minutes in the dark sobered me up very quickly. The pay-off was that a police car stopped to investigate, and gave me a lift back to the hotel. As it happened, it rained the next day and I didn't have to put my hangover to the test.

As soon as I knew that I wouldn't be staying for the Tests in Pakistan, I announced that I would be playing for Orange Free State back in South Africa for the rest of the English winter. Free State had spoken to me about it before the World Cup, but I didn't know whether someone might get injured in Pakistan, so I asked Free State to sit on it until I knew definitely that I would be available.

It was a delicate situation in many ways, because I knew Australia was going to file a proposal to the ICC that players with recent South African connections could be rejected by countries hosting Test series. I was well aware that I might have played my last game for England, but I still had hopes of a comeback because West Indies were touring England in 1988, and my track record against them was bound to count for something.

I was offered the chance to play for Free State as one of their overseas players, so I was not compromising my England Test qualification in any way. Before I signed the contract, I told the TCCB that if England had any injuries, I would be available if required, so I had cleared all areas of doubt.

As the Currie Cup rules were then, a province could play more than one overseas cricketer and I would be joining Alvin Kallicharran and Sylvester Clarke who had already signed. On 12 November 1986 Ali Bacher confirmed my registration, as he did with Neal Radford and Bruce Roberts who both played for Transvaal as overseas players, so I was not on my own.

I signed to play six Currie Cup matches, because I had to return to England in January 1988 to prepare for my benefit year. The first contact was made back in England before the World Cup by Mike Procter who had just signed to become Director of Cricket at Free State, and was happy to complete negotiations as soon as I knew England didn't want me.

I was a professional cricketer who was out of work for three months so, providing I did not contravene any registration regulations in South Africa or England, I reckoned I was as entitled to earn my living there as was any other business man. I got a lot of publicity when I arrived at Bloemfontein, and although I knew my own contract, I didn't know about other sponsored incentives on offer for various individual performances.

My first Currie Cup match for six years was quite something – especially as I had often been criticised with Western Province for not going on to big scores often enough. We played Eastern Province at home, and they had a strong side with Kepler Wessels, Mark Rushmere, Kenny McEwan, Dave Richardson, Dave Callaghan, Greg Thomas and Rod McCurdy. I went in at 48 for three – they had declared with 268 for seven – and everything I tried came off. I ended up with 294, then the highest score ever made in South Africa, and we won the game off the very last ball when Sylvester mowed McCurdy for six when we needed five to win.

Our captain, Joubert Strydom, helped me to put on 355 for the fifth wicket, and we were over £30,000 better off from a sponsorship deal with South African Breweries in conjunction with Holland Insurance. I've always considered myself to be a team man, so Mike Procter and the boys were thrilled when I put the cash into the team kitty. That's how I've always operated and I saw no reason to change because the amount was so big.

After a start like that, I finished top of the averages with 837 runs for 10 innings, two not-outs, with three hundreds and three fifties and an average of over 100. I agreed to fly back in the middle of February to play at Wanderers against Transvaal in the Currie Cup Final, but I was rolled over for eight and 33 and we lost by ten wickets.

Back in England for the 1988 summer, I knew I needed a good start to the season to get back against the West Indies, but I didn't get a big score before either the Texaco games or the first Test. I was a bit lucky to play at Nottingham, but not so fortunate when I was given out lbw for a duck to Maco Marshall to one which ... well, it did quite a lot.

I stayed in for Lord's where we lost, as usual. England have a poorer record at Lord's than at any other home ground, but there is no obvious reason other than that most touring sides love to play there, because of its sense of history. When I went in in the second innings, we were 31 for three, needing 442 to win, so it was just a matter of trying to save the game. I got 113 before I was run out, so

I felt a bit happier, especially as I'd been drawn into the Rothley Court fiasco which cost Gatt the captaincy. During the Trent Bridge Test, I went home on the Saturday night because we had the Sunday as a rest day. It seems that Gatt was set up, but it was beyond me how I could be dragged into it as I was at home having dinner with Dennis Lillee. I couldn't believe it when I was called to the hearing at Lord's. This was the one in which Peter May said afterwards that they accepted Gatt's explanation, and then sacked him. The press were door stepping, so I had to pass them twice on my way in and out of the hearing. I was told to say nothing by the committee, but I was only in the room for a couple of minutes to tell them that I was at home when it had been reported that I was at Rothley Court.

I've been to a few inquiries in my time and have had my share of fines, but never before have I had such a cast-iron alibi.

We lost the series 4–0, but I remember the fourth Test at Headingley because it was Robin Smith's debut for England. When I heard he was picked, I couldn't help thinking back six years. He had followed the same road as me from South Africa, and now here he was making his England debut on the same ground, and I knew how nervous he was. Not only because of a first Test cap, but because of worrying how he would be accepted into the dressing-room. I remembered how good to me were guys like Lubo, Both and Willis, so I went out of my way to try to settle him down.

The only difference was that it was a different hotel, where the accommodation was the log-cabin type, with two rooms to a building. I was in the next room to Robin and Cath, and when I heard them talking on the first night through the communicating door, I shouted for them to stop the sex and concentrate on the match next day. That started them laughing, and the giggling got so loud that anyone outside must have thought there was an ex-pat South African orgy going on.

We were put in to bat and when 'Judge' – Robin Smith's nickname because of his hair style – came in to join me, we were 80 for four and bang in trouble. That sort of situation in any Test match is a tight one, but when it is your debut as well and everything is new, it's as though your bat is like a matchstick and your feet are stuck in treacle. I knew he'd get a few bouncers, and after the first couple which he ducked and dived against, I went down the pitch and said, 'Come on, Judgie. Cath has just wet her knickers, so you'd better get some runs'. It worked because after he had hit a couple of fours and got a few more bouncers, he came down to me and said, 'I'm enjoying this. It's good isn't it?' I wouldn't say enjoyment was ever top of my list against the West Indies, but I could see how caught up in everything he was, and I was proud that the two of us, both born in South Africa, but now ready to die for England, were out there fighting together.

We gradually got on top – well, as much on top as you ever get against Marshall, Curtly Ambrose and Courtney Walsh, but then I tore a calf muscle, going for a quick single, so badly that I was out of cricket for a month. We had batted together for two hours and I was desperate to stay on, but Laurie Brown, our physio, said it was impossible. So I went off and that started a collapse in which the last five wickets went for 18 runs – and 16 of those came in the last wicket partnership between Foster and Dilley.

Laurie packed my leg with ice and put me on crutches, but it was such a bad tear, that I could do nothing but hobble around. The next day, it seemed to get a bit easier, and I had a bit of fun at the hotel. They had some geese in the grounds and I managed to get them into Laurie's room, where they crapped everywhere before he chased them out. 'You little bastard. You can treat your own leg now,' was what I got, so I threw my crutches away and batted second innings with a runner.

My right leg wouldn't take any weight at all, so I could only play forward, but I managed to stick around for well over an hour after coming in at no. 8. Curtly let me have a lot of bouncers, but no complaint from me about that. If I chose to bat when I was injured, he was quite right to treat me as normal. Micky Stewart paid me a nice compliment: 'What we saw from Allan today was typical of him. He was marvellous'.

I tried to make it for The Oval Test, but it was hopeless – although I did get back for the Lord's Test against Sri Lanka and ended the season well with 63. We won in the first over after lunch, but Judge and Tim Robinson got some stick from Gooch and Emburey in particular for not finishing the game off in the last over of the morning session. They were desperate to get away and go and play for Essex and Middlesex in the four-day games starting at The Oval and Hove. If we had won before lunch, they would have both been at the other grounds by the start of the afternoon play, but when

Robinson played out the final three balls of the morning with the scores level, they had to stay for well over another hour because of the post-match ceremonies.

It was adding insult to injury when Judge hit the winning boundary straight after the break, because the presentations were delayed until BBC television came back live – and that was fifteen minutes later because they were showing *Neighbours*. As it happened Essex were fielding and Middlesex batting, so both of them got away with it.

16
Captain of Northants

Most people thought when Geoff Cook stepped down from the captaincy of the Northants team at the end of 1988, that his successor would either be Nick Cook or Wayne Larkins. However, I was also keen to become involved, but my big problem was that I would be away a lot, always assuming that I stayed in the England side.

What convinced me to declare my interest was that there were several England cricketers who had captained their counties, such as Mike Gatting, Graham Gooch and David Gower, and they seemed to be able to manage it. I told Steve Coverdale, who was Secretary/Manager at the time and later Chief Executive of the club, that I was interested, although I knew he was keen on Nick, who was considered to be the front runner. The club also looked outside for a captain and I know that Chris Tavaré was approached, but Kent wanted him to stay, and Northamptonshire weren't prepared to use one of their precious contested registrations on him.

I knew I had at least five or six years left and, after eleven seasons with the club, I wanted to try to turn them from a team of talented cricketers into a winning side. The attitude needed changing in order to make everyone play for the side. I reckoned that the main difference between Geoff Cook and myself was that he wanted to do everything himself, but I wished to involve the other players.

I remember one incident in Geoff's period as captain in 1986. I was talking to Neil Mallender in one game, and Geoff shouted across to me, 'Leave the bowlers alone. If they need talking to, I'll do it'. I thought that was wrong, but I kept quiet after that and

Mallender moved to Somerset. Never once did Geoff tap me up for any input, but in my view the more heads that were involved, the better.

When I got the job, I made sure that the first thing I did was to talk to Nick and 'Ned', because they were bound to be disappointed, and I needed them on side if I was going to do any sort of job. Ned was all right about it, as I guessed he would be because he is such a laid-back guy. Cooky was different. He was much more intense and perhaps he had been led on to think he would get the job. I spoke to both of them at a farewell party for Geoff after the end of the season, and was pleased when, in the end, Cooky seemed to accept the situation.

My first year in charge, 1989, wasn't a great success, mainly because of Test calls and injury. I only played in eight of the 22 matches and found that when I came back after a Test match, I had to start all over again regarding a proper routine of time keeping and net practices. Ned was captain when I was away, but he wasn't strict enough to follow through with what I wanted.

I hadn't had much experience at captaincy, so I did a few things wrong in my first year. For instance, in one-day cricket, I didn't always get the bowling right regarding who bowled when and at which end. After each game, I tried to analyse what I had done, and was always looking for improvement.

I became depressed. I don't often quit, but I came close to it towards the end of that first season in charge. A couple of the senior players tried to talk me round, but what really convinced me I should stay was when Frank Chamberlain took over as Chairman of the TCCB, and Lynn Wilson got on the club committee and soon became Chairman.

Nothing against Frank, but I knew Lynn so well that I believed that we could work together and make the side into a good one. And a winning one, rather than one that flattered to deceive.

We had strengthened the quick bowling by signing Greg Thomas and Curtly Ambrose. We already had Winston Davis, because clubs could register two overseas cricketers even though they could only play one at a time. Thomas was my idea because I had seen him in the West Indies and knew he was sharp, but I hadn't realised how stubborn he was. He got 66 wickets in his first year, Davis took 50, David Capel 51 and Curtly 28, which was why I was disappointed we didn't win more than seven matches, even though we finished fifth – our highest finish since 1976.

As for the boy from West Wales, I will never forget what he said when I suggested that Dennis Lillee had a look at him to try to help him in one or two areas: 'No thanks, I'm bowling all right'. Nice one, Greg. I know how easily bowlers can get messed about with the wrong advice, but Dennis was not only one of the all time greats, but it didn't take him long to make his mark as a coach.

In 1990, I played in ten games, and had the same problem again whenever I came back after playing for England. But I was a stronger captain on my thoughts and discipline, because I had tightened up a lot about punctuality and dress. I was never too special at either, but knew I had to set an example if I was to get the respect of the players.

I set up a fining system for latecomers, in which the money went into a pool, and we had a party at the end of the season. That was another thing – I decided to distance myself a bit from the players. As an ordinary player, I enjoyed going out for a drink and a meal after the close of play, but I also knew that we didn't want the captain around all the time, so I deliberately stepped back a bit.

What I tried to do from the start was to encourage everyone to express themselves on the field for the benefit of the side. When I first got into the side, players like Peter Willey and David Steele used to play for themselves first and the side second, and their attitude rubbed off on younger players. There was one game when I was in with Peter and we had got maximum batting points, but I carried on playing my shots. Peter came down the pitch and said that I shouldn't be doing that because we couldn't get any more batting points. He told me to play for a nice not-out, but that is something I've never done.

We were nowhere in the championship in 1990, but we got to the NatWest Final after three cracking games against Nottinghamshire, Worcestershire and Hampshire. They were all high-scoring games, but I was most pleased with how I juggled the bowlers around in what were three tight finishes.

We beat Notts by 20 runs, but looked dead and buried against Worcestershire, when Botham batted and had the game as good as won, before the other players lost their heads. We were able to pressure them into some unnecessary slogs, and keep Both off strike, and finally won by five runs.

I'd known Both for more than 10 years, but I dared not say a word to him as we walked off. The steam was coming out of his ears, because he knew that they would win 19 out of 20 of such games – but this time it was the 20th.

The Hampshire game at Southampton was another which was running away from us when Gower and Marshall batted together and put off 141 in 26 overs. But I knew that 'Lubo' only played one way, which was the main reason why he rarely finished a one-day game off. There are times when you have done the hard work and you can cruise home without taking unnecessary risks, but Lubo would never throttle back. So I brought on our spinners, Cook and Williams, and it worked. Lubo holed out in the deep off Richard Williams, and Maco and Mark Nicholas went to Nick Cook. It still went to the last ball of the last over which was brilliantly bowled by Mark Robinson, and we won by one run to reach the Final against Lancashire.

As we prepared for the big game, I could only think back to the three previous Finals we had played in ten years, and the heartbreaking way we had lost them. I have to give Geoff Cook credit for getting us there, and I know how desperate he was to win something for our supporters. He was shattered when we became the first side to lose two Finals with the scores tied, because we lost more wickets than Derbyshire and then Yorkshire, in 1981 and 1987 respectively.

I helped to lose the other game against Nottinghamshire, also in 1987, when I dropped a couple of catches off Richard Hadlee in his last big match in England. So when we got to Lord's against Lancashire, thanks to that last-ball win at Southampton, I hoped our luck would change.

It didn't, mainly because the toss in the September Final is so vital, it almost makes the game a lottery. The record of sides batting first is so awful that it is unfair. The 1990 game was another one which was ruined as a contest and a spectacle by the usual damp Lord's pitch.

It was the most one-sided big match I have played in. DeFreitas got the first five of us in his first seven overs, and we did well to bat out our overs for 171. We had to get into them early, and if Curtly had caught Fairbrother off Cooky, they would have been 28 for three. As it was Neil hit 81 from 88 balls and we were having a serious drink at 6.15 pm.

I got a few surprises in my first couple of years as captain. Peter Arnold was one. He was Chairman of Cricket but I had no dealings with him and we hardly spoke a word before I became captain, and then I found him to be a fair, strong man who knew the game. It makes a big difference to a captain when he has a good Chairman of Cricket, and the New Zealander was just that.

Like me, he was frustrated that we had such a lot of talent in the club in the 1980s, yet we kept under-achieving, mainly because we hardly ever played together as a team. That was what I had to change, and I started with the batting order. Everyone has their own idea of where they want to bat, but you can't fit them all in. David Capel always thought he should bat higher. Rob Bailey wanted to bat at no. 3, whereas I reckoned he was better at no. 5, and one day I told the team that they should be able to score runs in any position.

Bailey is a good example of a successful county cricketer who was prevented from doing better for England because he is too much a front-foot batsman. He is one of the nicest guys in the game, and maybe that is part of the problem, because he needs a bit more aggression. He has to be a hard man at times, especially now that he is captain. I know he has said that he won't change, but I believe he will have to. I know I did, and the same applies to any cricketer when he first becomes captain.

Capel was different. Nice guy and he had more talent than Bailey, but he is too intense. If he could relax more and just play instead of worrying about it, he would have played more Test cricket. That isn't to say that you shouldn't worry about your game – but rather that you should use the worry as a spur and not a hindrance on the field. I know it's easier said than done, but that is the mental trick sportsmen must learn if they are to reach the top.

The average cricket supporter can't begin to understand what goes through a player's mind when he is about to start an innings or begin a bowling spell. We are like top golfers on the first tee. We know what we have got to do. We've done it thousands of times, but now it has to be done one more time without the player making a fool of himself. Tension is the destroyer and there is no simple way to control it. Without it, you become dozy. With too much of it, you do something stupid.

We never had a lack of batting talent, but the bowling was more suspect until we signed Greg Thomas and Curtly Ambrose. With

Winston Davis and Eldine Baptiste there for a while, as well as Paul Taylor, Capel and Curran, we had a strong hand of pace, and that is why I decided to do all I could to get grassy greentops.

The main problem was the groundsman, Ray Bailey. I could understand his reluctance to mess about with the square because, like all groundsmen, he regarded it as his baby. He also said that the responsibility for any action from Lord's, if he was reported, was down to him. I argued that he was employed by Northants, and I wanted to do the best for the club. If that meant pushing things to the limit, I was prepared to do it.

It was the way I wanted to go. Over the years it was a batting paradise at home, and we had too many players who couldn't bat on sporting pitches when we went away. That is one reason why I turned things around by demanding greentops. When I got a few moans from our batsmen, I told them it was a team game and we were doing the best thing for everyone by winning a few games. Ray kept moaning, but I was determined to keep the policy going, and we even put him on a bonus every time we won at home. Still he wasn't happy, and a couple of times we got the pitches I didn't want.

Of course this was going to affect our spinners, especially Nick Cook who was no. 1. He had to learn to bowl like a stock bowler, so he did not try to spin it. I should have understood his problems better. Also, I should not have gone public after our game against Essex at Colchester in August 1991. They got over 400 and then Peter Such and John Childs bowled us out twice, and I said, 'If Nick Cook had pitched the ball in the right place, we could have kept them down to 200. They bowled well and we didn't, and that was the main difference between the sides.'

I shouldn't have said that, but he got his best bowling figures of seven for 34 against Essex at Chelmsford in 1992.

Kevin Curran was another signing who some of the committee thought would cause trouble. I was told that his time at Gloucestershire showed he was difficult to handle, but I'd known him for years and never believed all the bad things I heard about a guy I knew was a genuine classy all-rounder. I said that I could handle him, and the club signed him – but not for the sort of telephone numbers that were widely quoted.

'Kippie' Smith, Robin's elder brother, rang me and gave me a burst when the news broke because he claimed that Curran had told

Hampshire he would join them; but that wasn't my problem, because we had acted properly and I knew we had pulled off a coup.

I never had a serious problem with him although Capel seemed to regard him as a threat. That was another example of the wrong attitude I was trying to get rid of. I wanted the best side for the club, and everything I did was aimed at that, even when I wrote in the *Chronicle & Echo* in my weekly column that we wouldn't lose any players to England. The club fined me £200 because the players moaned at what I'd written, but it was just another way of geeing them up.

The only problem with 'KC' was one he couldn't help. He had a back condition which flared up occasionally and it affected his bowling, although he would never use it as an excuse. Which is why we got more out of him with the bat than the ball. There was the odd spot of trouble in the dressing-room which I had to sit on, but usually it was when KC had told players straight that they hadn't performed properly.

Mike Procter joined us in 1992. After three years, I wanted someone there to do things my way when I wasn't there. I have to admit that I was wrong in the first place to believe that I could captain the side properly while I was still playing a lot of Test cricket. I tried with everyone who captained the side when I was away – usually Larkins or Cook – but everyone has got their own way of working, and it wasn't an ideal situation.

The club spoke to all sorts of people, including David Lloyd and Bob Cottam, but I was pleased when they took Mike Procter. Lloyd had too much media work to give up, but he has shown what he can do with England.

'Procky' was a great help to me in selection and with tactics, although I know he didn't go down too well with one or two players who thought he should have been more up-front with them. He was the sort of coach who waited for players to go to him rather than impose himself, and he ran into the same sort of problem when he became South Africa's first coach after the Test ban was lifted. I never felt the criticism was fully justified, because too many modern-day players want their hands washing for them.

Procky was a brilliant talker when you started him off, and exactly the right sort of guy to work with me. We won the NatWest in his first year, and that win over Leicestershire was the turning point for me as captain. I was hard on mistakes in batting and fielding, but I tried not to take away the players' licence to express themselves. I wanted them to work things out for themselves more often, and for the first time in my fourth year in charge, I saw a gleam of light.

That was also when I decided to keep away from the side after play, and I almost became a loner. Quite a change for me, and I bet that surprised Pat Murphy of the BBC. He did one of the first interviews with me when I was made captain, and I remember him saying that a leopard can't change his spots, so how could I captain a side when I was such a party-goer etc?

I can look back now and know that I got better at the job each year. I always had the playing credentials, but I had to tailor my character and I never stopped trying to learn. We wanted to offer Procky a long-term contract, but the chance to coach the South African team was too attractive for him to turn down.

That brought Phil Neale to the club, and I have to admit that he didn't go down too well. In fact, several senior players said they wished we had persuaded Procky to stay. Nothing against Phil, but he hadn't got the same spark. He was very efficient and a good organiser, but I soon found that he and I duplicated each other at team talks.

I had warned the club, as I was in South Africa when they signed him, that I was against it because I wanted Bob Carter who I knew was on my wavelength. Peter Arnold stood down as Chairman of Cricket when Phil came, and I knew that things would be more difficult. At least I persuaded the club to let Bob Carter attend every game after Neale left, and he was a terrific help to me because all the youngsters had come through the ranks under him. I wasn't anti-Neale, but we didn't have much in common, and maybe he thought I took too many chances as a captain.

He had two years with us, but I think it was the best for everyone when Warwickshire lost Bob Woolmer to South Africa and asked for permission to talk to Phil. Funny, in a strange way. We lost two coaches because of South Africa, and Procky lost all the way round. He could have had a long-term contract with us, but gambled with his country, only to get the sack after the tour of England in 1995.

I took my biggest gamble of all when I heard about Phil and Warwickshire. I told the club to let him go and I would take over. Everything. Coaching, Selection, Manager. It would be my seventh and last year as captain, and I wanted to sink or swim with my own efforts. I told the club that I would accept total responsibility for every aspect of the first team, and I was happy to be accountable, win or lose.

The members and local supporters must have wondered what they were in for, but I can look back on my final season with pride. I know we won nothing, but we gave it a full go and deserved to finish higher than third in the championship, and everyone agrees we got the rough end of things in the NatWest Final against Warwickshire.

There were several reasons for such a great season, starting with Anil Kumble and his 105 championship wickets. If we had signed the man we wanted to replace Curtly, Kumble would still be waiting to play in county cricket, but we missed out on Shane Warne when I thought we had put together an offer he couldn't refuse.

Left to himself, I don't think he would have refused because, from various sponsorship sources, he could have cleaned up nearly £150,000. The Australian Board put the block on, and I suspect they were right because of wear and tear injuries to his bowling shoulder and spinning finger – the third on his right hand. The Board did not want to run the risk of Warne being overworked and Austin Robertson, his agent, explained why we would have to look elsewhere.

When I came up with Anil, everyone thought I was crazy, but I had spoken to Azharuddin, and he told me all I wanted to know. I confirmed it with Sunil Gavaskar, and I was happy that two good judges who had seen a lot of him believed he would be a great success in county cricket.

He is a terrific man as well as a great bowler. He didn't smoke or drink, which is why Sunil's only reservation was about my influence. He told me, 'Lamby, after a season with you, I reckon he'll get off the plane in India with a woman on one arm, a glass of champagne in the other hand and smoking a cigar'.

I saw enough in our first game at Canterbury to know that we had to take advantage of the Board's policy of allowing the grass to be taken off at both ends to help the spinners. I went to the committee and told them what we wanted, but there was a big row concerning Ray Bailey. He was just as much against two-tone pitches as greentops, and it was a heavy meeting before I got my way.

Actually, the bare ends weren't particularly helpful to Anil, because he was not an orthodox leg-spinner. His stock ball didn't leave the bat, but was a top-spinner or googly which ran into the right-hander at quite a pace. I was told by 'Azhar' to make sure I got my best catchers in the bat-pad positions, and that's why we had such a great season.

As it has turned out since, I couldn't have wished for a better season to finish with, both from the team angle and my own. We competed as well as in any of my seven seasons as captain, and I had a good year with the bat.

I can look back on those seven years in charge of Northamptonshire and know that I improved each season. I also know that I left the club with a better team than the one I inherited, and that the players definitely had a better attitude. When my first season started, my priority was to win the championship. The club had never won it and for me it provided the biggest challenge of all.

If I was to assess my captaincy, I would say that I was a bit of a gambler, but I always worked on the principle that we were better off winning nine championship matches and losing nine in an eighteen-match programme, rather than settling for a few safe draws. I played cricket positively and never minded losing if we had a chance to win. My main fault was that I tended to be too impatient of other's mistakes, but I think I got through to them that mistakes were forgiveable if they were playing positively.

I tried to captain Northamptonshire like I live. No challenge is too big to duck … and you can't win them all.

17
Close call in the West Indies

The 1989 home summer was a perfect illustration of the best and worst in playing cricket for a living. Northamptonshire first. They made me captain to follow Geoff Cook, and I was desperate to repay their faith with a trophy. We won three of our first four championship matches, but lost the other one to Glamorgan at Swansea where Steve Watkin bowled us out in just over an hour for 61.

We needed to bounce back in the next match at home against Surrey, and only rain stopped us winning. I got a big hundred, 171, but their last pair held out, and we lost momentum after that. We still finished fifth, which was our highest placing since 1976, and we had a reasonable season in the Sunday League with eight wins and a joint sixth finish. We lost in the quarter-finals in both knock-outs, but the biggest disappointment to me was that I only played eight matches because of three injuries which also kept me out of the England side after the first Test.

I have been lucky with injuries in my career, but maybe I now had a rash of them because I was the wrong side of 30. That calf muscle I pulled at Headingley in 1988 was bad enough, but once I was picked for the Texaco games against Australia and scored 102 not out from 104 balls at Trent Bridge, I thought I was in for a great year.

My only innings for Northants between the Texaco games and the first Test at Headingley was that 171 against Surrey, so I couldn't have gone to Leeds in better nick. The first game of a series usually sets the pattern for what follows, and what a balls-up we made. David Gower was captain, appointed instead of Gooch by the new

Chairman of Selectors, Ted Dexter, but Lubo has since admitted that he was wrong to be talked into going into the match without our only spinner Emburey.

He spoke to several of us as well as the selectors, but it was his second term as England captain, and he should have backed his own judgement if he felt that strongly about it. The groundsman, Keith Boyce, also told him the pitch would not be that helpful to pace, but he was talked into the wrong decision – made worse by putting them in when he won the toss. Our four seamers were too similar in pace to bother the Aussies once they got in. DeFreitas, Foster, Pringle and Newport were the four, and they couldn't stop the Aussies rattling up 601 for seven declared. But once they batted on into the third morning and we finished the day at 284 for four, the game looked a certain draw. I was then 103 and 'Smithy' 16, and when I was caught on the Monday morning by David Boon off Alderman for 125, the game was nearly dead. We saved the follow on easily with 430 and, even though we didn't bowl well on the final morning when they declared, we had 83 overs to survive on what was still a good track.

To be bowled out in less than 56 overs for 191 was poor, and I accept my share of the blame when Boon caught me again off Alderman whose five wickets gave him 10 in the match. I passed 3000 runs for England in my 57th Test, but to lose a game like that hurt so much that everything else meant nothing.

The following Saturday I captained Northants against the Aussies, and that day was the start of the end of the season for me. I only played in three more championship matches and not again for England. Sod's Law said that after 'Boony' caught me twice in the Test match, I would injure a thumb in trying to catch him. It was a bad one, although not broken, but I couldn't risk it in a Test match. If I got another crack on it, I would be out of the match. So the selectors brought Gatt back.

I decided to play for Northants on the Saturday against Somerset, because assuming I would be fit for the third Test, I didn't want to miss an extra county match in my first year as captain. The thumb was manageable so I played also in the next game at home against Worcestershire. I got 55 in the first innings, but then my right shoulder played up so much I couldn't bat in the second innings and we lost by an innings with Both taking 11 wickets in the match.

I fell on my shoulder in the field and the pain was so bad that I knew it was serious. The problem went back three years when Lubo and I went to Portugal for a few days just after he was first sacked as captain. We were in the Douro valley up north, when we had a competition to try to throw lemons into a river from quite a way out. That was when I had the first twinge, although I had never had any serious problem until that game against Worcestershire.

The England side for the third Edgbaston Test was announced on the Sunday and I was named, but I knew I had no chance, even with a cortisone injection. I doubt whether there have ever been so many withdrawals from a squad, because 'Smithy' was also injured and Gatt's mother-in-law died on the eve of the Test, so he withdrew as well. Foster also got hurt, so the selectors rushed up Paul Jarvis, Tim Curtis and Chris Tavaré, who hadn't played for England for five years. Rain took 10 hours out of the first two days and the game was drawn, and that was the end of my international summer, and of most of it with my county.

I had actually got over the shoulder injury by the middle of July and came back against Leicestershire at Grace Road. There was still nearly half the season to go and three Tests, but I bust the top joint of my right index finger going for a slip catch, and that was that for another six weeks. As I'd missed an early Benson & Hedges match with a hamstring, that made four serious injuries in 10 weeks.

In July came the bombshell announcement of another England rebel tour of South Africa, and again I was one of the cricketers who benefited. Not just because the batsmen who went included Gatt and Tim Robinson, who played in that Ashes series, but also a senior player like 'Embers' who must have been a candidate for the coming tour of the West Indies, and the England vice-captaincy.

After such a miserable and cruel summer, I could hardly believe my ears when I was named as vice-captain under Goochie for the tour, which included a one-day tournament in India followed by the series against the West Indies starting in January 1990. As Northants also showed their faith in me by re-appointing me for a second season as captain, I was happier about my immediate future than for a couple of years.

The vice-captaincy meant a lot to me for several reasons. It meant that the selectors were happy for me to captain England if something happened to Goochie, and that was a big boost at the age of 35. I also respected Goochie as a player more than anyone, because of his ability and his approach. I can't think of another batsman who got more out himself than he did and, other than Allan Border, no batsman ever gave a better example to his team-mates. Secondly, I was determined to make my input a good one, because I reckon that in the series I'd already played against the West Indies and done well, we had the wrong attitude. Too defensive, with most of the batsmen seemingly resigned to waiting until the bullet with their name on came along. Stuff that. I wanted to convince them that a bit of fight-back was the answer. I don't mean cutting and carving, but a game plan in which you defended and defended until a short or wide ball came – and then you'd got to give it a full go. And just keep picking up the singles and rotating the strike.

I had had my first taste of the Cresta run in 1986, when Gower and I upset a few people at Lord's by getting into shape for the tour of the West Indies by some high altitude training of a different sort. I loved it, and, just before the 1989/90 tour, we went back, despite my injured shoulder, because there was going to be a special challenge race between Gower and Lamb.

There was a big party of us, with Lindsay, Simon Strong and Charlotte, Lynn Wilson and his wife Judy, and two other friends, 'Buff' Marshall and Rosemary. I had some good insurance, but my main problem was to avoid any publicity because of my shoulder injury.

Somehow the *Daily Mirror* found out about the trip, and Chris Lander and photographer Brendan Monks turned up. I managed to talk them out of taking pictures, even though Lynn put up a magnum of champagne for the Gower v Lamb race, but the start was a sickener for me. As with all those gun-shoots with Ian Botham, I fell foul of the rules.

The secretary of the St Moritz Tobogganing Club is Lieutenant-Colonel Digby Willoughby, MC, and he is a stickler for doing everything by the book. As in 1986, we were due to fly to the West Indies a few days later although Lubo was now going as a journalist. What a waste!

I was mad keen to win the Wilson champagne and fancied myself because I had a best time down the run of 48.37 seconds, while Lubo had never broken 50 seconds. What I forgot was that you have to take your toboggan from the shed at Junction 15 minutes before the start of the race. This is to prevent a competitor from heating the runners on the wagon to increase speed.

I was all wound up for the start which was officially announced by Digby Willoughby, and suddenly heard him introduce me with 'riding, but not racing, Allan Lamb'. That was it. I was disqualified and no matter how fast I went down, Lubo was the winner. He chose to go down gently in 88 seconds, and I lost the cup and the champagne.

Not often does a man get his come-uppance so soon, but Lubo did that night, or rather early morning when he lost a friend's Opel car. A party of us went out to dinner and after we drank the Wilson magnum, everyone now had the taste and bottles kept coming. There were nine of us including Lynn Wilson and his boys, Giles and Nick, and the *Daily Mirror* pair, 'Crash' Lander and Brendan Monks. After we left the restaurant, Lubo announced he fancied a spin on the lake, and I was all for it until Lindsay put the block on.

She was five months pregnant with Richard and as we were catching an early train next morning to come home, she insisted we went to bed.

Lubo took the Wilson boys and the *Mirror* pair with him and spun the car in all directions. 'Crash' didn't fancy it in the least and so Lubo drove him and Brendan on to the hotel. That should have been that, but he then persuaded Giles and Nick to go back and have one more spin.

He flung the car all over the lake, but then made the big mistake of trying to leave the ice at the wrong place. As he said later, he learned two crucial things within the space of about three seconds and 50 yards. 1. The grey bits in your headlamps are where the ice is not as thick as you hoped. 2. Brakes, on ice, don't.

When they got out of the car, the front wheels were through the ice and he was stuck. The boys pushed while he tried to reverse, but the car wouldn't budge. They walked up to the road and tried to persuade a local taxi-driver to help them, but he said he wouldn't go on the ice in his cab for any amount of money, so Lubo locked the car and said he'd sort it out in the morning.

Except that it was virtually morning then, and within a couple of hours Simon Strong wanted the keys to run us to the railway station. He finally woke Lubo, who took a few minutes to remember where he had parked the car. When he remembered, he asked the hotel manager, Heinz, to check that it was all right.

Heinz had to tell him that while there was a nice hole in the ice, there was a distinct lack of an Opel car. Not a sign – it had gone straight to the bottom, so perhaps I used the wrong word when I said that Lubo got his come-uppance. More like gone-downance.

The police were called and although Lynn didn't want his kids involved, the papers got hold of the story, even though they were wrong about who was in the car. They wrote that Lubo had two blonde girls with him, not knowing that it was Giles and Nick. The car had to stay where it was for a few weeks until the ice thawed enough to pull it out.

When we got to the West Indies, at least Lubo said to me, 'I wish now that you had never been disqualified from the Wilson Cup, although maybe I would still have sunk the car.'

My other memory of the Cresta Run was in 1986/87 when Simon Strong was in charge of the British bobsleigh team. He wanted publicity for them and reckoned the press would come if Lubo and I went down the run with them. It was one of the most exciting things I've ever done. In order to get to the top of the run at Cervine we went by helicopter and lifts. We met the other teams as well, including the Russians who showed everyone a thing or two in the 'piss-artist' stakes. They were gold medal class, even though their number two was sent home after throwing up the morning after the night before. In case anyone thinks that was a bit drastic, I should mention that it happened in the toboggan, halfway down the run, and his back two team-mates got the lot. As the one said to me after he cleaned himself up, 'Why should I get his own back?'

We had an inexperienced squad for the West Indies tour – Goochie and I had 130 caps between us and the rest 65. I know how shattered Both was to miss out, especially as he says he was approached about his availability by Stewart and Dexter, but I was glad that 'Ned' Larkins had been picked. I knew he'd never just stand at the creases and suffer, and I was sure that if we could get the right sort of spirit going, we could win the series.

We had a good warm up in India where we competed in the Nehru Trophy with India, Pakistan, Sri Lanka, Australia and the West Indies. We were there for two weeks and lost to Pakistan in the semi-final after qualifying by winning three out of five games. It was a useful exercise in getting the party together and I was now confident about the series in the Caribbean. For the first time in my period with England, we actually planned a proper pre-tour preparation, including a magnificent fitness assessment by John Brewer at the National Human Performance Centre at Lilleshall. Our hearts were wired, pulses monitored and we were given individual programmes and targets for the two months before we flew out.

I have never been fitter, which made it even more of a sickener to pull my left calf muscle on a gentle five-mile jog back to the hotel in Barbados from the ground. To make matters worse I hadn't got a cent on me, but the taxi-drivers knew me and gave me a lift. It was only a minor niggle and I stayed in one piece for the rest of the tour.

I enjoyed the responsibility from the moment we landed. I was on the tour committee with Goochie, Micky Stewart and Peter Lush. I didn't get off to the best of starts, because I got on a plane trip around Jamaica, and we were a bit later getting back than I expected. I rang the hotel where the team meeting was about to start to say that I wasn't far away, but I got an old fashioned look when I walked in.

The Jamaica Test match was one of the most memorable in which I have ever played. It shook the West Indies rigid when we bowled them out for 164, and I was determined we would ram home the advantage. All my 10 Test hundreds had come in England, and the 132 I got at Sabina Park gave me more satisfaction than any other. I batted for over six hours, one of my longest innings ever, but it set up our first win against the West Indies since 1974, and we won by nine wickets.

The second Test in Guyana was completely rained off and then the Trinidad game was drawn after we were robbed by a shower on the last afternoon, followed by some of the most blatant time-wasting I have ever seen. We only needed 151 and had the game sewn up at lunch when we were 73 for one, although Goochie was out of the game after being hit twice on the hand by Ezra Moseley.

Against the local weather forecast, it rained for half an hour, but when we re-started, we wanted 78 from 30 overs. Light in Trinidad goes quickly, so their captain, Dessie Haynes, deputising for Richards, set about slowing things down to what was almost a dead stop. What with sending for sawdust and some of their bowlers – Ian Bishop was one – getting halfway through their run-up and then stopping because they said it was too slippery, we only got eight overs in the first hour.

I went in at 79 for three and watched helplessly as I realised the umpires were powerless to stop what was now little less than cheating. Lloyd Barker and Clyde Cumberbatch did their best, but Dessie knew they could only report him to the ground authority after the match, and by then he'd have saved the game. Which he did. Of the supposed minimum of 30 overs, we got 17, and the last four of those were in light that was unplayable. When Jack Russell and David Capel finally had to come off, we only wanted 31 from 13 overs with five wickets left, but someone might have got killed if we'd stayed on.

I'm not going to whinge, because we tried the same sort of tactics in the next Test in Barbados, but what happened in Trinidad stopped us going two up with two to play.

As it was, and on their favourite Kensington Oval, they knew they had a chance in what was my first game as captain of England, because Goochie was now out of the tour. It was quite a lively week in Barbados, with a one-day international played two days before the Test. We lost the game, but I saw one of the worst and most astonishing incidents I have ever seen in cricket. As we walked off the field and Gladstone Small was met by Gordon Greenidge on the step, Gordon suddenly grabbed Gladstone around the neck and there was quite an outburst, but we stepped in and broke it up.

It followed on some chat earlier, when we thought Gordon nicked one but was given in. We've all done that, but to see one player physically attack another, and in public, was shocking. Afterwards, somebody said Gordon actually deserved to be congratulated for finding Glad's neck. Most of the press missed it, but there was an inquiry and Gordon was warned about his future conduct.

The itinerary was such that we played the fourth and then the fifth Test, in Antigua, on a back-to-back basis and, as Easter came in the middle, we had two rest days in two Tests in five days.

We played four days in Barbados before the rest day, but only one in Antigua because of Good Friday. My captaincy debut was not great, even though I got another hundred. My problem was that we couldn't stop the West Indies scoring at well over three an over, so after three days they had scored 446 and bowled us to for 358. I tried to slow it down on the fourth day, but we weren't so good at it, and they declared in time to have a sprint at us and get three out. Rob Bailey will argue forever that he wasn't out when Viv appeared to intimidate Lloyd Barker into giving him out – supposedly caught down the leg side – after it seemed he had said not out and called over.

Robin Smith and Jack Russell were marvellous on the final day, but Curtly Ambrose cut loose with the second new ball and we lost in the final 15 overs of the match. I had put them in, so copped the expected criticism, but I've always backed my hunches and I wasn't going to change now.

Now it was 1–1 and all to play for. Lubo was on the tour as a journalist, but he had played in the island game in Barbados, in case we needed him. The more I thought about it, the more I was sure that he should play in the decider, and I was so sure I could talk the others into it, that I told him privately that he was likely to play.

My view was that it was a crunch Test, and we must pick the best side we could. Micky and Goochie wouldn't have it, because they reckoned that he could disrupt the side. They made the point that even though Goochie was out of it, we should stick with the original party. I argued that if you wanted one batsman to play for your life in one match, would you pick Gower, Bailey or Hussain? That is nothing against the other two, but Lubo had done it all and I was positive that my side would be better if he was in rather than writing about the game.

I argued right to the bitter end – even when everyone was out on the ground for practice, including Lubo himself. When I knew that they wouldn't budge, I had to tell him in public that he wasn't playing and I know how hard it hit him. He didn't say much, but he didn't have to. Micky and Goochie might argue that I had no right to tell him that he was going to play, but I was the captain and surely that should have counted for something.

It is history now – they won by an innings and took the series 2–1.

I stayed as vice-captain back home against New Zealand and India and got a couple of hundreds against India, including one which gave me a lot of satisfaction because of a Raymond Illingworth remark when I obliged Anil Kumble in our first innings with his first Test wicket. 'Illy' said something about me being nearly the worst batsman against spin ever to play for England, so when I got a hundred in the second innings I couldn't help but salute the commentary box first.

Lubo was now back in the side and an unbeaten 157 at The Oval meant they couldn't leave him out for the Australian tour, even though I knew Goochie was still not keen on including him. We all have blind spots about players, but I can't remember a captain in my time so set against a top player as was Goochie with Lubo.

It was a combination of things, but mostly because the captain was obsessed with training, fitness and hard work. I've nothing against that, but Goochie's real blind spot was that he never accepted that that approach did not work for everyone. Particularly someone like Lubo who has always been his own man. You've got to pick him and let him run free. That's not to say he's ever been bad for team spirit, because he hasn't.

Anyway, once he was picked, I suppose he and Goochie were an accident waiting to happen. The captain and manager were too blinkered in their approach to practice. I spoke to Laurie Brown about it, but it made no difference. Even the young Atherton had his say. When Goochie had a week off up the Gold Coast and then, when he came back, said 'Come on, work hard', Atherton replied with, 'Not all of us have had a week off'".

The first whiff I got of the Tiger Moth flights in Carrara was when Lubo asked to borrow 240 dollars. I hadn't got it, but borrowed it from 'Lushy' and only later did I find out that the manager's cash had financed the flip. I was batting with 'Judge' when the two Moths came in low, the one just missing the pylon. McDermott was bowling to me, and when play stopped I saw the wings dip and Lubo wave to me.

The disciplinary meeting was inevitable, especially as Lubo admitted he'd gone back for a photograph. I told him that he was deep in it, because as a member of the tour committee, I sat at the hearing. The other three, Goochie, Lush and Stewart wanted to send him home. All I could do was to suggest that they fine him for leaving the ground and, in the end, they agreed to do him and John Morris £1000 each.

There had already been a bust-up between Lubo and Micky when he was criticising the team and Lubo objected. If the Tiger Moth wasn't the last straw, the Adelaide Test was, unfortunately, when Lubo holed out to fine leg off McDermott just before lunch. Goochie was entitled to go crackers, but the only thing that was said was when Lubo came into the dressing-room and asked me what was for lunch. I knew that that was just his way of hiding his feelings, because he didn't need telling that he'd just fallen for the three-card trick.

Everything that could have gone wrong did. Like when I jogged back to the hotel in Ballarat after getting a hundred and pulled another calf muscle so badly I missed two Tests. It looked stupid and it was. Hands up, I should have known better, especially after the same thing had happened in Barbados a few months earlier.

By the time we got to Perth, the series was lost, and so was a lot of the dressing-room spirit. Micky warned me that I was drinking too much and I should slow down and pace myself. I told him that I was fine, but it seemed to me that my time in the vice-captaincy position was running out.

I had four series as number two, and enjoyed the involvement. My input was positive, but I still say I should have been listened to about Lubo playing in Antigua. As for the Australian tour, the management must take some of the blame for isolating him as they did. He got two of our four hundreds in the Tests. Surely, once they picked him to do just that, they didn't expect him to sweat it out at training every day. He was a senior player and a former captain, and deserved better. This was the tour which finally convinced me that Gooch and Stewart got it wrong by over-doing the daily grind of nets and training when we weren't playing.

The rumours started flying at the start of the 1991 season at home, but all I wanted was someone to tell me straight what my position was. I had dinner with Gooch at the Swallow Hotel in Birmingham where we were staying for the first Texaco game against the West Indies and I asked him point-blank whether I was still vice-captain.

I didn't know that the decision had already been taken, but could tell he was flustered. 'Haven't you been told yet?' When I told him nobody had said a word to me, he said that there must have been a misunderstanding. I waited until the third one-dayer at Lord's and then tackled Micky Stewart and Ted Dexter about it. What I didn't know then was that the press had already asked Dexter about it and he said that no decision had been reached.

They tried to tell me the same thing, but in truth they didn't have the guts to tell me the truth. I'm an expert on bullshit – I've dealt in it a bit myself – and I knew I was getting a big barrow load of it. I lost respect for all three of them – the captain for not being the first to tell me and the other two for trying to lie to me by saying that no decision had been taken when I knew it had.

I wouldn't have minded if they'd come up front and said that my lifestyle wasn't right for a vice-captain of England. Or they wanted a younger man, or even they just wanted a change. They even tried to soften it by saying that they had decided not to have an official vice-captain that summer, but if one was needed on the field, I would probably do it. That was like lighting the blue touch paper and I told them what they could do. But to avoid telling me the truth hurt a lot. I already sensed that Gooch wouldn't have Gower in the side again, and now it seemed that I was next in line for the chop.

I have never felt so bitter about anything to do with England – not even with the ball tampering the following year. They didn't seem to realise how proud I always was to play for England. If they had, they would have told me the truth and not let the matter become public and messy.

The other complaint I have is that they rarely go to the right people for advice when it comes to a marginal selection for a tour. For instance, they asked me about 'Ned' Larkins for the West Indies and I said he should go. But nobody said a word about him going to Australia and I would have advised against because he was in no sort of form, averaging only 28 in championship cricket. Also, nobody bothered to ask me about Capel and Bailey going to the West Indies. If they had I would have said no to Rob Bailey because of the bouncier pitches as he is mostly a front-foot player.

I played in four Tests against the West Indies in 1991, but never got going, so it was a relief to be picked for the winter to play three Tests in New Zealand before the World Cup. Alec Stewart was named as vice-captain, and I thought we had a great chance of making my third and last World Cup a winning tournament. I went well in New Zealand, with 338 runs in five Test innings, including 142 in Wellington, and we won 2–0. We beat them 3–0 in the one-dayers, but I was only picked twice in the World Cup. In the final against Pakistan, I was going well with 31, and so was Fairbrother and we had put on 72 in 14 overs, when back came Wasim Akram and he bowled me and Chris Lewis with two bananas in two balls and Pakistan went on to win by 22 runs.

On a memorable and dramatic autumn summer evening, Pakistan had won their first World Cup Final, while England had lost their third chance of winning it.

18
1992: Suspension and Fines

My final year in international cricket brought me my last two Test caps against Pakistan. I played in the first two Tests of the five-Test series and scored only 54 runs in three innings. In the second, at Lord's, I was bowled by Waqar Younis who, when he has conditions in his favour, can deliver the most lethal inswinging yorker in cricket.

With a low arm, he lets the ball go close to the stumps, with it apparently heading straight towards the left foot of first slip. In its last few feet of flight, and going at 80mph and more, it swings sharply in to the right-handed batsman, sometimes moving as much as two feet in the last three yards. Bowled against that initial off-side line, it accentuates that swing even more, and the batsman has got no chance of adjusting his stroke. Scientists have proved there is a certain point beyond which the human eye cannot provide for an adjustment, and Waqar has the talent and control to pitch beyond that point, which is why he is such a devastating bowler.

I also played in all five one-day internationals, scoring 144 runs including two fifties, and I was still hoping to be picked for the tour of India in 1992-93 but, as with the vice-captaincy issue, Graham Gooch tried to soften the blow the wrong way by saying that the selection policy was to concentrate on youth. Gower and I were not chosen, but Gatting and Emburey were, which didn't add up.

For me, however, the season was overshadowed by the fourth Texaco one-day international, played at Lord's on 22-23 August.

The game was held over from the Saturday, when Pakistan scored 204 for 5 in their fifty overs, because of rain, which is why the Lord's pitch and outfield was unusually lush and green for that time of year.

We hadn't smashed the ball around into the fence and hoardings, so there was no way the ball would become naturally roughened in the first 25 overs of use. Except, just after I went in before lunch on the Sunday, at 72 for three, the ball started to swing violently. I couldn't believe it – until Fairbrother was bowled by Aqib Javed. I then watched the Pakistanis huddle together and Aqib was definitely scratching the ball. When we walked off at lunch time, I told both the umpires, John Hampshire and Ken Palmer, that they had to do something. I asked them to have a good look at the ball, which was nowhere near 30 overs old, and I told them that there was only one reason why it had started to swing.

Micky Stewart asked me what I had been talking to the umpires about and, when I told him, he went to see them. I didn't know it then, but they had called the match referee, the former West Indies batsman, Deryck Murray, and the decision was being made to change the ball because of illegal interference.

It was only when I got back in the middle after the break, that 'Hamps' told me that they had changed the ball, but he asked me not to say anything. Some hopes of keeping it quiet, especially when Micky told the team and Both took matters into his own hands. Like me, he was totally brassed off and frustrated by the amount of tampering we had seen the Pakistanis do during the series, and also by the fact that we knew our Board knew but had not made any official objection. That is why 'Both' rang the press box to alert them, and when I left the ground after we lost by three runs, I was happy that the whole truth would finally be printed the next morning, when both sides would be at Old Trafford for the final one-day game.

Micky had told us that a statement would be made after the match, so bearing in mind what the umpires and Micky told me, I was happy that, at long last, the truth would be told.

Like hell. I couldn't believe it next morning when all I read was a statement from the Pakistan management that the ball had been changed because it had gone out of shape. I checked again with Micky, who confirmed that it was changed under Law 42 (5), which deals with illegally altering the condition of the ball*. That was good enough for me, but when I was first approached by Chris Lander of the *Daily Mirror* to go on the record, I honestly thought that the TCCB would tell the truth. I should have known better. They dodged, ducked and dived, as though they and not the Pakistan bowlers were guilty of something.

When nothing appeared from them next day, I told Micky that if they would not make a statement, I would. He said he was finishing anyway, so I must make up my own mind. I did, which is why I struck a deal with the *Mirror* where they would give me plenty of space and the £5000 fee would go to the Cystic Fibrosis charity.

I was accused then, and since, of doing it for money, but does anyone really believe I would have sold a story like that for £5000? It was worth much more, but I was only interested in pinning the Pakistanis for their cheating. All of the England players had moaned about it during the summer, but couldn't do anything until something official was done. Now it had been by Hampshire and Palmer, so I reckoned the public should know that we weren't just a bunch of whingers. We were fed up with Pakistan breaking the law for cricketing profit. Wasim and Waqar are brilliant bowlers, and it sickened me all the more to have to pin them publicly. But why should I stay silent when I had been the central figure of the first official case of ball tampering in international cricket? Everyone in authority had bleated for years that they wished they could take action to stamp out ball tampering.

I was now in deep trouble on two fronts – with the TCCB, of course, and with my county, as I knew I would be once I had decided to go ahead and tell the truth. People can argue as much as they like about my motives, but the facts are simple. Every word written with the *Daily Mirror's* Chris Lander and Colin Price was the truth.

***Law 42 (5). Changing the Condition of the Ball.**
Any member of the fielding side may polish the ball provided that such polishing wastes no time and that no artificial substance is used. No-one shall rub the ball on the ground or use any artificial substance or take any other action to alter the condition of the ball.

In the event of a contravention of this Law, the Umpires, after consultation, shall change the ball for one of similar condition to that in use prior to the contravention.

This Law does not prevent a member of the fielding side from drying a wet ball, or removing mud from the ball. See Note (b) **Drying of a Wet Ball**. A wet ball may be dried on a towel or with sawdust.

Had the official ICC statement about the Lord's Texaco Trophy match in August 1992 told all the facts, I would have been satisfied, but when I read that, yes, the ball was changed by the umpires, but no reason was given, I blew my top. That was a cop out, and the real reason why I went public. As soon as I read it next morning before the final one-day international at Old Trafford, I decided I would blow the story.

As soon as I decided to take the plunge, I telephoned Ian Botham's solicitor, Alan Herd ('Herdy'), and asked him for advice, because I knew I would be up for the high jump. He was brilliant. He drew up a short letter contract and a legal indemnity which was under our total control, but although I was never going to be at risk financially I could still be suspended, and that was a big enough worry in itself.

It seemed to me that if the TCCB moved quickly enough, they could hold a disciplinary hearing and suspend me to coincide with our NatWest Final game against Leicestershire.

I attended a cricket committee meeting at Northampton on the Tuesday, two days after the Lord's game, but I didn't stay long. The meeting had hardly started when my mobile telephone rang in my brief case. Rather than answer it there, I left the room, and it was a good job I did because it was the *Mirror* telling me about the first article. It sounded so sensational that I asked for them to fax it to me at home and went straight there.

I know I was prepared to go public, but I could well see what a story it had turned into, so I rang the club and Lynn Wilson and Steve Coverdale came round. As soon as they saw it, they said it was so explosive I had to get it stopped, and we rang the *Mirror* sometime after 7 pm. It was too late. They told me the first editions were being printed and they would be on sale later that evening.

It didn't take long for the lines to buzz. We started a three-day game against Middlesex next day and I was out with the players having fielding practice when I was called in to the club office. They'd never had a disciplinary meeting at Northampton according to Lynn, but he told me he had called an emergency meeting of the Chief Executive, Steve, the coach, Mike Procter, and the Chairman of Cricket, Peter Arnold.

I knew they were afraid that the TCCB might suspend me and stop me playing in the NatWest Final, which is why they acted so quickly. They told me I was in clear breach of my contracts with them and the

TCCB, and they proposed to fine me a maximum twenty-sixth of my salary, £955, and I would be suspended for the following Sunday League match against Warwickshire and the three-day game against Yorkshire, starting Monday 31 August, the week of the NatWest Final.

My TCCB contract prohibited me from commenting without permission for two years after the end of my last contract, but how they could ever enforce that I don't know. It's just another example of how the Board tries to run the game by secrecy. They gag players, they dodge any issue that needs firm handling, and they don't believe that the public should know anything. I had been aware of that for years, but the ball tampering issue proved it right up to the hilt. Everyone suffered, including the umpires. Several had reported incidences of ball tampering in 1991 and 1992, yet no action had apparently been taken.

Not only does that tell the players that they can get away with no punishment, but it also deters umpires from reporting because they know nothing will be done. I will never understand why the issue of ball tampering creates so much fear with the authorities and the lawyers. The game will be ruined if that attitude persists. The lawyers seem to think that anyone accused of ball tampering is cheating and that could be actionable. Until cricket shakes off that approach, the game will lurch from one crisis to another. What's more, the mutterings among the players will fester until we get to the point where the game is played in the worst possible spirit.

Even the press gets caught up in the same muddled thinking. Sometime later Jeff Powell of the *Daily Mail* wrote an article in which he nailed me as 'a South African mercenary who contended that England's enfeebled and now mostly discarded Test players would have been champions of the world – if only in one-day cricket – had the opposition bowled straight instead of crooked'.

He lumped me in a group of whingers which included rugby international Jeff Probyn, and the England soccer manager Graham Taylor. He wrote that people like us put British support 'down there among the wimps, the whiners and the spiritual dead men'. He then went on to say, 'Whether or not the Pakistanis are nit-pickers and ball tamperers, they have nourished a regeneration of verve and technique which ought to be the envy of Lord's'.

Herdy read the article once, issued a writ on my behalf and the

Mail settled for £7,000, plus an apology. That mattered a lot to me because, whatever faults I've got, whinging and moaning are not among them. Yes, I speak my piece if I have to – and sometimes even when I don't – but I have always gone on to the field and fought it out. The point Powell and others miss is that the Laws are there to be adhered to. I didn't create the one that governs the state of the ball but, as a batsman, all I ask for is a fair deal. Wouldn't a bowler reckon I was cheating if I got away with using a bat an inch or so too wide?

The whole point about cricket, even when played the hard way, is that it is played *fairly*. If the law allowed a ball to be peeled like an orange, then I'd have had no complaints, but I did this time, because I considered the series was settled by unfair means. We are all in it for a living, and why should international careers be affected by something illegally done by the bowlers? It is like throwing; it gives the bowler an unfair advantage and either it must be stopped or the law changed.

I will show how the TCCB double-dealt in the next fifteen months leading up to my court case with Sarfraz Nawaz, how they refused to co-operate until legally forced to with certain items of evidence and how they pressured players and umpires not to go to court. But, why shouldn't they speak? I still don't know what the Board was afraid of, because the truth is the truth, and the umpires in the Lord's game state that, in their opinion, the ball in question was tampered with and so they changed it, and that should have been the end of it, not the beginning.

Anyway, back to the beginning. Northants had bounced me for the financial maximum, and they hoped the suspension would keep me available for the NatWest Final. Lynn Wilson called the players together before the start of the Middlesex game and told them what had happened. The suspension cooled a couple of them down, because both Alan Fordham and Nigel Felton were a bit up tight as they reckoned I'd only done it for cash.

That was also a possible problem with the public, so the club put out a statement that the fee would go to charity, and I wanted to see out my two-year contract and stay as county captain. Fine, except for the fact that Chris Lander was interviewed by Pat Murphy the next day on BBC Radio 5.

When Murphy asked Chris how much I had been paid, he replied,

'We can hardly divulge that, but it is a substantial amount of money. When the contract was entered into, we knew the risks he was taking, so did he. As you have heard, he has already been fined and I think the contract absorbed that possibility'.

Alan Herd went ballistic at that answer, as he did with the next one. Murphy asked if part of the deal was that the *Mirror* would pay any fine incurred at national and county level. Lander went straight in again. 'I think you know we didn't do that. What we knew is he was likely to be in trouble, and so we have made it worth his while'.

Namely, that I had been paid a huge amount – big enough to pay any fines and be in pocket. The rest of the interview was supportive, particularly when Murphy asked Lander if my international career could now be on the line. 'It would be sad, in fact scandalous, if Allan Lamb's career was affected by this and he was made to pay such a penalty for having the courage to say something that cricketers around the world have been wondering about for a very, very long time'.

Scandalous or not, it happened. I never played for England again, and that still hurts.

Alan Herd told me that it would now be doubly difficult to maintain a stance of no payment after the Lander interview, but the fact that I paid the fee to charity shows I got nothing out of it. It might be argued that my profit was the knowledge that the legal indemnity ensured I would not be out of pocket, but I still ended up not making one penny out of the story.

So it was the end of my England career. Coincidence? It could be, just as one day a pig might land on Jupiter, or English cricket officials might adopt a policy of open government. In my time, the authorities have ducked and weaved, and by doing so they let down the players, the umpires, the public, themselves and, above all, the game of cricket.

Before the NatWest Final, Alan Herd wrote to TCCB Secretary Tony Brown saying that I was guilty of breaching my contract. Also, any request from them regarding production of documents, including my *Daily Mirror* contract, would have to be carefully considered. A letter from the Board's solicitors, Slaughter & May, asked for them, but Herdy stuck a flea in their ear by saying that the *Mirror* indemnity letter meant that documents would not be available, unless ordered to be by a court of law. The legal battle lines were already being drawn, but I had the Lord's final to concentrate on first.

What a start I had to the game. I was coming back from nets about 10 am, and walking though the Long Room carrying my helmet and gloves. Somebody pushed a piece of paper at me and I tried to flick it off before I dropped it in the bin without thinking anything more about it. I didn't think anything was up until Mike Procter and Bob Carter walked me to the pavilion door on my way out to bat. What I didn't know then was that they were trying to prevent me being served with a writ, but it was already too late – the damage had been done. I only knew that when Herdy asked me one question later: 'Did the piece of paper touch you?' I told him it had and he said that was all it needed to serve someone a writ.

Which is what it was from Sarfraz Nawaz, the former Pakistan fast bowler and my ex-Northamptonshire colleague, suing me for libel because I had written that the methods used by the Pakistanis were the same as those he showed to me when we played together for Northants.

So now I was in two lots of soup: a pending disciplinary hearing at Lord's within a few weeks, and a High Court case later on. Somehow, I got through the rest of the season, starting with Northamptonshire's second-ever win in a Lord's final. We won easily by eight wickets and I got in in time to hit 24 not out after Alan Fordham and Rob Bailey settled the game with a stand of 144, and I had lifted my first trophy in my fourth season as captain.

We had one four-day game left against Leicestershire, and our win by six wickets meant we finished third in the Britannic Championship. I got a duck in the first innings, but hit one of my quickest hundreds in the second when we chased 290 in 73 overs. I managed 122 off 167 balls and we won with 19 balls to spare. That pleased me, and so did a quiet word from one of the umpires, Don Oslear. Remember, he was the third umpire in the Lord's Texaco game three weeks earlier, and he knew the pressures I was under. It was nice to know, he said, that I could put everything to one side to play an innings like that. I reckon one of my main strengths in life has been my ability to push any trouble on one side if I'd got a job to do. As I see it, there's no good in worrying until the time comes for action. What's the point of making your life a misery, particularly when other people are trying to do it for you? I suppose that's all down to my family background and the way I was brought up, when I had to fight my corner. My folks were always good to me and fair as well, but they made sure nothing came easily. I know sister Brenda reckons I got away with things she never did, but I was still taught to value the right things in life, like honesty and loyalty.

Also, as I stopped growing at about fifteen, I was usually shorter and smaller than my mates, which meant I had to push harder than they did at games. And my size didn't help when I started going into pubs, because I would be pushed quickly on to a bar stool so that my lack of height wouldn't make the bar staff suspicious.

The TCCB disciplinary hearing was fixed for 23 September, thirty-one days after the match at Lord's and exactly twenty-eight days after the *Mirror* article. That is quick work by their standards, and what a farce everything was. The TCCB asked Herdy for relevant documents, including the *Mirror* agreement, and was refused. The Board then said that the failure to produce them could be interpreted any way they wanted, which was a veiled threat that I had something to hide.

Herdy had represented Both so often at disciplinary hearings that he was like a season ticket-holder at an Elizabeth Taylor wedding, so he worked out our tactics. It takes a lot to surprise Alan, but he was amazed – and relieved – to hear that it seemed that I was only going to be charged with a breach of contract. He thought they would add in a charge of bringing the game into disrepute, or making derogatory public statements, so he told Tony Brown that I would be pleading guilty.

Whatever I got as a fine or suspension should only take about half an hour to decide, because the committee and their lawyers should have met beforehand and sorted out what they would do.

Straightforward? An open and shut case, quickly disposed of? It might have been anywhere else but Lord's, but nothing was going to stop a procedural farce that cost the TCCB much more than was necessary, and wasted so much time that a serious case involving Surrey could not be heard by the same committee members, because too many of them had to leave at lunch time.

I can still hardly believe what happened, but I was able to take it all in because, as with Both, Alan insisted I say nothing and that he do all the talking.

The three of us walked into the room, me, Alan and his colleague Mark Mulholland, and the Chairman, Eddie Slinger, introduced the rest of the company: Dennis Silk (MCC), Donald Carr (Middlesex), Tony Cawdry (Yorkshire), Alan Wheelhouse (Nottinghamshire), Neil Wadey (Sussex), Alan Moss (Middlesex), Geoff Cook from the Cricketers' Association, the two legal representatives from Slaughter & May, Howard Jacobs and John Bramhall, and Tony Brown from the TCCB.

That made fourteen altogether, including four legal beagles to talk their way through a mountain of paper. I couldn't believe what was laid out, including what Mr Jacobs in his opening address described as 'the blue velo bound papers which are not as formidable as they look'.

Not much! It must have cost a small fortune to prepare and produce a bound document which ran to 42 pages. God only knows what the legal charges are per hour, but that one item must have cost over £1000, and we hadn't even started the hearing. While the chairman ran through his introductions and put Howard Jacobs in to bat first, I had a glance through the bible.

There were ten clearly numbered sections, starting with a 'Diary of Events'. The first page listed the ball change, my unauthorised *Mirror* article and the fact I had been fined and suspended by Northamptonshire for not getting the article vetted by them. Then came a list of correspondence starting with the Board letter of 28 August asking for documents, including my contract with the *Mirror*.

The final two letters itemised were dated 4 September and 14 September from Alan Herd, pleading guilty on my behalf and confirming that no papers or documents would be made available. I'm not a great fan of court-scene films, but I started to enjoy what went on, especially when I noticed in Herdy's first letter that his plea of mitigation 'would not take more than 30 minutes'.

Well, he had to wait longer than that for Jacobs to complete his opening address. There is a 27-page transcription of what was said and by whom, including Herdy getting a dig in that, although the documents were requested, my presence was not. Then, tongue in cheek, he said, 'I assume it is perfectly in order for Mr Lamb to be here and hear what happens'.

The chairman said, 'I would have been upset had he not been

here'. It was like a game of tennis, with Herdy holding his first service game easily. His next point was in the same vein. He acknowledged that I was aware of my playing contract with the TCCB, including the block on me making any comment without permission.

I couldn't see his point, until he followed in with, 'Presumably, Mr Lamb would not have been here today had he made a form of comment which praised any individual cricketer or the performance of the Pakistan team. Had he made that sort of comment without permission, would he be here today?'

The answer from the opposition was that the article might not have been printed, so that was another first serve in for Herdy, who now started to open up. He emphasised that I was not making a profit, nor would there be any form of newspaper contract in the future. He then referred to a press conference given by Micky Stewart after The Oval Test match, where he'd started to speak about the Pakistan bowlers and the fact that they got so much swing, before he shut up.

This he brought in to show that what I had written was not exactly a shock to anyone. He also said that I had been sued by Sarfraz Nawaz, and could be by anyone else in the Civil Courts, although no other writs had been received.

Good stuff, I thought, as I looked around the table and wondered what the ex-cricketers there were thinking, like Donald Carr, Alan Moss, Geoff Cook, Dennis Silk and Tony Brown. Never mind their official positions, they knew what I was talking about, especially Tony Brown, who knew all about the reports on alleged ball tampering filed in the previous year or so by umpires like Don Oslear and Chris Balderstone.

And what about Geoff Cook, my former team mate at Northamptonshire who played more than I did with Sarfraz? The club must have known I was telling the truth, but I appreciated that they could do nothing other than deal with my breach of contract. After all, I didn't have to prove whether what I said was right or wrong – I had knowingly broken my contract about making unauthorised statements.

Then things got technical. Alan Herd referred to the Board's 'request' for documents, as opposed to 'requiring them'.

Eddie Slinger then said that if there was a difference in the two words, then 'I think this committee will formally require you to produce them'.

My man wasn't having that. He said that any documentation between the *Mirror* and me was private, and there were certain legal restrictions to prevent him from producing it to a third party. He agreed that the committee could place any construction that they saw fit on any non-production.

It sounded like an academic point ... until he said that he had written to the ICC's solicitors, Simmons and Simmons, asking for a copy of the Match Referee's report. They had refused, saying 'it is a confidential document'. Another nice one. He then outlined the cost to me so far, with the club fine of £955 plus £243 in lost bonuses in the games I missed, as well as other possible lost bonuses. Worse than that, he said that I had not been selected to go to India and quoted remarks of Ted Dexter, then chairman of selectors, who said 'this incident has happened and it is part of Allan Lamb's record. The whole affair is bound to be considered when the Indian side is picked'.

Herdy finished at a gallop. He said I had never been disciplined in 14 years in county cricket and that I had never considered joining the Mike Gatting 'rebel' tour of South Africa in 1990/91 because all I wanted to do was to continue to play for England.

He then asked for nothing worse than a reprimand, which was a bit like a nicked, known pickpocket claiming he was doing a public service by lightening the weight carried about by his victims. He did a brilliant job, but I knew I would be bounced. It was just a matter of how much, or even if I got a suspension.

The Chairman asked if I wanted to exercise my vocal cords, which brought a quick 'No' from my legal ventriloquist. Now what?

Howard Jacobs went back to the non-production of documents. 'What is the legal basis for your refusal?'

Herdy certainly lost me with his reply. 'If I explain the legal reason, I will be breaking the very legal reason for the non-production'.

More ping-pong, with Jacobs claiming that if I had entered into any restrictions, that would be inconsistent with my obligations under my TCCB contract.

That got a dead bat. 'The last thing I want to do is to upset this committee, but I have already made my submission on this point and I don't think I can really add to it'.

So he'd said nothing, but seemed to have got away with it, because Jacobs then switched attack, or so I thought in my ignorance of legal debate.

'Mr Herd, are you aware of any arrangement or understanding, even if amounting to less than a legally binding commitment, which could provide for any payment or other reward arising out of the article?'

'No, I'm not'.

'And, are you aware of any indemnity arrangement, by which I mean were this committee, for example to levy a monetary fine...?'

Namely, would the *Mirror* pay any fine imposed by the committee?

Herdy nipped in like lightning. 'You're really drifting into the very documentation that I am saying is something I can't discuss. I have already made my submission here, so I am unable to answer that'. I thought I could wriggle in an argument, but this was in a different class.

Donald Carr wanted to know if my club had only punished me for a breach of contract, and was told they had. No charge of disrepute. The Chairman wanted to know if I felt justified in what I'd done and was told by proxy that I thought I had done something for the greater good. I suppose it was for the best that I did not utter one word from start to finish, otherwise my replies might not have been so carefully worded as were those of Herdy.

Then a leading question came from Alan Wheelhouse which asked whether I thought I had given the board a smack in the eye. I might have said that it wouldn't have hurt anyway, because their eyes were already closed, but my man tip-toed through quietly.

'It was done to reveal a situation he felt should be revealed. It was not intended to land the Board in trouble, land the ICC in trouble or embarrass officialdom. He felt that a wrong had been perpetrated and he wanted to reveal it. I have had those instructions ever since I've been involved in it'.

So far a lot of sparring, but the digging suddenly got deeper, not about possible rewards for me, but about the whole issue of ball tampering and its effect on the England dressing-room.

The Chairman asked if I had made a formal complaint to Micky Stewart on 23 August, and he was told that my conversation during the lunch interval constituted just that. The timing of my first conversation with Chris Lander was then established as less than 48 hours after the incidents, on Tuesday 25 August at Old Trafford.

I could not see why this timetable was discussed, because the hearing only concerned my breach of contract, not my reasons for it, even though mitigation was something of an issue. What came out next was my conversation with Micky Stewart at his farewell dinner as England manager. I told him that I was so wound up about it that I was going public. All he said was, 'Do what you like: I'm no longer England manager after tomorrow'.

That seemed to make an impact, because there was no follow-up, and Alan Moss came in on a different tack.

'Can I ask Mr Lamb, Mr Herd, did Northants play Pakistan this year?'

'Yes'.

'Did he detect any tampering with the balls during that match?'

'No'.

Nor did I, but we were bowled out twice in 51 overs and 63 overs, losing the first five wickets cheaply in each innings, the first three to the new ball each time.

'Mossy' then asked if I had 'asked Mr Gooch, the England captain, to put it in his captain's report, or did he assume he would do that?'

From Herdy: 'My instructions are that Mr Gooch was also complaining about it, presumably in the privacy of a dressing-room, and Mr Lamb therefore assumed he would put it in his match report'.

Moss's point was that a captain's report would have been the best way to deal with the suspected ball tampering, not through a national newspaper. He also acknowledged what had been said about Micky Stewart.

Had I been able to speak, I would have made the point that I didn't trust the Board to do anything, even if it had figured in Goochie's report. I knew they'd taken little or no action about the same bowlers in county cricket, and also that they'd ignored the John Holder/Mervyn Kitchen match report 12 months earlier, when Gooch was warned about ball tampering by his players in The Oval Test against the West Indies.

Although I didn't know whether or not that Lord's game figured in the captain's report, I don't think it would have made any difference to what I did with the *Mirror* – not after that weak ICC statement from Deryck Murray in which he decided not to give any reason why the ball was changed.

Dennis Silk was next to bat. He asked point-blank if I understood that my failure to disclose my arrangements with the *Mirror* could affect the hearing adversely, 'that the world might think that failure to make a statement about that was because there was a large source of money available to him through it'.

For the first time, I was glad I had nothing to do but to continue my audition for Madame Tussaud's. Herdy agreed that such inferences could be drawn, but insisted that I was only being charged with breaking three regulations, not for failure to produce documents. 'He is here for a disciplinary hearing over not getting permission for his statements'.

Chairman Slinger wasn't going to let go that readily. 'Isn't it right, though, that the purpose of that regulation is so that this committee can get at the truth? Isn't that the whole purpose of having that regulation?'

Tricky, I thought. Or, as Eric Morecambe would have said, 'Get out of that'.

Which only shows that what was a bouncer to me was a long hop to Herdy.

'I don't know the purpose. I didn't draft the regulation'. Slinger repeated the question, stressing that the regulation about providing documents was to help the Board find out the truth. Wouldn't Mr Herd agree with that?

'Yes, and I must say I have had the pleasure of being before this committee when that regulation was not there. I believe someone told me that it was introduced about two years ago and, as I said earlier, it is a very widely worded regulation. It could cover private correspondence, totally privileged in a legal sense and, Mr Slinger, you have the misfortune to be in my profession as well, so it does cover a range of documentation that no court of law could force to be produced'.

Now I knew why I was wearing the Herd gag. It was like going into battle wearing a suit of armour that nothing could dent. Dennis Silk tried again.

'I was merely suggesting that a cynical person might say that this was a good way of making a lot of money'.

'That is a risk Mr Lamb accepts he runs. I know there has been some cynicism about what I said about him and his family not profiting, but that is the truth'.

Silk: 'My only point is that if you were prepared to reveal the documentation, all these things could be blown away'.

'I accept that and I do understand, but that is all I can say'.

That was the end of Silk, but he was quickly followed by one of the opposition pros, John Bramhall, and he chased Herdy up about the documents.

'Mr Herd, you've informed me that one of the reasons why you will not produce the documents is that there is a clause in the contract with the *Mirror* forbidding their disclosure to third parties. We have discussed that in numerous telephone conversations and possibly agreed that in entering into that contract with the *Mirror*, Mr Lamb put himself in the position where he was going to be in breach of the TCCB regulations, because he was either going to have to breach that contract with the *Mirror* by disclosing those documents to this committee, or breach an existing contract with the TCCB by being unable, so you say, to produce the documents to this committee'.

Then came the crunch question.

'Is it reasonable for the committee to infer from what you are saying as well that there is an indemnity clause in that agreement with the *Daily Mirror* holding him safe from any penalty that might be imposed today by this committee?'

Herdys' dead bat didn't exactly splinter, but the ball didn't rebound very far. 'I can't say what is reasonable and unreasonable for this committee to infer. I have to rely totally upon the integrity of this committee, which I do totally'.

The Chairman tried next. 'I think possibly this is something of which we know nothing. Is it in fact the case that there is a contract with the *Daily Mirror*?'

'Yes, I suppose you could call it a contract'.

'And then we ask you specifically, is there an indemnity clause in that contract which is a protective one?'

'I am unable to answer that'.

From Mr Slinger, 'Very good', which seemed to me to mean the opposite. Then, 'Does that contract provide for any financial payment to Mr Lamb or to his benefit, or to the benefit of anyone with whom he is connected?'

'No'.

'Thank you. We take that from you as a solicitor of course, Mr Herd'.

'Thank you'.

Herdy had two more shots to play. Asked if he had anything else to say, he said: 'I see the tape recording being taken. Does that mean there is a transcript available afterwards or not and will it be available?'

Having been satisfied about that, he then asked the committee to 'take into account Mr Lamb's previous record, his loyalty to his country, the fact that, maybe misguidedly, he acted out of a sense of moral obligation'.

That wasn't his second shot at the end of what I have to say was a great innings as my runner. That came when the Chairman asked if we would 'be good enough to retire and leave the committee to consider...'

'Well I would retire if knew where to retire to'. I don't think I'd have dared to go that far – that was about as cheeky as me giving my prefect's badge back because I wouldn't give up beer.

Out we went, but not for long. I reckon that was because they knew that they wouldn't get the documents, and so they'd more or less made up their minds how much to fine me in the open and shut charge of breaking my TCCB contract. I'd never tried to deny that – well, I couldn't, could I? While we were waiting, Herdy made the point to me that he thought that the committee, even if only privately, had some sort to sympathy with me, otherwise surely they'd have charged me either with making derogatory statements or bringing the game into disrepute.

Back in we went, and listened to Mr Slinger deliver the verdict. He pointed out that my breach of contract 'was deliberate and flagrant, and Mr Lamb is an experienced player and he has acknowledged that he was fully aware that under his contractual responsibilities he was forbidden to make a public statement. We have taken into account that he has an exemplary record, his contribution to the game both to his county and nationally, and we have also taken into account the fine and suspension already imposed by Northamptonshire for breach of his contract with them'.

I listened and started to feel hopeful that the fine would be small one. It wasn't the money that was important, because of the *Mirror* indemnity, but it was more a matter of what I saw as justice that I shouldn't be hit hard for what I'd said. After all, Alan Smith had tried to say the same thing in his original draft statement as Chairman of TCCB on 23 August, which Deryck Murray then changed to delete any reference to the real reason why the ball was changed – namely under Law 42 (5), which deals with illegal changing of the state of the ball.

I should have known better. 'The decision of this committee is that a fine be imposed of £5000 with a £1000 contribution towards the costs of the case. There will be a reprimand and a severe warning as to future conduct. You will know that under the terms of Appendix C of the Regulations there is a right of appeal against that decision'.

I could hardly get my breath. A total of £6000 for speaking the truth, even though I wasn't allowed to do so under my contract. I could have swallowed it a bit easier if I'd been done for disrepute, but I hadn't. I know Herdy felt differently, because he thought the committee had tried to guess the figure I'd be getting from the *Mirror*. They were fairly sure that the documents not produced indemnified me but they couldn't be certain.

It would have been easy for me to accept it without quibble, but I'm not made like that. Herdy kept telling me that I'd been charged and found guilty of a clear breach of contract, so I had no come-back because the law was the law.

Stuff the law was my answer. I've been done for doing other people's dirty work, and I didn't see why I shouldn't appeal. It seems that I was on my own with that, because I could tell that Herdy wasn't that keen. He felt he'd done his job at the hearing and successfully kept the committee in the dark about my arrangements with the *Mirror*.

And there was always the possibility that an appeal could increase the penalties. Lynn Wilson certainly thought that could happen, but all I knew was that I wanted to have a go. Whether the fine was increased or reduced was not going to make a penny difference to me, but I wanted the public and the rest of English cricket to know what my motives were for linking up with the *Mirror*.

The next few days were a nightmare.

I was due to go to play for Western Province early in October, so I had to act quickly. I wanted to appeal, but seemed to be in a minority.

Lindsay was particularly strong about it. The *Mirror* had made a big thing about paying my fine in a spread with headlines 11 inches deep, and Lindsay feared this might influence the appeal body to suspend me.

My county officials were also keen I should let the matter drop, and both Lynn Wilson and Frank Chamberlain tried to dissuade me from lodging an appeal. Frank spoke to me after dinner one night early in October at a partridge shooting party in Berkshire. He said he wanted to speak to me privately, so we took a bottle of port into another room.

What he told me certainly made me think about the whole episode. It seems that he had been speaking to someone in Anglo-Pakistani diplomatic circles who had just come back from Pakistan, and he thought that things could get heavy. I asked him in what way, and he hinted at threats (not from the TCCB) to me and my family. He even said that there could be race riots in the Midlands if I went ahead with the appeal, and told me that it was such a sensitive issue that it would be better for everyone concerned if I let it go without any further action.

I was very confused. Instinct told me that I had been unfairly treated by the TCCB, but I dared not take a chance and put my wife and kids at risk. Whispered threats like that disgust me, and had they been levelled at me only, I would have ignored them and gone ahead with an appeal.

The fact that the original ball tampering incident was not nailed in the match referee's report started a hornet's nest among the lawyers and politicians which succeeded in gagging the TCCB and the ICC. What a shambles – and all because Deryck Murray decided against explaining why Ken Palmer and John Hampshire changed the ball in the Texaco game at Lord's.

The last date for an appeal to be lodged was 20 October, twenty-eight days before the hearing if I wanted one, but I had more or less decided against it when I got a bombshell of a telephone call from Alan Herd.

He told me that Surrey had been given a suspended fine of £1000 for admitting ball tampering. It isn't often I'm at a loss for words, but I could scarcely take in what I was hearing.

I had written about it and copped a £5000 fine, but they had done if four times – maybe more, but they had been caught and reported

My first touch of Northamptonshire's first trophy. The Benson and Hedges Cup
after we beat Essex at Lord's in 1980.

Left My first Test hundred in my third game
for England v India at The Oval, 1982.

Left Second Test v West Indies,
Lord's 1984. On my way to 110,
my fourth hundred for England
and my first against the
West Indies.

Right A hot day in Delhi. Wicket-
keeper Syed Kirmani and Dilip
Vengsarkar are the onlookers
during the second Test against
India, 1984.

Above The 1987 World Cup Final v Australia in Calcutta. I sweep Tim May, watched by wicket-keeper Greg Dyer, during my innings of 45. We eventually lost by seven runs. I batted at five despite begging the captain and coach to send me in earlier before the run rate climbed.

Below On my way to 125 against Australia in the first Test at Headingley, 1989. Ian Healy is the wicket-keeper. We lost by 210 runs after an astonishing collapse on the last day.

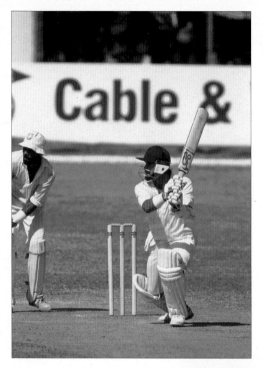

Above My trademark square drive. First Test v West Indies, Kingston 1990. Jeffrey Dujon is the wicket-keeper.

Above right My best innings for England. First Test v West Indies at Kingston in 1990 which we won by nine wickets – our first win against them for 16 years. Robin Smith is my partner.

Right We celebrate the historic win in Jamaica.

Right After starting the 1990 series in West Indies so well with the win in Kingston, we finished on a low with successive defeats in Barbados and Antigua under my captaincy. Ian Bishop gives me another 'smell the leather' delivery at St John's, Antigua. Definitely not one bouncer an over in those days.

Above About to be launched, along with Gower, Smith, Fowler and Botham, on the Kawarau river in New Zealand.

Left Top catch that gave me a huge thrill. Eat your heart out, Beefy!

Below In serious training Down Under with Lindsay, 'Lubo' and his future wife Thorunn.

LA PIROGUE
BIG GAME
FISHING

ANGLER	A LAMB
FISH	MARLIN
WEIGHT	200 lb
TACKLE	130 lb
SKIPPER	VITAE
BOAT	MOANA
DATE	30.12.94

Left Friend and foe. Sarfraz Nawaz was a great servant for Northants but later turned against me in the High Court.

Left Nothing is too much trouble for our star import, Curtly Ambrose, who might be asking if there is any chance of a bowl!

Below left My first trophy as captain of Northants after beating Leicestershire by eight wickets in the NatWest Final of 1992.

Below Anil Kumble was another excellent 'overseas' player for Northants, claiming 105 wickets in 1995 and nearly winning us the Championship.

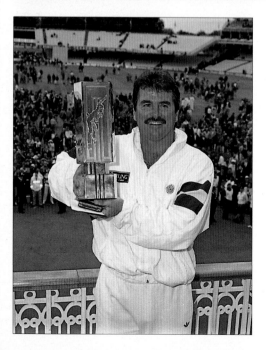

Above History in the making. South Africa's first Test after readmission to the ICC in November 1991. Ali Bacher, Kepler Wessels and Mike Procter work out how to beat West Indies in Barbados, 1992. It was not to be as West Indies won from an impossible looking position on the final day.

Above England tour of Australia 1990. Micky Stewart and I talk things over before the Brisbane Test where I captained England for the first time following Gooch's hand injury.

Middle right Ted Dexter, then Chairman of Selectors, who said before the party was picked to tour India in 1992/93, that my breach of contract after the Lord's Texaco game against Pakistan in August 1992 would be taken into account. He was right. I never played for England again.

Right One of my last appearances in international cricket with 'Both' against Pakistan in 1992.

Above Richard, demonstrating that there is another bottom-handed batsman in the family.

Above At home with Katie-Ann.

Above The most nervous of all my debuts. Edgbaston, April 1996 and my first appearance in the Sky Television commentary box. Quiet start! Shaun Pollock took four wickets in four balls and marked his home debut for Warwickshire with 6 for 21.

Below Happy families. Three reasons why I'll always be a winner.

four times – in two years and got a fine of what amounted to about £90 for each player and even that was suspended for two years.

It didn't make the slightest difference to my rage – and there's what it was – to be told that they had received the maximum allowed by the regulations governing the procedure under which their case was dealt. Even now, four years on, I can't come to terms with what happened.

It seems that the original idea was to hear my charge and the one against them at the same disciplinary hearing, but that went out of the window because of the amount of time they wasted in dealing with me. As a result, when it came to lunch time, most of the disciplinary committee could not stay, and so the Surrey case was delegated to what they call a Summary Panel.

That panel is drawn from the full disciplinary committee, but its powers are severely limited as a result. So £1000 was the maximum fine they could impose for a fourth instance of the most serious cricketing offence in cricket. That shows how weak and inept the TCCB is when it is faced with a need for strong action. To think that one county club had been reported for cheating by John Holder and Barry Dudleston eight days before my article in the *Mirror*. And those two umpires did their duty, just as Chris Balderstone and Barrie Leadbeater did in 1990, and Don Oslear, Bob White and Barry Dudleston did again in 1991. Surrey were warned by letter in 1991 about how severe the consequences could be.

That is the joke of the century. I assume the Surrey captain, manager, coach and players were warned, yet there they were again within 12 months, only this time there was one difference. The game against Leicestershire at The Oval in the middle of August 1992 was the only one of the four reported games in which Waqar Younis did not play.

When I calmed down sufficiently to speak, I told Herdy that I had to appeal, never mind the threats Frank Chamberlain told me about. I couldn't treat them as fairy tales anyway, because I'd had a stack of letters after the *Mirror* article. There were dozens from Asians hoping I would die, but plenty from county members and the general public supporting what I'd done. I've done a few things in my life that I've regretted, but the *Mirror* episode is not one of them.

I'd had a bellyful, and so had the rest of the England dressing-room. And what about those umpires who'd done their duty and then been let down by the TCCB? It was only after that summer that I began to understand how much the umpires felt let down. I remember asking Barry Dudleston in the Lord's Test against Pakistan to have a look at what the fielders were doing to the ball. When he told me he'd got enough on his plate without bothering with that, I was disappointed. Now, I understand, because he had sent in a report the previous year after the Surrey game against Yorkshire at Guildford and nothing was done.

Don Oslear was the other umpire, and he has told me how let down he and the other umpires felt during those two or three years. He even warned the TCCB in 1991, when Surrey were reported, that if no action was taken, the board was storing up trouble for itself in 1992. I know players always moan about the authorities, but the facts in this case are undeniable.

The TCCB kept promising the umpires support if they reported any player or team, yet when they did, they did nothing. It is the TCCB's fault that the 1992 season festered until the boil broke at Lord's. They condemned the England team and the public to a series that should have been a cracker, but which was soured for everyone by the terrible spirit in which the games were played.

The ICC are just as guilty. Look at their appalling performance at Old Trafford when Roy Palmer was harassed and bullied by most of the Pakistan team led by Javed Miandad. I have never seen anything like that on a cricket field, and I hope I never do again. I've done my share of sledging on the field, and I've had the odd go at an umpire, but I can't imagine any team I've played in or any captain I've played under who would stoop to those sort of tactics.

I don't believe the ICC could have cocked things up more, from the moment they appointed Clyde Walcott to be match referee, apparently not knowing that he couldn't do all the match because it clashed with the ICC's annual meeting at Lord's. Talk about left hand and right hand.

As a result they put Conrad Hunte in as deputy, and he just bottled it. Irrespective of any so-called provocation from Roy Palmer – there was none anyway – the Pakistan players involved should have been bounced good and hard. Although I can't imagine any England side misbehaving like that en masse, I'll bet that if it did the English board would clamp down hard. I remember Graham Dilley being done twice for relatively mild stuff compared with that Pakistan performance, and Chris Broad and Keith Fletcher were both in trouble for hitting down their stumps when they were out.

Yet the only ICC action at Old Trafford was a joint letter of warning to both sides, England as well as Pakistan. No wonder Gooch went mad when he was told about the letter just before the start of play on the final day. The incident in that Aqib Javed over to Devon Malcolm was a disgrace, and so was the response of the referee and the ICC. They had all the television evidence they wanted, yet chickened out of their responsibilities to the game. What makes every country in world cricket so afraid of Pakistan?

Hunte fined Aqib half his match fee, but only reprimanded Intikhab Alam for breaking the Code of Conduct by talking to the press about the decisions taken. So what did Intikhab do? He repeated the comments and was reprimanded again, this time by ICC.

Thanks to this spinelessness, the trouble created in the third Test was carried over and made worse in the fourth Test at Headingley because of more allegations about ball tampering. Micky Stewart brought it up before the start of the Leeds Test, because the trouble at Old Trafford overshadowed everything else. Also one of the balls used by the Pakistan bowlers in England's first innings at Headingley was sent by the umpires to the match referee, Clyde Walcott, again. All he said was he could see nothing to take action upon.

That was the game when England collapsed from 270 for one to 320 all out, with a ball that ended up having 113.5 overs of use. The second new ball was available long before England lost their second wicket at 270, but there was never any chance of it being taken. Not when the old one suddenly started to swing like a boomerang for Waqar, and he turned figures of none for 104 to five for 117 in 28 deliveries, with three clean bowled and two lbws.

And they weren't exactly tail-enders he rolled over – Alec Stewart, Graeme Hick, Chris Lewis, Derek Pringle and Neil Mallender. Just like in the second of that series at Lord's, where we went from 197 for three to 255 all out, with the hugely swinging old ball doing me, Both, Chris Lewis and Phil DeFreitas. And in the second innings we went from 108 for two to 175 all out, with Wasim and Waqar getting six of the last eight in a rush, with five bowled or lbw as were three of Waqar's last four wickets in the first innings.

Nine of their 13 wickets were unassisted, and that is remarkable for top Test batsmen, especially when the ball is old. That's the background for the Lord's Texaco game, and what spurred me to do what I did. As far as I'm concerned, that was all down to the authorities and how they let everything go unchecked, both in that series, and in the two or three previous seasons in county cricket, despite Surrey having been nailed officially on four occasions.

As soon as that suspended £1000 fine was announced, everything changed. Not just with me but Northamptonshire as well. The same day, Lynn Wilson sent a letter to the TCCB's Chief Executive Alan Smith, which was short and to the point. After detailing the club's fine and suspension, he wrote:

'The subsequent additional fine imposed on Tuesday last by the Disciplinary Committee is regarded by some as excessive, but what is more alarming is the way the Summary Panel dealt with Surrey's admitted transgression of ball tampering under Law 42 (5) on Thursday.

'The imbalance in fining an accuser six times more, plus suspension of five playing days, compared with the guilty who "suffered" a £1000 suspended fine is an area where Northampton-shire require a full explanation. I am coming under daily pressure from the media to comment and I need a quick and speedy response, otherwise I shall have no alternative but to make a statement.'

Copies were sent to Frank Chamberlain as Chairman of the TCCB, Steve Coverdale and Peter Arnold of the club, Peter Bromage and Eddie Slinger of the Disciplinary Committee and me.

The press had a go as well, with Donald Saunders in the *Daily Telegraph* making the obvious points already included in Lynn's letter. The headline was 'Silencing the sacrificial Lamb'.

He began: 'Those who cling to the belief that fair play is an essential ingredient of cricket will surely have been dismayed by the disparity between the severe penalty imposed on Allan Lamb and the paltry suspended fine with which Surrey escaped when they appeared last week before disciplinary panels of the Test and County Cricket Board.

'Now we are left to conclude that talking to newspapers about controversial incidents in an international match is a far deadlier sin than cheating in the County Championship.' He went on to say that the secrecy surrounding my hearing and the reason for the ball being changed in the Lord's game left too many questions unanswered.

'All cricket authorities should understand that they are selling a product to paying customers. Those customers have a right to know whether they have bought a genuine article or been fobbed off with damaged goods.'

Ray Illingworth weighed in with another important point, saying that 'the authorities don't have to name any names which might prompt legal action. All they have to do is to state that the umpires changed Pakistan's ball at Lord's under Law 42 (5) governing unfair play'. (*See footnote on page 176.*)

'But the situation now is that the umpires have not been backed up, and that is a recipe for chaos in the game. If a sport cannot administer its own rules properly and is forced into silence over a simple matter of what happened during the actual playing of a match, there is something terribly wrong. It is made even worse when here in England we have been prepared to tackle offenders in domestic cricket like Surrey, but will not make a stand at Test level.'

Except it was not much of a stand the TCCB made about Surrey, was it? By this time in early October, I'd been re-appointed club captain, with Lynn telling me that the committee had no reservations at all about the disciplinary hearings at Northampton and Lord's.

I wasn't quite so sure, because I had heard that there were some committee men who thought I should go. Perhaps it was the news about Surrey that turned them round. And although I had plenty of public support, I had my critics as well. One of the members, Roger Walters, wrote to the Northampton *Chronicle and Echo* and said that 'the prompt action of the County in suspending and fining Lamb is to be applauded as it demonstrated that no man is bigger than his team'.

I had a busy couple of weeks, including going with Lindsay to Mauritius for six days on holiday, followed by three days in Zimbabwe doing charity work with a project called Dreamflight, which sends terminally ill kids to Disneyland.

Then it was off to Cape Town for the season with Western Province, while Herdy processed the appeal. I flew back on 13 October for a couple of nights to present the *Mirror* cheque for £5000 to my favourite charity, the Cystic Fibrosis Trust. Unlike Both, who had been involved with leukaemia charities for at least 15 years, I'm a new boy because I didn't know anything about the disease until my youngest, Richard, was born on 6 May 1990.

A month later, I had reported to Trent Bridge for the first Test against New Zealand, when Lindsay rang me to say that Richard was going to have tests to see if he had cystic fibrosis. She was shattered, and so was I when I found out what the implications were. The disease is hereditary and comes from a faulty gene. Twenty years ago, kids didn't live to five years of age. Their bodies don't digest fat, and the breathing is badly affected because the mucus which forms on the chest can't be dispersed normally. There is no cure, but medication, antibiotics and physiotherapy can ease it and life expectancy now is much greater, somewhere around thirty. I offered to pull out of the game, because Lindsay was so upset, but she told me to play and get on with it. I did, but was in a hell of a state – so much so that I knew afterwards I shouldn't have played.

I got a duck, lbw to Hadlee, but nothing seemed important until we knew the results of the tests 10 days later. Richard was clear, and I was so thankful that I decided to try to help kids who weren't so lucky. That is how the idea came to have an annual cricket six-a-side competition on the Althorpe estate, and it has gone so well that already the Trust has benefited by £200,000.

I have never looked for personal kudos out of it, but I know that my name in cricket has helped, which is why I try for as much publicity as I can. You just never know in life, as I soon found out when the young lad of my county colleague, Richard Williams, was born with the same problem.

After I presented the cheque, I flew back to Cape Town, where I got off to a reasonable start with a double hundred against Northern Transvaal and 134 against Transvaal. The appeal date was 20 November, and Herdy was more confident after that letter from Lynn to the TCCB. He'd told me earlier that Lynn had advised 'put aside pride and prejudice because of the pitfalls involved', but he thought the letter showed a big change of heart and that would be in my favour. Whatever the club officials might have thought originally about the appeal, there is no doubt that once they heard about Surrey, they helped me in every way possible.

On 11 November they sent Herdy their submission for the appeal, and asked for it to be circulated. The Appeals Committee was made up with an independent Chairman, Judge Desmond Perrett, a representative of the Cricketers' Association, David Graveney, plus three people nominated by the Council, one of whom to be connected with the Board. They chose Messrs Ingman, Pocock and Elliott and they had to consider these points made by my county.

When I was suspended by the club, that robbed them of my services in a key game against Yorkshire. I wouldn't know what difference I might have made but we drew the game, whereas the 16 win points we missed would have put us in second place instead of third at the end of the season. The club had therefore deliberately handicapped themselves by suspending me, although they were hoping that swift action would stop a suspension from the board which could have kept me out of the NatWest Final.

The submission then detailed the public reaction to my action.

'The public reaction to the penalties we imposed has frankly astonished us. When first penalised by the club, the wave of sympathy and support for Mr Lamb was overwhelming. At the same time, criticisms levelled at the club by the general public, members and supporters were quite revealing. Mr Lamb was given a standing ovation every time he walked on to the pitch and received applause virtually every time he touched the ball.

'The volume of letters he received in support was remarkable. Likewise we were surprised at the amount of critical correspondence that we, as a club, received following the action we took. That public support was, if anything, intensified after the Board's Discipline Committee hearing when a penalty was imposed which many regarded as excessive. Long-standing members have threatened to resign their membership. Several sponsors have indicated they are considering withdrawing their support in protest. It is quite clear that there is a real danger of "martyrdom" in this case. Many have found it hard to believe how severely Mr Lamb has been punished in comparison with penalties that had been imposed upon others within cricket and by other sporting bodies'.

No direct reference to Surrey, but that was dealt with fully by my barrister Tim Grice at the appeal. Another farce really, with both sides represented by counsel, and all because of how the TCCB 'stuffed up' the two hearings involving Surrey and me. The appeal committee had the problem of being fair to me, but not being seen to condemn the discipline committee for the fines they'd imposed.

The day of the hearing, I was playing for Western Province against Natal at Newlands, but play was washed out, so I had plenty of time to think about what was happening back in London. I was more wound up than if my money was at stake, because as I went back over everything from when I batted before lunch in that fourth Texaco one-day international, I knew I'd been let down by the authorities.

They should have given the right reason for the ball being changed, but they didn't. The other thing that made me anxious was that mine was the first appeal held since 'Beefy' was suspended for two months after admitting smoking pot way back in the early Eighties.

What they came up with was a reduction of my £5000 by £1000, with another £2000 suspended for two years, and the £1000 costs awarded against me was halved. As I keep saying, the money was irrelevant, but the whole point of my appeal was to show the public that I'd not been treated fairly, and the way that Surrey were dealt with, compared with how I was, was a disgrace.

In round figures, my total £6000 fine by the TCCB was reduced to £2500 but the statement said that my original fine was not excessive. They reduced it because 'the Committee should have taken more account of Lamb's unblemished record'.

They also said that I had a 'reasonably held sense of grievance' about the Surrey fine, so at least some of the damage done to me had been put right. The English press now came on to me, and none of them thought that the verdict was over generous. Alan Lee in *The Times* said I had 'secured a significant victory when, on becoming the first player for six years to take a disciplinary appeal to the Cricket Council, he succeeded in almost halving his punishment'.

There it was, at least a part admission that what I had done was understandable. If only the TCCB had done their job properly in the first place.

What a legal year I was in for. Between the date of the Lord's match on 22 and 23 August 1992 and 19 November 1993 – a total of 454 days – I would be disciplined by my club and the county's cricket authorities. Then I would win an appeal against the TCCB, thanks partly to the backing of my county, before I would have to prepare for a nerve-racking High Court case brought by Sarfraz. I reckon I've always been pretty resilient, but the lead-up to that court case was something different from anything else I have ever experienced.

There was hardly a day when I was not in contact with Herdy and his assistants about one thing or another, but what disgusted me more than anything else was the attitude of the TCCB.

They really wanted a two-way bet. They kept up a public pretence that they had nothing to do with the case, yet they monitored every move and attempted to obstruct every request made to them for production of umpires' reports and the ball used in the Lord's Texaco game. However the Sarfraz libel writ was couched, it quickly became obvious that the one-day international, and my actions in drawing the attention of Ken Palmer and John Hampshire to the ball, would be the focal point of the trial.

Everything was interlinked with what I had written in the *Mirror*, and the Board was determined that they would not be seen to be involved. What a joke! They spent thousands and thousands of pounds that should have gone back into cricket. I will show how they leaned on cricketers and umpires not to help me, and they would have succeeded but for friends and colleagues like Both, Robin Smith, Don Oslear and a few others. I have a long memory and I won't forget those players who I asked to help me and didn't.

It was a year that I would not wish on anyone, but if Sarfraz wanted a fight, I was certainly not going to back off. However, I didn't realise that I would be fighting the TCCB as well.

19
Problems with Sarfraz

The 1993 season was the first one as captain in which I was available for Northamptonshire every match, now that it seemed I'd finished my England career. Once I was not picked to go to India, I guessed that that was it, especially after Dexter's remarks before that tour that my actions in the Lord's one-day international and afterwards would stay on my record.

I played in every championship match and had a reasonable season with 1046 championship runs at an average of 40. We finished fifth in the Refuge Sunday League, an improvement from 1992 of eight places, and reached the semi-final of the Benson & Hedges Cup, so I had plenty to think about.

The Sarfraz writ got a lot of publicity – his advisers made sure of that. They announced during the NatWest Final: 'Sarfraz Nawaz, the well-known Pakistan international cricketer, has issued proceedings for damages for libel in the High Court against Allan Lamb, the English cricketer and his former colleague at Northamptonshire. It concerns allegations made by Mr Lamb in an article published by him in the edition of the *Daily Mirror*, dated 26 August 1992. Any enquiries should be addressed to Mr A. Karim of Karim solicitors.'

Dear old 'Sarf'. I was still playing international cricket and his last Test match was in 1983, but he was 'the well-known Pakistan international cricketer', while I was 'Allan Lamb, the English cricketer'.

So what had I written in the *Mirror* that got him steamed up? Nothing I reckon, until one of his legal acquaintances thought that he could sue me for libel, because of this. I wrote, 'At Lord's on Sunday, the other England players and I watched the Pakistanis tampering with the ball just as they have all summer. When I went out to bat I saw them up to their old tricks, so I alerted umpires Ken Palmer and John Hampshire.

'I pointed to a few scuff marks on the ball and told the umpires; "Keep your eyes on those and you'll see them get bigger". Sure enough, by lunch the scuff marks had grown alarmingly. The trick is disguised at the end of each over, when they know the umpires are most likely to inspect the ball, by smearing sweat over the roughened surface so the new scratches stain red from the leather.

'It was an old trick first shown to me a dozen years ago by my old Northampton team-mate, Sarfraz Nawaz. He was a genuine swing bowler, but he learned the trick to help him bowl on the concrete-hard surfaces of Pakistan.'

That was it. That was how I came to touch what turned out to be a writ before the Lord's Final against Leicestershire in 1992, and that is why the build-up to the High Court case, fourteen months later, certainly opened up my eyes about a few officials and players. I was lucky in having Alan Herd to guide me through what was a legal minefield, because the case was being brought only on my reference to Sarfraz, but we needed to widen it out to include the events of the Pakistan tour of England in 1992.

As soon as I knew there would be a court case, I believed that all my England mates who played in that series would help me out. I had stood up and told the truth, and now was their chance to support me and show how I knew they felt about the ball tampering. I had heard enough moans from them over the years, especially in 1992, so I was sure they would help me.

Wrong, wrong, wrong. I didn't want to subpoena them, because I thought that would be unnecessary seeing as they were mates. I didn't even feel it was necessary to ask them, because I was sure they would come forward without hesitation. The ensuing silence was deafening. In the end, only Gooch and Gower were subpoenaed, but by the opposition, who never used them anyway. I know that Herdy spoke to Gower before he was subpoenaed, and he got the knock-back, mainly because 'Lubo' insisted that he'd got nothing to say as he did not play in the one-day game at Lord's.

I didn't buy that for one moment. It was dodging the issue to claim that, because he had no concrete evidence, there was no point in him coming to court. He might have believed that, but I reckon it was a cop-out. It's true he didn't play in the Texaco game at Lord's, but he did play in the third, fourth and fifth Test matches at Old Trafford, Headlingley and The Oval. I also know that the players in the England dressing-room at Old Trafford went ballistic during that game, and not only because of the Roy Palmer incident.

In fact, the England players felt so strongly about the ball tampering that went on in that game that Micky Stewart brought it up at the pre-match briefing at Headingley. It was supposed to have been a peace meeting after all the commotion at Old Trafford, but Micky raised the question because the Palmer issue had over-shadowed everything else.

Gower was part of that, just as he was at Headingley, when England went from 270 for one to 320 all out with a ball that appeared to be over 100 years old. In fact, Gower was stranded with 18 not out while he watched Waqar bowl Hick, Pringle and Mallender and nail Lewis lbw for two runs between them – all batsmen beaten by banana inswingers at top pace with a ball that had not deviated at all in the previous six hours. Also, he must have known that the ball was sent by umpires Ken Palmer and Merv Kitchen to the match referee, Sir Clyde Walcott. Never mind that Walcott sent it back and did nothing. Gower was part of that England side which, for the second game running, knew that something suspicious was going on.

What's more, even if Gower could not swear on oath that he had seen any of the Pakistanis actually scratching the ball, he knew that the ball was changed under Law 42 (5) in the Texaco game, and he could have come to court and voiced his suspicions. He should remember that I went in to bat for him over the Tiger Moth incident on the Australia tour where, as vice-captain, I sat in on the first hearing involving the management. They wanted to send him home but I persuaded them to fine him instead. I could have sat back and said nothing then, because I was junior to the captain, Gooch, and manager, Micky Stewart. I'm not looking for eternal thanks from Gower, but he should have remembered things like that when he decided to stay away from my court case.

There were other players as well who kept their distance. Herdy approached Derek Pringle at Chelmsford, but he was another to dip out, apparently as a result of some legal advice which he had taken. Neil Fairbrother and Alec Stewart were other two players who particularly disappointed me. They had played for years with Wasim and Waqar, so they knew the full story. Yet, when it came down to supporting an England mate, it seems it was never a contest. Many of the England players had plenty to say at team meetings to Micky Stewart, yet they headed for the hills when it came to going on the record. I've had a big go in this book at the TCCB for lack of guts, but the same applies to a lot of my fellow cricketers. They talk one game in private and another in public. I know I might be impetuous in some of things I say and do, but at least I can live with myself. Some of those players cheated themselves as well as me.

In my opinion, there was no reason at all why Graham Gooch should not have supported me in public. I had been his vice-captain for a couple of years, and had always given him my full support. Now he had a chance to do the same for me, and he could have been as big a help as Ian Botham, Robin Smith and Don Oslear. As captain, he knew what happened at Old Trafford, Headlingley and especially at Lord's in the Texaco game. He didn't play in that Sunday match but he was present, and he did play at Old Trafford the following day when the whole ball tampering debate started to boil over after the Pakistan manager said the ball was changed because it went out of shape and the TCCB refused to put the record straight.

Don't forget, Gooch had been called up at The Oval for the same thing by John Holder and Merv Kitchen in 1991 against the West Indies. He had as much as anyone to say at our team meetings during the Lord's Test in 1992 when I asked umpire Barry Dudleston to watch what was going on. Yet after all that, Gooch kept quiet, when he should have been the first one to go public with me about it all. If the TCCB leaned on him, he should have told them to get lost. I was a member of his team, and that team had been done down – both by the ball tampering and then by the weak way the authorities dealt with the problem. He's another one who talked a big game in private, but backed off when it called for real guts to support me publicly. I am not trying to pretend that he was a big mate of mine, but Gooch and I played nearly forty Tests together, and surely loyalty counts for something.

Gooch preached loyalty all the time, yet I reckon that by staying quiet, he was actually disloyal to me. And so really was Gower, even though he might convince himself that he was justified in staying quiet. He *knew* what was going on, as I did, and should have come to court to say so, just as Robin Smith did, and Both would have done if the trial had not collapsed. We all have to live with our actions. I am comfortable with mine; only Gower and Gooch know whether they feel the same about theirs. I know I would have supported them had it been the other way round.

As for the court case itself, the main issue was not the money involved – either the costs or possible damages against me, because of my indemnity agreement with the *Mirror* – but that Sarfraz's writ meant my whole reputation was on the line. If I lost the case, I would be shown to be a liar, and also to have pointed the finger unfairly at an old friend and colleague.

Once my *Mirror* article appeared, the reactions came thick and fast. How about the joint claim of Waqar and Wasim that they had never been charged 'by an umpire, official or administrator with having done anything illegal'? What about those Don Oslear reports concerning Surrey, three of which were about games in which Waqar played?

I know he did not name a player, but simply said that illegal tampering had gone on while Surrey were in the field. And each instance just happened to follow an explosive, wicket-taking burst from Waqar with an old ball.

Waqar and Wasim then got personal in the same statement, published in the *Daily Telegraph* on 27 August 1992. 'We are amazed that a fellow professional has stooped so low as to make such unfounded comments in the papers. We can only guess at Allan Lamb's motives for his article in the *Daily Mirror*, but we hope that they are nothing to do with money or even worse our nationality'.

There it was, finally, out in the open. The hint of racism. Why is it that you can moan about Australians, West Indians, South Africans, New Zealanders, Indians and all the others, and never get accused of racist remarks? But say what I said about one aspect of their cricket, and then it is only because they are Pakistanis.

I suppose Shane Warne, Tim May and Mark Waugh only accused Salim Malik of offering them bribes because he was a Pakistani, and they'd have kept quiet had an alleged bribe come from a cricketer from another country. Like hell. The Pakistanis must think everyone else in world cricket is stupid.

I started off the 1993 season short of runs, making only 13 and 3 against Warwickshire at Edgbaston and 8 and 14 against Gloucestershire in our home match, but I recovered a little with 46 against Oxford University and 37 not out in a one-day match against the Australians, which we won on scoring rate.

Alan Herd also started slowly in his attempt to drag from the TCCB the help he needed for me, such as the umpires' report from that Lord's game and the ball which was apparently locked in a TCCB safe.

He and Francis Neate of Slaughter & May ping-ponged their way through a series of letters, with the TCCB determined to avoid any involvement. So much so that a letter from Herdy, dated 17 June, said that Tony Brown had been subpoenaed because 'I have asked if the TCCB would produce the reports voluntarily, and have been told that the Board was not willing to do so, hence the subpoena'.

Regarding the ball, the letter said, 'The Defendant is required to give particulars in respect of the ball that was changed on 23 August 1992 to "indicate how the ball was illegally damaged and by whom" and to indicate "at the point in time that the ball was changed, what condition it was in, and whether there were any scuff marks on one side of the ball".'

The asked-for reply was twelve days later, 29 June. You can't give the hurry-up to the legal profession. Again, it was a knock-back, repeating Mr Neate's request for copies of the pleadings in the action. Herdy had already refused unless he was given a good reason, which was then given in the letter. Mr Neate said that he wanted to 'advise my clients fully about the implications of the subpoena which you have served. It would seem to me self-evident that anyone receiving a subpoena in relation to an action to which they are not a party is entitled to be given a full explanation of the issues in the proceedings and the relevance of the subpoenaed evidence to those issues.'

Then came a little bouncer. 'I will, of course, be pleased to reimburse to your firm the cost of copying, should this be a concern.'

I'm not sure how much a word those sort of remarks cost in a letter, but it seemed to me to be becoming more and more of a game. What was I getting into?

The next letter on my behalf was dated 8 July, and Herdy rammed home the point that Tony Brown was only needed to identify, formally, the items of evidence. The reports and the ball were clearly relevant, and Herdy insisted that as 'Mr Lamb is the defendant, might it not be better to ask the Plaintiff or his Solicitors for copies of the proceedings?'

He then got to the heart to the matter. 'Your clients have been unwilling to produce documents voluntarily. You also told me yesterday that your clients have advised Counties having membership of the TCCB to request the employees and members of such counties not to provide any statements or other evidence to any of the parties involved in the current litigation; the TCCB being a body having control over cricketers, umpires and other officials involved in the game of cricket.

'If you would give me a cogent reason why your clients still wish to see the pleadings, then I will consider the position thereof. This would of course have to be on the basis that both Mr Lamb and ourselves received a full indemnity from you in respect of any claim arising out of publication of any of the pleadings. In the meantime, I have asked for the right to view the Reports of the two umpires who officiated on the 23 August last year and the report of the third umpire, Mr Oslear, without asking for copies of all three reports and await hearing from you with your response.'

I would make two points about the correspondence so far. How can the TCCB insist, as they continued to do, that they had nothing to do with my case, when those letters are full of 'my clients' and 'your clients', and what about the fact that they had instructed all the clubs and their employees not to provide any statements or other evidence?

The longer the summer went on, the more disgusted I got at what was not just non-co-operation. It was downright obstruction. After all that happened the previous year, and despite the result of my appeal, the TCCB were at it again. It was as though they were guilty of something they wanted to cover up and hide. They can't blame anyone who accuses them of being gutless, or an administrative shambles.

I have only played my cricket in England under the control of the TCCB, but players of the 1950s and the 1960s say how much worse things have become since the Test & County Cricket Board was formed in 1967. It sounded a good idea then to let the county clubs run their own professional game, but the result has been disastrous.

No wonder we have disappeared from the top layer of international cricket. Everything suffers when there is no respect between players and the authorities, and their attitude towards me in that period of fifteen months between August 1992 and November 1993 is typical of a set of officials whose first instinct is to run from trouble.

It must be the system, because I'd seen 'AC' in a different role as England manager in 1984. Mind you, I'd also seen Tony Brown in the same position in India and the West Indies.

When I was told about how determined they were to withhold all assistance to me, I couldn't believe it. They knew that apart from my original breach of their England contract, everything that had happened was because of the refusal of them and the ICC to release the facts of 23 August 1992. And even my *Mirror* article was only written out of sheer frustration once I knew that the match referee's report only told part of the story.

If someone, starting with Deryck Murray, and then progressing to include officials for other bodies, had spoken out on what was purely a cricketing matter, I would not have written the article, and I would not have been fined and suspended by my club. I would not have been further fined by the disciplinary committee, nor would I have had to instigate an appeal. And, most important of all to me now was that I would not have been dragged into High Court by Sarfraz if they had been strong enough to deal with the reported cases of ball tampering from 1990 to 1992.

I could tell things were hotting up because it only took Francis Neate six days to reply. It was mostly legal stuff concerning the right of 'my clients' to challenge the subpoena on the grounds of 'relevance or admissibility', but he then went on to make a different point.

'Your client is being sued for libel because of public statements which he made in breach of his contractual obligations to my client. Those matters have already been dealt with, nevertheless your client remains subject to the obligations of the contract in question, as well as remaining a registered cricketer subject to my clients' jurisdiction. In these circumstances, I find it strange that he should be seeking to justify the alleged libel which he uttered in breach of his obligations to my clients, to produce in evidence documents which they regard as strictly confidential, and the production of which in evidence would of itself, amount to a breach of my clients' regulations'.

I once read that it was firm policy on one of the Murdoch newspapers in Australia that journalists must never write a sentence of more than nine words. That sentence contains 63 words. Not only that, but it makes the claims that the TCCB's regulations are more important than the law of the land.

Several other letters were exchanged in the next three months, without Herdy getting very far. We knew that players and umpires were being discouraged from appearing in the case, yet still the TCCB said the case was nothing to do with them. I was getting nervous as the date of the trial drew nearer. During the summer, I'd managed to push most of it to the back of my mind, but from the middle of September onwards, there was no escaping that I was right in the thick of things.

I'm grateful to those people who did offer help. Micky Stewart made available various tapes from which we wanted to produce a montage of examples of the ball apparently being interfered with. Also, he told us what to look for, especially when the bowlers were walking back to bowl. And Don Oslear refused to be persuaded by Francis Neate to take no part in my case.

By this time, we wouldn't have settled out of court for any sum of money offered. We wouldn't have entertained one penny, not now that the affair had gone this far and I had seen the performance of the TCCB.

Alan Herd and Francis Neate had several telephone conversations about a possible settlement and various other matters, and another letter went to Slaughter & May on 4 October. 'There will not even be a token payment – irrespective of costs.'

That established one thing, and the letter went on to settle another. The TCCB were desperate that the case be dropped, which is why the question of a settlement was raised. These paragraphs followed:

'Whilst I appreciate that your clients are concerned to protect the welfare of cricket, I think it right to state that there is a view that the essence of cricket is not protected by any form of cheating. One of the reasons my client published his comments is that he felt that he and others had made many complaints to officials of the TCCB, but nothing was seen to have been done. In particular in respect of the 23 August match, a statement was issued by the Pakistan officials which my client felt did not represent the truth.

'It is only Sarfraz Nawaz who has sued in respect of Allan Lamb's comments. Sarfraz retired from first class cricket I believe in 1984. As it happens, on Friday evening I met Brian Moore of Edward Lewis and Co, the solicitor who issued a statement on behalf of Waqar Younis and Wasim Akram on the day of publication of Allan Lamb's comments. I know Brian quite well, and he told me that since he had first received instructions from Wasim and Waqar, he has heard nothing further.

'Sarfraz has stated in connection with other legal proceedings that he is on income support of £42 per week. As of course you know, one cannot get legal aid for a libel action. You will also know that the solicitors acting for Sarfraz are Messrs Karim, who also act for the Pakistan Board of Control.

'The only way I can see this matter being resolved, other than by the Court, is for the Plaintiff to discontinue. It is an action between a private individual Plaintiff and a private individual Defendant. It is Sarfraz who brought the action, not Allan Lamb, and unless Sarfraz is persuaded to discontinue I am afraid there is nothing I can do to help your client's position. I will certainly not make any approach to Karim of any nature, as I do not want to do anything which might be wrongly interpreted as showing a weakness from the defence point of view.'

Francis Neate's reply was immediate. 'I do know quite a lot about the underlying facts and I have to say that I am not convinced that your confidence in your client's case is entirely well-founded. My clients' view is that it is not in the best interests of the game of cricket for this kind of dispute to be fought out either in the press or the courts. Whoever wins the court case, the only real winners will be the press who will have a field day reporting the proceedings regardless of whether or not your client is justified and regardless of the truth.'

That last sentence says a lot. Namely, if I won, I would not gain anything – not in reputation or satisfaction. And what about the public? Wouldn't they gain something by knowing the facts which the authorities had gone to unheard of lengths to suppress? Also, what about his remark that the press would enjoy themselves whether or not I was justified and regardless of the truth? Relations between the TCCB and the media are governed by that sort of attitude, with neither trusting the other.

Then came the crunch paragraph, and another one which said more than just the words used. 'Furthermore there is a serious risk that the court hearing and more particularly the press reports of it will serve to exacerbate relationships with the Pakistan Board of Control and with the Pakistani community in England as a whole. These are both matters of legitimate and serious concern.'

I thought, 'There goes that song again'. I'd heard it from Frank Chamberlain and now I knew why. That meant that the TCCB were prepared to put up with virtually anything rather than stand up for principles which are right at the heart of life, never mind cricket. Again, I wondered why it is always Pakistan that frightens our authorities off.

The letter finished with an even more significant paragraph. 'So far as the other side is concerned, it may be that we could bring some influence to bear, but I would certainly hesitate to use up all the slender reserves of goodwill we have in pursuing an impossible goal. If all I am asked to do is to persuade them to surrender, then that would be a waste of time'.

Just as it was a waste of time trying to persuade me to settle out of court. By even mentioning that, a year after my Cricket Council appeal, the TCCB showed how they still couldn't understand anything I'd said or done.

Herdy was even quicker off the mark.

'I thank you for your letter by fax this afternoon. There is not much I can do but for the avoidance of doubt, please let me make it clear that I have not asked you or your clients to try and persuade anybody on the other side of anything. For reasons I understand, the approach as 'honest broker' came from you.'

The case was now 41 days away and they were the longest six weeks of my life.

Although I was nervous at the thought of the trial, I was confident about the result. After all, I had never accused Sarfraz of cheating. All I did was to say that he had shown me the trick of making an old ball swing, so the more I thought about it, the more I wondered why he was suing me for libel. Whoever advised him must have thought he had a case, but we couldn't see it.

The other thing was that he was being represented by the same legal firm that handled the business of the Pakistan Board of

Control, and I couldn't help thinking that maybe Sarfraz had been put up as a sort of stalking horse. If he won, then that might have opened the door for Waqar and Wasim to follow him in, but it seemed strange that a year after they had first threatened to sue me for the *Mirror* article, we had heard nothing.

Herdy kept going with Francis Neate right up to the start of the case. He was keen to pursue the chain between Sarfraz in the early 1970s and Waqar and Wasim twenty years later. That is why he wanted the TCCB to produce whatever evidence there was from the Lord's game. Namely, the umpires' reports and the ball.

Just four days before the start of the action, Francis Neate refused point blank on what he saw as strong legal grounds. Whether he was right or not is not the only thing that matters. I was being accused of libel by Sarfraz and if the TCCB had any understanding of what I'd done and my reasons, surely they would have helped where possible. Especially as by helping me with these items, they would not be doing anybody down. Yet their refusal, never mind whether legally justified or not, was robbing me of some crucial evidence. Who were they protecting?

Mr Neate's letter asked for Alan Herd to withdraw the subpoena concerning the reports, the ball and two other balls used in the Headingley Test 1992, which Don Oslear had kept and photographed, despite various requests from A C Smith saying 'Please can we have our balls back?'

The argument was that the ball was an object and that cannot be subpoenaed, and also that a person not directly involved in the case (i.e. Tony Brown) cannot be compelled to produce such an item of property as evidence.

That dealt with the cricket balls, and he wrote that 'the TCCB will only release the umpires' reports pursuant to an order of the Court'. By that he meant 'pursuant to the subpoena at the trial and not before, and the TCCB will only produce the reports if it is satisfied that the reports are relevant to the issues in the proceedings. We are currently considering the question of relevance and whether to challenge the subpoena on this ground. I also note that the subpoena served on Don Oslear purports to require production of two cricket balls and obviously the same considerations will apply as are stated above. You will of course appreciate that the two balls concerned are the property of the TCCB.'

You couldn't get a much clearer statement of intent, that the TCCB were determined that they would make nothing public of the events of 23 August 1992 and afterwards. What a shift of policy. AC had been keen when he prepared a draft statement on that day for Deryck Murray to say that the ball had been changed by the umpires because of malpractice. OK, so he was overruled by Murray on that day, but what about later? Why refuse to produce something which would confirm, for the first time officially, what had happened? It is no good him hiding behind the ICC Code of Conduct which prohibits comment on a match referee's decision. This was a court case, so why the brick wall?

There seem to be only three alternative answers. They did not want to help me. Or, they wanted to protect themselves. Or they wanted to protect the Pakistanis. I cannot believe either of the last two theories, because the TCCB had nothing to protect themselves from, except for the reaction of the Pakistan Board of Control and their players.

Which only leaves the fact that they did not want to help me. Nice isn't it, when your country's cricket board backs off on a matter like that? I am not one to hold grudges, but nothing in my twenty-four years playing first-class cricket has made me so bitter. I know I broke my contract by writing in the *Mirror*, but the important facts are surely that the ball was changed because the umpires believed it had been interfered with, and that the Pakistanis pressured men like Deryck Murray and John Stephenson to say that the ball was changed because it had gone out of shape. That would have been untrue, and the TCCB know it. Yet, when they finally had a chance to nail that lie and several others, they refused.

Why? I suppose I'll never know the answer, but the officials concerned have got to live with that, not me. They lost whatever reputation they had among cricketers for integrity and showed that they can't be trusted.

Herdy confirmed to Mr Neate that we would withdraw the subpoenas concerning the balls. He wrote that 'the events of the 1992 tour were of relevance in establishing what it was that the Plaintiff was suing about, and indeed that my client's newspaper publication was basically concerned about the events of 1992. The relevance of the umpires' reports is that the Defendants have been ordered to provide particulars of the condition of the ball that was changed on 23rd August.'

I have used only a few extracts from a file of correspondence that made me realise why costs are so big in court cases. And yet the TCCB were spending thousands of pounds in blocking me, while they tried to maintain they were not involved. What I do know is that the bills were a waste of time and money – money which could and should have gone back to the counties as an extra share-out.

Herdy handled everything for me, including my witness statement which I worked long and hard to get right. I probably altered half a dozen drafts before I was satisfied, but it was my first experience of the High Court and I didn't want to make any stupid mistakes. I wondered about how I would get on when it was my turn in the witness box. Would I stand up to cross-examination, and would I be able to field questions that might be loaded? In the end, I tried to push it out of my mind, because I reckoned that if I just stuck to the truth, then nobody would be able to trip me up on any serious matter.

My witness statement was seven pages long and I detailed various occasions on which I saw the Pakistanis apparently gouging and generally interfering with the ball, including the Lord's and Headingley Tests and the one-day international at Lord's. I set out my conversations with the three umpires, Ken Palmer, John Hampshire and Barry Dudleston, who stood in the two games at Lord's, and also with Micky Stewart in both matches.

Also I put down what Sarfraz said to me in the Karachi Test in 1984 when he had me caught at short-leg off a real boomerang with the old ball. I said to him, 'You're still using that same method you showed me', and he laughed and said, 'Yes, Lamby, I am the best'. But none of my remarks had directly called him a cheat, and that was what he was suing me for.

As for Imran, I told about a chance meeting he had with Robin Smith and me on the Wednesday before the start of the Lord's Test match against the West Indies in 1991. 'Judge' and I were sitting at a pavement table outside a wine-bar in St John's Wood, when Imran saw us as he was walking past. He came and joined us for a chat, and he asked Robin how Aqib Javed, then playing for Hampshire, was doing.

Robin said, 'Very well – he was doing a good job for us but had got warned on numerous occasions for tampering with the ball'. Imran replied, 'Yes, I've told him to be more discreet when he does it.'

So to the hearing, with Lindsay and me deciding to travel each day by train from Kettering. The next few days were going to be very interesting.

20
The Hearing

The hearing started on Monday 15 November 1993, with a crowded press area. My QC was David Eady, with Andrew Caldecott (now a QC himself) as his junior counsel; Jonathan Crystal acted for Sarfraz, with Justice Otton in charge. Each day was a long one once we'd decided to travel by train. It meant getting up at 6 am to catch a train about 7 am, so that we could go to Alan Herd's office before we got to court at 9.30 am.

Both Eady and Crystal had been involved in two high profile cases. Eady had been advising the Mirror Group Newspapers over the Princess of Wales' gym photographs while Crystal had acted as counsel for Richard Branson in his fight with British Airways. As for 'Sarf' and me, we never spoke throughout the four days. It's a shame when something like that happens between two former team mates, but we were only in court because of him. The press were there only for one reason. They wanted to know why the ball was changed at Lord's 15 months earlier, but they had a long wait before they got the answer in what was the first big case involving cricket since the Packer trial in 1977.

The jury had nine women and three men, and I wondered how much they understood on the first day when Sarfraz explained how he held a cricket ball to make it swing. A ball was given to each juror and the Judge entered into the spirit of things by saying, 'We will open from the pavilion end'.

Sarf explained about the legitimate means of obtaining reverse swing involving spit and sweat on one side of the ball with the other side being allowed to roughen and deteriorate by being hit around.

I'm well aware that is the legal method, but that sometimes takes more time than the fielding side has got, which is when the helping hand using finger nails etc comes in.

I was accused of having double standards by Mr Crystal, who made a big point that I'd never had a word to say about Sarf and his methods in the six years I played with him for Northamptonshire. That was easy to answer. It was because I never played a county match in which anyone, his team mates or the opposition, suspected anything. I believed that what he showed me he used only on the rough wickets of Pakistan. The court was told that Sarfraz had suffered 'an appalling libel, he had been vilified and even called the Godfather of Cheating by some people'.

It was my turn in the box next day, and I was very apprehensive on the train going down. When I was called, all I seemed to see was a mass of wigs and media, and I found taking the oath was much worse on my nerves than taking guard in a Test match. The Judge must have seen how nervous I was and we had a couple of laughs in my first half hour of testimony. Every time I spoke I bent down so that my mouth was close to what I thought was the microphone, but it turned out it wasn't, so Justice Otton put me right.

The next thing was that because I was obviously going to be in the box for a few hours, he suggested that I sit down. 'If I do that, nobody will see me,' was my reply so away we went. I think I was lucky going in after Sarfraz, because I reckon he was a lousy witness, and I knew that if I just concentrated on the truth and let nothing budge me on the main facts, I would be bound to make a decent impression.

Another thing that helped me was that Mr Crystal did not seem to know much about cricket and I thought he waffled a lot. I made the most of my five and a half hours in the box, spread over Tuesday and Wednesday. I named Waqar, Wasim, Aqib and Aamir Sohail as the four players I saw interfering with the ball during the Lord's Test match.

It is funny how some things get to you more than others, and it might surprise some people what gave me more offence than anything else in the trial. I know that the idea is to ruffle a witness, but it stuck in my throat that I was accused of being a whinging pom and a bad loser. Anyone in cricket the world over will tell you that I am neither.

I also named Martin Bicknell as an English player who had been reported for ball tampering, and emphasised how much concern had been caused by the practice since 1990. I told the court of all my conversations with umpires during the two Lord's games and I repeated that my only reason for deliberately breaking my TCCB contract was that no ICC or TCCB official would deny the lie by Pakistan the day after the match that the ball had been changed because it had gone out of shape. I can't repeat often enough that an official confirmation of the facts would have killed the matter stone dead. And if the TCCB were afraid that they might have been sued for calling the Pakistanis cheats, why were they unafraid to accuse Surrey of the same offence? I know they only administered a slap on the wrist, but the charge of ball tampering was the same as Ken Palmer and Hampshire accused the Pakistanis of when they changed the ball.

Again, why is everyone afraid of the Pakistanis?

The trial got enormous coverage in the nationals, with the odd cricket correspondent in the press gallery. After my first day in the box, Colin Bateman of the *Daily Express* wrote: 'It was one of England batsman Allan Lamb's toughest innings as Jonathan Crystal, who probed away, had Lamb fending off several deliveries as nasty as anything he had faced in his illustrious career. Under cross-examination, Crystal asked Lamb why none of the 17 umpires and match referees used during the series had reported them. Lamb said they were gagged by Lord's and scared of losing their jobs'.

By that, I didn't mean that the TCCB sent the umpires official letters telling them not to report ball tampering. I'm not that thick, but I do know all the umpires on the first-class list, and there wasn't one in the early 1990s who believed they would get backing if they reported – not after what happened, or rather didn't happen when, among others, Don Oslear and John Holder did report sides with Test bowlers in them, and they both believe it counted against their career record.

I said in evidence that, 'There is no way an umpire will stick his neck out and jeopardise his chances. John Holder did and he never had another Test. Test matches double the umpires' fees. They are the peak of their job'. My first day in the box ended in a hurry, when Mr Crystal asked me if I was calling Martin Bicknell a cheat.

As the *Express* put it: 'This remark from Crystal brought an admonition from Mr Justice Otton. At that time, the prosecution suggested that Lamb had had enough, and the Judge replied: 'Well Mr Lamb has played longer innings than this one, but there seems to be an appeal against the light, so we will stop there'.

Things were hotting up now, and the third day, the Wednesday, brought out a great deal in my favour. I had to finish my stint, and stood firm when Mr Crystal accused me of inventing the conversation with Sarfraz about him showing me how to give the hurry-up process to obtaining reverse swing. The *Daily Mail* reported that I 'glared at the lawyer, and said, "are you calling me a liar? I do not accept that".'

We had a video to look at, in which Chris Cowdrey would try to interpret 54 filmed instances of irregular treatment of the ball put together from BBC Television tapes of the 1992 season. But before that, two of my former county colleagues, pace bowlers Alan Hodgson and John Dye, would give evidence about their experience of playing with Sarfraz.

Alan made an impressive witness, as he told about a couple of incidents in a charity game at Stamford in 1991. 'I took a wicket early in my final spell and Sarfraz said "well bowled". He took the ball off me and started scratching it up one side: "This is what we do Hodge".

'I got another wicket and Sarfraz asked me if the ball was swinging. I said a bit and he started scratching it up right in front of me. He was scratching away and saying, "This is the way we do it now". He told me not to shine the ball but to scratch it up one side'.

John Dye went the other way, testifying for Sarfraz and saying that he'd played in the same game and saw or heard nothing. Fine, until he was asked where he was fielding when Sarfraz and Hodgson were talking. 'Fine leg'. That was him gone, with all three stumps wood-peckered.

'Hodge' made clear that he had never seen Sarfraz do anything like that in a county game when they played together for 10 years. Wayne Larkins was another good witness for me. He said that 'Sarfraz told me about scratching the ball 12 years ago. I asked him at the end of one particular day why he didn't take the new ball, and he told me he would rather bowl with the old one because it swung more. He also told me that he achieved this by dampening the shiny side with spit, and scratching or scuffing the rough side. But I never saw him do this in a game'.

John Young of *The Times* wrote about that particular day's evidence, and ended with another bull point from 'Ned'. He wrote: 'Questioned by Mr Eady, Larkins said he had never known a bowler to achieve reverse swing without the ball being tampered with'.

Then came the video, with Chris Cowdrey in devastating form and a jury that must have been close to becoming totally bemused in the first two and a half days. The *Daily Telegraph's* David Millward wrote: 'Mr Cowdrey, who was capped six times by England, said, "Before I saw this tape I had heard stories of people picking the seams and so on, but having seen the tape, this was more irregular than anything I have ever seen before".

'The video, showing incidents of alleged ball tampering involving Younis, Javed and Akram, was taken from Test matches at Lord's, Headingley and The Oval. Cowdrey highlighted several incidents during the second, fourth and fifth Tests which apparently showed the three bowlers using thumbs or fingernails to scratch the ball'.

What made as big an impact as anything were the now famous remarks of Richie Benaud. Seeing Aqib Javed digging deep, he said, 'Whoa, steady on', followed by 'Jesus' when he mistakenly thought he was off microphone. The *Telegraph* wrote: 'Benaud was in Australia and unable to give evidence in person on behalf of Lamb. He explained his astonishment by saying that ball tampering gave the bowlers an unfair advantage and "was against the spirit of the game".

'In a *News of the World* article during the following Test, Benaud said that what he had seen – Aqib working on the ball before tossing it back to Waqar – "rocked me back on my heels".

'He wrote that "perhaps it was just another praiseworthy method of removing grass seeds embedded in the leather or fixing a ball that had gone soft". But it astonished him to the extent that he let go with "Whoa" and invoked the name of the founder of Christianity.

'Of that incident, Cowdrey told the jury, "Aqib has got his thumb and he has just gouged the ball, it is very blatant".'

I thought that each day had got better for me since Sarfraz started the case off in the box on Monday. Tuesday and Wednesday morning, I'd done all right, and then Cowdrey, Hodgson and Larkins were terrific on Wednesday. Now for the fourth day, because we'd got some big guns lined up – 'Beefy', 'Judge' and umpire Don Oslear.

Guess what? Beefy was late, and so couldn't go into the box when his turn came. He'd been delayed flying to Heathrow, and only got to court an hour or so before lunch. Judge gave some powerful evidence, including saying that he had played in every international match last year against the Pakistanis, and constantly saw bowlers and fielders interfering with the ball illegally. He named three players in particular, Wasim, Waqar and Aqib, who he said were always using their finger and thumb nails to scratch and roughen one side of the ball. He also said 'in all the matches I played, I saw something going on, and I complained to the umpires three times and I also raised it with Micky Stewart'.

Robin did well, because he gets a bit nervous when he has to speak in public, and he got a big shock later in the day when the Judge asked him to stand up. He looked as though he'd been caught cribbing at school and went red as he got to his feet. We all wondered what was coming next, but all Justice Otton wanted to do was to congratulate him on his selection for the tour of the West Indies and to wish him every success on behalf of the jury and everyone else in court. That came at the end of the case, but there was plenty of drama either side of lunch before that.

Don Oslear was called next, with Beefy still in the middle of an attempt on the lap record from Heathrow to Court 14. I had to admire Don because I knew what unfair pressure was put on him by the TCCB. He knew that they had blocked our request for reports and the ball, and Mr Francis Neate had seen him a few days before the start of the trial. But still Don Oslear resisted everything they threw at him, because he was like me – he'd had enough of the TCCB and their cover-ups. This was the first time I'd tangled with them, but Don had had half a dozen experiences over the years where he had reported various offences by players – mostly ball tampering – only for the Board to remain silent and do nothing, except for those ineffectual letters to Surrey.

In his evidence to David Eady, he answered a question about any irregularities he noticed with the ball during the Headingley Test match in his position as the third umpire: 'I did, sir. In my opinion the ball was beginning to be scoured on one side by an outside agency. In my opinion it is not possible to scour a ball like that by legal means'.

I knew that Don had taken the ball to the match referee, Clyde

Walcott, after England collapsed from 270 for one to 320 all out with Waqar suddenly taking five wickets in 38 balls after he had got none in the previous 178. Ken Palmer and Merv Kitchen were the umpires, but once the ball was returned to them with little apparent support from the referee about any tampering, they took no further action. Maybe that is why Ken Palmer and John Hampshire told Deryck Murray at Lord's that they were going to change the ball, but did not ask his permission.

The *Telegraph's* David Millward wrote up Don's evidence in this way. 'Mr Oslear flatly contradicted the explanation given at the time by the Pakistan team manager, Intikhab Alam, that the ball was replaced because it was hammered out of shape. Mr Oslear, who also accused the Pakistanis of scouring the ball during a previous Test at Headingley, was at the Lord's lunch time meeting in which the two umpires and Mr Deryck Murray examined the ball.

'Mr Oslear said: "The ball on that occasion had lines cut across it on one side. It was not as deeply scoured as it had been at Headingley. But I felt it was the start of an attempt to scour the ball". He added that the ball was changed on the instructions of the umpires, John Hampshire and Ken Palmer'.

Go on, I wanted to scream. Tell the court the official reason for the change. At long last, despite every despicable move by the ICC and TCCB officials to stay quiet in 15 months, good old British justice was about to defeat them. In came Mr Eady with the killer question. 'Mr Oslear, was the ball changed under Law 42 (5)?'

Don's answer only took a split second, but in that time I felt a wave of relief, like when I've gone for a big hit and know as soon as I've made contact that it's six. Or the odd time I sink a long putt at golf and know I've canned it when the ball is still a yard or more from the hole. Go on Don, let 'em have it.

'Most certainly sir'. There it was. Under oath in a court of law. The one fact that the entire cricketing world had been denied knowledge of by the men who were supposed to have the greater good of the game at heart. I looked at Lindsay and she nodded and smiled.

Don was magnificent. He must have known he was running the risk of ruining his own career, but he never wavered. The *Telegraph* report said, 'The court heard that the Pakistani manager was told that the ball could not have deteriorated as quickly unless there had been some outside intervention'.

Of course it couldn't – the damn thing wasn't 30 overs old, whereas the Headingley ball had had at least three times as much usage. Also, it was a damp and lush outfield after the rain which caused the match to be spread over two days.

'Once the decision was taken to change the ball, Mr Alan Smith, the TCCB Chief Executive, was summoned. Pressed by Mr Eady, Mr Oslear added that Mr Smith took the decision not to give journalists an explanation why the ball had been changed'.

By that, Don did not mean that AC agreed with no explanation being given in the match referee's statement, but simply that he had no power to expand on it afterwards. Maybe, but that still didn't stop the Board's Media Relations Manager, Ken Lawrence, from dropping some pretty broad hints about the facts. He'd been a journalist for years, so he knew that an unofficial briefing would help the press to write the proper story, not one based upon speculation. Just co-incidence, I suppose, that he was replaced within a few months in what the rest of the press termed surprising circumstances.

So was Don Oslear, although the TCCB insist that they didn't move any goal posts when they denied him a contract in his 65th year, because his birthday was before the start of the season. There have been at least half a dozen precedents in the last 20 years concerning umpires who continued to stand after their 65th birthday.

Don's evidence caused such a flutter with Mr Crystal and his colleagues that we recessed for lunch early. Don still had to be cross-examined, so he couldn't speak to anyone as we went over the road to a couple of pubs. I was looking forward to the re-start, because I reckoned that the morning session had put us miles ahead.

When we got back into court, there was a delay, so I chatted with Beefy and Robin. Beefy is usually ahead of the game – any game – and after about an hour sitting there, he said to me 'something's happened. I reckon they might have pulled out'.

Bulls-eye. They proved what a waste of time the whole thing had been by withdrawing. As far as I was concerned that meant I'd won, but you can never beat someone like Sarfraz in an argument. On his behalf Mr Crystal explained why the case was dropped, and had the cheek to say that it was because Sarfraz accepted that I had never accused him of cheating. What in the name of Langebaanweg and

Scaldwell, where I now live, was the reason he brought the case? Because he said I'd libelled him by accusing him of cheating.

The exact quote from Mr Crystal was that 'Mr Lamb had acknowledged that in the games he played with Sarfraz, the bowler played within the Laws of Cricket and did not cheat and Mr Lamb does not and never has suggested otherwise'. I suppose if you read between the lines, there is no mention of games involving Sarfraz other than those I played in – which were only a small percentage of his overall career. Mr Eady said on my behalf that I stood by my newspaper article which I wrote in good faith and also stood by the evidence that I had given in court. Namely, that Sarfraz did show me the trick of obtaining reverse swing with an old ball, and I had seen the Pakistan bowlers frequently tampering with the ball on their 1992 tour of England.

And the biggest bonus of the lot – the one that finally made worthwhile the 15 months of brushes I'd had with the TCCB and then Sarfraz. Lindsay was happy and relieved, because we'd both been under a big strain at home in that time. It wasn't easy to stay normal in front of the two kids and she was terrific in her support all the way through.

Sarfraz was first out of the court and immediately started to claim a victory. As we were originally awarded costs I'm not sure what sort of victory it was. He brought the case. He dropped it, and the court landed him with an order for £100,000 costs. As it happened, the *Mirror* agreed to pay our half, to avoid any trouble in obtaining the £50,000 from Sarfraz.

The money side was unimportant to me, and not just because I was indemnified. I had fought to defend myself against every one who threatened my good name by questioning what I'd said, and also my right to say it. Lindsay felt just as bitter about the TCCB as I did, and she made an important point when she stated that I was effectively their employee. I can understand them nailing me for breaching my contract with them, but once that was finished with at the appeal, they had no possible justification for refusing to help me where they could.

The Chief Executives of ICC and TCCB, David Richards and Alan Smith, were forced to say something after the trial in response to some tough questioning from the national press. How about these two?

Richards: 'Match referees' reports are confidential and, for the system to work, they must remain confidential whatever period of time has elapsed'. Great that. The system didn't work, mostly because of his precious confidentiality. His comment about my trial was fair enough – or rather his 'no comment', because he said, 'ICC will make no comment on legal advice'.

As for AC, he trotted out: "Our solicitors were in court this week and I shall be getting a full briefing about it in the morning. But the outcome does not affect us directly because it was contested privately by two individuals'. In which case, why were the Board's solicitors in court every day?

The rest of AC's statement was no better. 'We tackled the issue of ball tampering more than 12 months ago. The Board's principle concern has been to support its umpires and, in particular, to preserve the confidentiality of its reporting systems with them and the finality of their decisions'.

Tell that to Don Oslear and John Holder. What support did they get? Or the other umpires who reported illegally damaged balls?

Mr Crystal seemed to me to get his knickers in a twist when he explained that Sarfraz had withdrawn because he was now satisfied I'd never accused him of cheating in games that we'd played together. He said, 'If you play on the same side as Mr Lamb, you can cheat, because he ain't going to complain about it. He never did, not in all the years they played together. But when England play Pakistan he does not want any cheating on the other side. What double standard is that?'

Actually it is only double standards if there was cheating in those games with Sarfraz, so did Mr Crystal infer that there was?

We gathered in a wine bar and celebrated. Beefy had come all that way for nothing, and I kidded him with: ' A great help you were'. Back he came: 'You stole my thunder, you little shit, so there goes my job as a government representative in Pakistan'. Robin was a lot more confident now it was all over. 'As I was the last player in the witness box, I feel I have played a large part in this. They must have been petrified of my evidence'.

Not half as much as he was when the Judge asked him to stand up in court to wish him well in the West Indies. Justice Cotton seemed to enjoy himself, particularly when the evidence got technical. His final act was to announce what he would do with the ten cricket balls used for demonstration purposes. He said: 'I'm keeping one, there are six for the jury and that leaves three. I can think of no better beneficiary that the Royal Courts of Justice cricket team'. Before we left court, Lindsay threw me a ball a juror wanted signing. She said, 'Don't scratch it, Lamby. I don't want to see another scratched ball in my life'. There was an answer to that – two in fact – but I kept quiet.

It was all fun and laughs after it was over, and a few of the next morning's newspapers treated it lightly with headlines like 'Stumps drawn at High Court as judge takes ball home', and 'Sarfraz declares before Botham can take the crease'.

But there was a very serious side to it, and I was pleased to see a newspaper like *The Times* turn their correspondent, Alan Lee, loose on to the implications of the events before, during and after the case.

The headline was 'Game's rulers courting the wrong arm of the law', and what an opening paragraph, considering it was written in November 1993.

'At the time it was made, the decision by the International Cricket Council to award the next World Cup to the sub-continent seemed perverse and prejudicial. The events of the last fortnight have offered nothing in the way of reassurance, either that the game's ruling body acted advisedly, or that its flagship competition will proceed smoothly in two years' time.

'All concerned have been in the dock, figuratively and almost literally'.

After going on to voice misgivings about the 1996 World Cup, Lee said this about my court case:

'Pakistan's standing in the fair-play league was dealt another blow by the umpire, Don Oslear, confirming what many people already knew or suspected to be the real reason the ball was changed during the controversial one-day international at Lord's.

'That it had not been made public before is a matter for the conscience of the ICC. Its appointed officers chose to remain silent, inviting the worst and most prolonged form of speculation which eventually led to the High Court. It was a silence which spoke of fear and weakness, provoked by the belief that Pakistan would either take legal action or abort the tour, maybe both if the truth was told.

'The image of cricket has sustained some needless damage in recent days. Much of it could have been avoided by firmer leadership when circumstances demanded that tough decisions be taken and broadcast'.

Herdy got a good quote into the same newspaper. 'We sub-poenaed the TCCB to see the ball and the umpires' reports, but they simply did not want to do it. The board are very concerned about the image of cricket. That phrase occurred a lot in my dealings with them. I said to them that it might be better for the game's image if any form of cheating were revealed.'

Even now, nearly three years later, I can't help thinking what a mess it all was. My county's first reaction was to fine and suspend me. The TCCB added another heavy fine, and the ICC just hid. For years, and especially in 1992, players have been trying to get the authorities to take cheating seriously but, for years, the authorities just turned a blind eye.

The Editor of *Wisden,* Matthew Engel, wrote this in the *Guardian*: 'Much of the evidence this week has been riveting. Open court has brought out far more detail about ball tampering than cricket would ever have permitted left to its own devices. In that sense, Mr Sarfraz has done the game a service. And his failure to sustain the case will make it easier for cricket to conduct its own open debate. If it can bring itself to do something so uncharacteristic'.

Nice thought Matthew, but nothing changes, nor will it unless English cricket's top officials are either changed, or made to speak out by the clubs. Beefy had a go, but the board are more likely to make Phil Tufnell their press officer when he retires than listen to the likes of Both. He went into print with: 'Once and for all why don't you tell the world officially what the Pakistanis were up to in the summer of 1992?'

He also asked the Pakistanis 'to censure their guilty bowlers, or for Pakistan to even be banned from international cricket until they do take action against the culprits'. At least he was speaking from the strength of playing in that Lord's one-day international, when he said: 'We were told the ball had been changed because it had been tampered with. Then we were told not to say anything'. One quick call to the press box was what Beefy thought of that sort of instruction from on high.

Ken Lawrence went into print to defend AC, but seemed to confuse himself, with this in the *Daily Telegraph*: 'What has to be remembered is that ICC match referees were new to English cricket in 1992. No-one was quite sure of their authority. Umpires were supposed to be still in control of matches, but if they opted out of a decision and left it to the referee, it was felt that the issue had passed from TCCB to the ICC'.

Except the umpires did *not* opt out of a decision, so the matter did *not* pass from TCCB control to that of the ICC. I accept that the match referee's statement is his own, and he did not have to accept Alan Smith's draft, but that did not stop AC putting the record straight later. Or even if he, personally, didn't want to do that, he could have organised sufficient co-operation with Herdy to ensure that the facts were made public, as he had wanted to do on the day of the match.

Ken Lawrence seemed to agree with me. 'I suspect that, given similar circumstances again, a different view might be taken today. But in the confusion that reigned on that Sunday in August 1992, the match referee's ruling against Smith's statement was, with considerable reluctance, accepted. Our belief then was that Smith's words would have saved a great deal of trouble. I am in no doubt about that today.'

And those words of AC? All Lawrence would say was: 'He wanted the truth told, briefly but clearly'.

We held a press conference at Northampton on the Friday, and Alan Herd and I again said how disappointing it was to find so many players we approached put under pressure by the TCCB not to appear.

I note in my cuttings that I picked out 'Judge' for refusing to bow to pressure. 'Robin is currently an England player and at the peak of his career. I admire that guy. He's got character and guts. He showed up every other cricketer who didn't come forward, even though they knew what was happening'.

Lindsay had a big go at the Board at that press conference. 'I think the TCCB owe Allan an apology. I'd clear out the lot of them and give a young man a chance. I knew Allan was telling the truth and I never doubted he would come out on top'.

The point was also made that there was no settlement on the basis of shared costs. Costs were awarded to me against Sarfraz. Martin Johnson, then of the *Independent* before he moved to the *Telegraph*, made several points about Pakistan and their touchy relationship with the British.

He referred in print to Javed Miandad as a 'streetfighter', meaning to be complimentary about his batting qualities when the chips were down. His lawyers took a different view, thinking that Johnson was inferring that Javed went around beating up people on pavements. After my case, he wrote, 'As always, the "sit tight and say nothing approach" by the ICC and TCCB has merely made things worse. As far as Pakistan are concerned, cricket in England is run by arrogant racists. As far as England are concerned, Pakistan cheat. Today, the two countries are as far apart as ever'.

Anyone who thinks that Johnson is stretching a point should note this nice little remark from the Pakistani tour manager in 1992, Khalid Mahmood. 'I think there has been a element of racism in what's been going on. It can't be a coincidence that it's been between two South Africans, Allan Lamb and Robin Smith, who want to have a go at us'. And Beefy and Don Oslear? Or perhaps British racism is different from South African racism. No wonder Pakistan cricket is always in a mess with administrators like that running it.

Even Sarfraz jumped on the same rotten bandwagon. He did a piece with Colin Bateman in the *Daily Express* in which he said, 'The court didn't understand all this. There were nine young girls on the jury who didn't know the difference between a football and a cricket ball. We should have had a multi-racial jury, instead we had 11 English people. And most of those were women who kept looking and smiling at Lamby and Robin Smith and Botham. That's understandable. They are national heroes but it was not a serious court case – that's why we stopped it'.

AC's statement after the end of the case included this sentence, which again shows a complacent attitude that is destroying goodwill with players and umpires. He explained that the TCCB 'would have produced whatever was required by law, but it could be that umpires would refrain from mentioning anything controversial if their reports were subsequently made public'. Most of them stopped doing any such thing well before my court case, because their reports were sat on, not acted on.

The *Mirror* kept on having a go at the TCCB, but they just sat tight. Perhaps they hoped it would die a death. Now, they know better.

21
The Press and Broadcasters

I've always refused to take the press too seriously because they usually deal only in highs and lows. I know sometimes we players pretend we don't read the real rough stuff in the tabloids, but you can't help knowing what has been written. I only get bothered when I know my family has been hurt by the headlines, but it seems there is no escape from this in English cricket.

I honestly believe we have the worst press in the cricketing world. Hardly any of them could write a proper cricket report, even if their editors wanted that ... which they don't. They hunt together on the Test circuit, each one anxious that he doesn't miss anything. There is not one tabloid that takes a different view during a Test match or on tour, and if you've read one you've read them all. The broadsheets are different, but even they now seem to have got caught up in a world of quotes. That's a poor way to fill columns, and it shows that the correspondents concerned haven't got an opinion of their own that's worth a light.

As with most things in life, the approach of the press and the media in general has changed since I first got into cricket. Particularly in the tabloid papers, which are now in such fierce competition with each other, anything seems to go. When I started with England in 1982, men like Peter Smith, Pat Gibson, Peter Laker and Chris Lander were completely trustworthy. You could have a drink with them, and talk about all sorts of things which happen on a tour. Late nights, parties and so on. Normal bar room gossip if you like, but they would never let you down by revealing anything that was said.

It started to go wrong on the 1984 tours of New Zealand and Pakistan, when the *Mail on Sunday* sent their heavy newsmen to Lahore to try to dig the dirt. The same happened a couple of years later in Barbados when 'Both' was put through the press wringer. They can argue that we are public figures, therefore we are fair game for anything they print, but that is just cant.

The split between them and us came when Smith and Gibson told us that they were all coming under increasing pressure to report everything if they travelled with us. They also told us that we could expect set-ups, and that was when the England teams made it a matter of policy to keep our distance. It led to a lot of bad feeling, including some of us refusing interviews, and I now see that that was taking things too far. To be fair to Smith and Gibson, they told us that one of the reasons the tabloids changed was because Both had then become one of the most publicised cricketers of his time, and never seemed to be out of the headlines.

I felt sorry for him, because I spent a lot of time with him and know that when he walked into a pub or a restaurant, there was always someone who wanted to be clever and try him out.

It is easier to say now that I have retired, but the players have got to swallow the rubbish and still try to promote themselves and the game with the more responsible journalists.

There has never been any trouble with most of the broadsheet correspondents, or someone like John Thicknesse, then of the *Evening Standard*. At least they wanted to concentrate on cricket matters, and we never had a problem about a confidence being broken. It is always difficult on tour, because the newspapers insist that their reporters stay in the same hotels as the players and also travel with them.

The pattern on tour nowadays is always the same. The manager meets the press and lays down the guide lines for co-operation, and everyone is happy until the first sensational tabloid story comes back from England. The players then close ranks and the management looks for ways to be unco-operative regarding press deadlines back home. It soon becomes like kids in the playground, with both sides looking for tit-for-tat. A shame, but that is the way of the modern world, and I don't see any solution.

It is different at home, because we don't see so much of them, and often they don't stay at the same hotels anyway. As for criticism, it has never bothered me if it was justified and thought through properly. What a reporter should do more often is to try to work out why a batsman or a bowler has played badly and made obvious mistakes. We are only human, and we must have bad days when we do silly things and don't know why. What I have learned in my brief time in the television commentary box is to try to put myself in the mind of the players, and try to work out why they do certain things. I often went in to bat to try to grab the initiative. Sometimes it worked and I was a hero, and sometimes it didn't and then I would be blasted for playing an irresponsible stroke.

If I had to make one judgement on England's cricket writers, it is that hardly any of them know the game or attempt to learn enough about it to write a proper cricket piece. They will argue that the public gets the papers they want, otherwise nobody would read them. Therefore they write what their editors ask for, which means the cricket content of a tabloid report is smaller than that of the broadsheet.

My favourite cricket correspondent? It has to be John Woodcock, now retired from *The Times* (but still contributing). He not only knows the game but has a feel for it, and that is very rare. There are now more ex-Test cricketers writing, but I'm not convinced yet about some of them. I'm in the same position. When we played we moaned all the time about criticism, and now we are called on to do the same thing, and I can understand the players grumbling about double standards.

Geoff Boycott in particular comes in for stick, because the players reckon he is always having a go. It couldn't have been right for him to coach the players and then have a go at them behind the microphone. I know he argues that if he sees a mistake, he is entitled to point it out. But he has such a heavy repetitive style that I can't take him. One instance which upset us was when he had been coaching the players, and then outlined on television the best way for the Aussies to get Jack Russell out. He kept hammering home that they must go round the wicket to him.

Both is criticised for going too much the other way and never picking a player out for a mistake. But my number one is Richie Benaud. The players respect him because of his own Test record, and for the fact that he always tries to understand why they have done something, even if it has turned out wrong. I suppose it is second nature for him, because he was such a brilliant thinking captain, who was always trying to put himself into the shoes of the opposition and work out what they wanted him to do least of all, and then he would do it. David Gower is now well established with the BBC but personally I reckon 'Lubo' should commit himself more. Too often, he takes the middle road when the situation is crying out for a strong view, one way or the other. He has more to offer than just being a fence-sitter, but that is what he often is at the moment. On radio, Jon Agnew has done well – probably because he is young enough to talk to the players on their level. As for myself, I am treating it as an experiment which might work. If it does, fine. If not, it won't be the end of the world. All I ask is that if I do make something of it, and if I start the 'Boycs' approach of too much 'I did this or that', that someone tells me there and then.

22
Selecting the Greatest

I am lucky to have played with and against some of the greatest cricketers in the history of the game. We all hear about the past, and how the game was better then, but the fairer thing to say is that it was different. You can't compare cricketers from different eras, because the game changes. Also, it is difficult to say that Sir Richard Hadlee is a better fast bowler than Dennis Lillee, Jeff Thomson, Michael Holding or Malcolm Marshall, because they are different types. The same with batsmen – Clive Lloyd, Viv Richards, Barry Richards, Sunil Gavaskar and so on. All among the all-time greats and each is the number one in a particular aspect of batting.

My 79 Tests have brought me close to them all, and they all pass my ultimate test – which is how they perform when it matters and the chips are down. Put another way, all the cricketers I rate don't sit back and react to the events of a game. They usually set the pattern themselves. Imposers. Enforcers. Call them what you like, but they are or were all great players and great fighters.

I'll start with Hadlee, because the fact that he got better and better as he got older shows that he never stopped thinking about his cricket. He was a better bowler than Botham but not a better batsman. A good comparison between him and Both is that both batted the way they did because they were worth their place as a bowler. Their bowling ability gave them an open cheque to blaze away with the bat, and I count them as the two best all-rounders in my time in Test cricket.

Imran was different. He swung the ball more at a greater pace than anyone else, but as a batsman was more of an anchor man – perhaps because he was captain. He was always one step up the ladder of life ahead of other cricketers, and gave a new meaning to the word 'arrogance'. He didn't just look arrogant, his manner was arrogant. What I admired most about him as a cricketer and captain was how he ran Pakistan cricket the way he wanted. He wouldn't tolerate interference from anyone, often said and did things to his Board which would have meant the sack for most of us. Imran was a great cricketer and a great captain, perhaps because he really was as superior to the rest of us as he seemed to think. You could laugh and joke with him, but anyone who claimed to have got close to him on the field or in the dressing-room is fooling himself.

Malcolm Marshall was probably the most dangerous bowler of the lot to face, because he swung it both ways at top speed. He was difficult to pick up because his action was one in which he ran through the crease, rather than jumping on to the back foot and rocking back before coming through like Imran, for instance, or Lillee and Thomson. I only caught those two on the way down, but I saw enough to know what great bowlers they were at their peak. Lillee was probably the most aggressive of the lot with a perfect action. 'Thommo' was the quiet one, with a unique slinging action that got it to your end quicker than most.

For sheer effort, Willis was the best. He never gave up, and considering the trouble he had with his knees, he achieved miracles for England. Sylvester Clarke and Garth Le Roux were two who were top of the hostile brigade. It is not sheer pace that counts, but an ability to hurry you and hit the top of the bat instead of the middle. I have heard a few moans about Clarke's action, but I never had a problem with it. He also had a great change of pace, and I don't mean anything obvious like a much slower ball. He varied his pace much more subtly – and only occasionally did he let fly at top pace.

Joel Garner was another one with hostility. I know he got steep bounce because of his height, but the hostility thing is something that is mental as well as physical. Bowlers like Joel lope in and bowl well enough – then suddenly they find an extra gear from somewhere, and it shows in their follow through which takes them closer still towards the batsman. Curtly Ambrose is another like Joel. He uses his height well, and can never be classed as an out-and-out quick, but not too many batsmen get on to the front foot against him. Not if they want to enjoy their evening meal.

For sheer pace, Michael Holding was tops. He had a magnificent approach and action, and was so perfectly balanced through delivery that his wonderful hand action would produce unplayable deliveries – as 'Boycs' will testify after that historic first over in the Barbados Test in 1981.

Courtney Walsh is much like Hadlee, in that he has got better as he got older. There's a bit of Willis in how he keeps going, day in day out, and I rate his 300 plus Test wickets as one of the best performances of my time.

Then there was Colin Croft, who delivered the ball from wider off the crease than any other bowler I have ever faced. Already near the edge of the return crease, his left foot would splay towards gully, and the line of his stock ball came at you from mid-off's right hand. That caused two problems. He would draw you into playing at stuff which was too wide; then every now and again, he would hold one up from leg to off and the angle made that sort of delivery a real killer.

He wasn't the most placid either – almost anything would wind him up and then batting was like being at the wrong end of a coconut shy. Even his own team mates weren't safe. Viv told me that once 'Crofty' went through the crease at him in the nets. He became a pilot but, as Viv said, 'If I am ever on a plane and I hear, "This is your Captain Croft speaking", I'd head for the emergency exit.'

Kapil Dev was a great bowler, but in a totally different way. For most of his career, he carried the Indian attack, but despite their pitches, he kept getting good players out. Also his batting puts him into the same all-rounder bracket as Both, Hadlee, Imran and Procter.

Wasim Akram's batting is dangerous, but not in that class, and he is the finest left-arm fast bowler I have faced. Like Marshall, he runs through his delivery stride and he can swing it both ways – not only at speed, but also from over or around the wicket. He is an amazing bowler, and I rate him even more dangerous than Waqar. He doesn't swing it away much, but his inswinging yorker is unplayable when everything is right for him – including the ball. I have to include Sarfraz as one of the best four Pakistani bowlers I have played. Forget the High Court case, because that was all about ball tampering and swing, but 'Sarf' used to hit the seam more often than any other bowler. Up to a point, you can adjust to swing, but never with seam if it is pitched well up.

There are plenty of other quicks who were terrific bowlers, although perhaps a bit behind those I have already named. Geoff Lawson was one, and Rodney Hogg another. In my book, they were both better bowlers than Craig McDermott, with none of them in the class of Lillee and Thomson. Hogg was a skidder – like Marshall – and his bouncer was often more troublesome than that of taller bowlers, because it came at you as a throat ball. They all had aggression – in fact I can't think of an Aussie quick who wasn't nasty with a ball in his hand.

Their sledging used to get to some batsman, but it just made me more determined, and because I always got an earful is one reason why I loved playing in Australia. Another was the great arenas and crowds in Melbourne and Sydney. They would get a hate campaign going when you walked in to bat, and I loved that. Merv Hughes was another sledger who thought you'd insulted him if the ball missed the middle of the bat by a millimetre.

Oddly enough, he never gave me much of the verbals – maybe because he knew he couldn't get to me. The Aussies tend to target players, and they went for Graeme Hick and also Robin Smith. I told 'Hicky' to try to relax and ignore them, but he found it difficult to do, so he kept copping that Merv moustache from about a three foot range. Another thing that didn't help Hicky was the one bouncer per over in county cricket for a few years. As a result, he found he couldn't cope for his first few years with England when the quicks whacked it in short, especially the West Indians.

Some people believe that one of his problems was that he couldn't play Test cricket until he was 25 and therefore he was too set in his ways to adapt easily to the extra quality of bowling. Well, I was three years older, but the bouncers were a free for all in my early days, whereas Hicky was on rations.

A lot of county cricketers get upset by sledging, and those who do get a lot more once the word has gone around. As I've said, I don't mind taking or giving it within reasonable bounds. Occasionally a player or a team goes over the top, and then I'll respond accordingly. Roger Twose got heavy with Kevin Curran in our marvellous four-day game at Edgbaston in 1995, and Umpire Kenny Palmer had to step in. Warwickshire are dab hands at it and Dermot Reeve got them doing it in a subtle way. Often the remarks will be across a batsman and to each other but, indirect or not, they make sure you know what is being said about you.

In my time as county captain, I kept a grip on these things, mainly because I knew when matters got too serious, but that all went out of the window at Edgbaston. I remember telling the guys, 'Right. They started it so it's a free for all – but try not to overstep the mark'.

I've mentioned the top bowlers I saw – now for some of the batsmen. I've got to start with Viv Richards, if only because of his attitude and approach. He never wore a helmet as a message to the bowlers: 'You aren't good enough or quick enough to hit me'. It was pure arrogance, but it worked. More than any other batsman, Viv set out to intimidate. He was a murderer of a batsman, and there might have been better ones in history, but never one with such an aura about him.

Arrogance of a different sort belonged to Javed Miandad. Where Viv butchered bowlers, Javed wore them down with accumulation and had a wonderful hand-and-eye co-ordination. If Viv was an enforcer, Javed was an adjuster. He could get fiery on the field, but I never had any trouble with him and found him easier than Imran to speak to off the field.

The real hard man of international cricket when I started was Clive Lloyd. He pioneered the four-fast-bowler tactic after his side was smashed 5–1 by Lillee and Thomson in Australia in 1975/76. He was in charge when Edrich and Brian Close were battered at Old Trafford in very poor light in 1976, although I wouldn't argue against the idea that if you have four fast bowlers, then use them. What I couldn't swallow was his defence in saying that he always left it to the umpires, and if they saw nothing wrong, then that was that. I remember the fuss he made when 'Dickie' Bird cautioned Malcolm Marshall for intimidatory bowling at Edgbaston eight years later. Lloyd raced from first slip and let Dickie have both barrels.

The one batsman whom I would have wanted to bat for my life was Allan Border. He was a crisis player, and reacted to tough situations better than anyone I have ever seen. We all think we are mentally tough, but nobody could touch 'AB' for all he went through as batsman and captain for 93 consecutive Test matches in 10 years.

His predecessor, Kim Hughes, could play, but wasn't in the same class. Talking of class, the batsman who had it all was Greg Chappell. He was on his own as the best Australian batsman I saw, although we played on his arrogance a couple of times when we bounced him out in 1982/83.

After him, I have to put Dean Jones and Mark Waugh ahead of good payers such as David Boon and Steve Waugh. The first two are top drawer. Jones has a stack of aggression – in fact he has a fast bowler's temperament, always ready with a chirp. Tom Moody is more of a front-foot player than most Aussies, which is why he averages under 40 in Australia and over 50 in England.

'Boony' was a great fighter and as tough as they come. He was one of the cricketers who helped form a new, hard side under Border after Hughes stepped down. For a few years, they'd lost their strength of character when several of the top players went to World Series Cricket. But once they got their Shield and Grade cricket back on track, they became tough again, and there is no doubt in my mind that they have the strongest domestic cricket in the world.

The Currie Cup used to be like that – every game was like a Test match and that is what breeds the right sort of toughness and aggression. As shown by Ian Healy, another hard man who is never short of a few words, as was Rod Marsh before him.

Behind Clive Lloyd and Viv Richards were the two best openers in my time – Desmond Haynes and Gordon Greenidge. I don't use the word awesome much, but Gordon was just that. Devastating. I like to hit the ball hard, but I was a powder-puff compared with him. 'Dessie' was a complete opener. He could play off front and back foot and had enough patience for the whole side. The only other batsman I really rated in my time was Richie Richardson although the strain and stress got to him in the end. Another non-helmet man, he was impossible to contain when he was in.

Only Martin Crowe of the New Zealand batsmen I played against could make you blink occasionally. If a severe knee injury hadn't got to him in the early 1990s, he would have scored a lot more runs, but 17 hundreds in 128 innings is one of the best ratios in modern cricket.

I've already discussed Javed Miandad, who was in a class of his own, and I suppose Zaheer Abbas and Mohsin Khan were the next best players. 'Zed' was as run-hungry as any batsman I saw, and was able to indulge himself at a time before Pakistan made up into a serious winning side, away as well as at home.

There aren't many spinners I consider to be outstanding. I only played against Shane Warne once when he was still at the Academy, so I can only go on what I have seen on television. He is one of the biggest spinners I've seen, and is also wonderfully accurate. His record in the last three years is the best in the world, and if he stays fit, he should break all records. In my time, Abdul Qadir was the best. He mesmerised batsmen, and I reckon I was doing well if I read 40 per cent of his deliveries. He had so many variations, including two googlies, and with a natural fast bowler's temperament, he was easily the most aggressive spinner I played against.

All this is leading to me playing selector. Sole selector of the best side I can pick from players of my time, and if Qadir is in, I have to go for the safest wicket-keeper with the best pair of hands. Easy. Bob Taylor first and the rest nowhere. He made everything look easy, and he was an artist.

My team – and thank God it never has to play, because it would be quite a lively dressing-room – would come from this squad: Gordon Greenidge, Graham Gooch, Greg Chappell, Viv Richards, Javed Miandad, Allan Border, Ian Botham, Richard Hadlee, Malcolm Marshall, Bob Taylor, Dennis Lillee, Abdul Qadir and Wasim Akram. That 13 would cover all options for the captain – and who is the captain?

As I said, a lively-dressing-room, and I want someone who would face down any star name who shot his mouth off. I have picked seven Test captains, but my choice is Allan Border.

Now who better for them to play against than my best South African team picked from players I played with and against between 1972 and 1995? Eddie Barlow, Barry Richards, Peter Kirsten, Graeme Pollock, Lee Irvine, Kenny McEwan, Clive Rice, Mike Procter, Denys Hobson, Vintcent van der Bijl, John Traicos, Garth Le Roux and Allan Donald. Irvine would keep wicket, and if I picked two spinners, Big Garth would have to go, because Donald is now one of the best fast bowlers in world cricket.

Captain? It is a toss up between my first captain, Eddie, and 'Ricey'. Both hard men, and both cricketers who would fight until they dropped. I think I'd lock them in a gym with a boxing ring, and the winner would do for me. As for who would toss the coin, I still see them both from time to time, so I'm not stupid enough to give an opinion.

Two great sides, and which one would I rather play for? Put another way, which set of bowlers do I think would be marginally easier to face? Whisper it quietly back in South Africa, but I would rather play for the other side, even though Vintcent split my head as a kid, and even though Allan Donald has bowled me out more than once. As the game can never be played, I suppose I can claim that I would smash a hundred in each innings against both attacks. The trouble is that I still play the odd charity game – as do those bowlers – so let me settle for being twelfth man for both sides once the final teams are picked.

23
Enforced Retirement

Monday morning, 15 April 1996 was the time when I said my final farewell to first-class cricket as a player. It was one of the saddest occasions in my twenty-four years in the game when I drove to the county ground in Northampton to tell the players that I was forced to retire because the Test & County Cricket Board would not accept my registration. The reason was this very book, but more of that later.

I have never been an emotional cricketer, but I was full to the top as I said my goodbyes to the players and thanked them for everything, both as captain for seven years and as colleagues for 11 years before that. Normally a dressing-room is full of chipping and banter, but the boys knew I was struggling to control myself.

I had to make it short, and then drove home hardly able to believe that it was all over. I was glad that Lindsay was out with her Mom, Biddy, who had flown over from South Africa to stay with us during April. I sat in the empty house and thought about the finality of it. I still had to go back into the dressing-room one more time to empty my locker, and I would be watching some home games, but now I was on the outside looking in, and I can't remember when I felt so down and depressed. From school to Claremont, to Western Province, Northants, England, Orange Free State and the other sides I had played for, I thought of them all as I realised that, apart from benefit and charity matches, I was finished.

Having gone so close in 1995 to the club's first ever county championship, I wanted to go out with a bang and give the new captain, Rob Bailey, a bag full of runs to help him in his first season as official club captain. I averaged over 50 in 1995 and knew I was worth my place, but now Lord's had done me.

It started when I was out of contract at the end of the 1994 season. I wanted a two-year contract, but Steve Coverdale said that the club would only offer me a one-year agreement and that on a match-to-match basis. I was disappointed in that, because I knew I still had plenty to offer, so I refused it. They then came back with a proper contract, but which meant I played no Sunday League cricket. However, I wanted to sort out this book and its publication date, because now it was mid-January.

Alan Herd warned me that there was a snag. I signed the original book contract in January 1993, after which the TCCB changed the players' undertaking regarding the procedure for dealing with articles and manuscripts for books. They introduced a clause 3 (d) which called for any proposed public comments to be submitted to them, *before* they went to the publishers.

The old rule called for clearance by a player's club and/or the Board before publication, but they could not ask for the material before it was sent to the publishers.

The exact wording is this: 'Any cricketer or umpire must notify the county cricket club or Board as soon as any contract is entered into and should keep them informed of progress, including providing drafts and proofs as and when they are prepared, and before they are submitted to a publisher, newspaper or any other body of concern'.

As I had already signed my book contract well before that new clause was put into the undertaking, it was impossible for me to comply. My book contract called for the company to receive drafts and proofs, and not after they had gone somewhere else for approval. Catch 22. If I complied with the undertaking, I would break my book contract. If I kept to my book contract, I could not sign the undertaking. And no player who refuses to sign that is allowed to be registered.

The background to what is a sore subject among players is that prior to this new clause 3 (d), any book by a player would be vetted by someone like Donald Carr, Tony Brown or AC Smith, but only after the final proofs were forwarded to them by the publishers.

The blue pencil would come out and, usually, the passages objected to by the Board would be deleted. There have been exceptions, in particular the book by Mike Gatting about his tour of Pakistan in 1987, in which he had the famous run-in with Shakoor Rana.

He was told to amend the chapter about the incident in Faisalabad, but the publishers refused. They tried to out-flank Lord's by putting that chapter under the name of the lady ghost writer, but the TCCB weren't having that. 'Gatt' was pulled in front of the disciplinary sub-committee and bounced for £5000, despite insisting that he had tried to persuade the publishers to follow the Board's instruction.

An earlier case along the same lines concerned Chris Old in his first season with Warwickshire after he moved from Yorkshire. He signed to do a couple of articles with the *Sun*, but when he saw them, he knew that they would never be cleared because of the way that the journalist concerned, Ian Jarrett, had jazzed up and personalised them. The newspaper refused to alter anything, so he told Alan Smith, then secretary of Warwickshire.

He went spare and tried to prevent publication, but the paper refused to play ball, so Warwickshire immediately fined Chris £1000. When the TCCB doubled that and suspended him as well, the Warwickshire chairman, Cyril Goodway, resigned in protest at what he saw as official criticism of him and the Edgbaston committee.

I know that players have to have some sort of restriction against sounding off, but the present rules are not the answer. The introduction of clause 3 (d) might have followed my case after the Lord's Texaco game against Pakistan and my *Daily Mirror* article, but what should surely have counted in my favour was the fact that they brought it in *after* I signed the book contract.

Northamptonshire decided to bring the matter out into the open. Steve Coverdale wrote to Lord's at the end of January to tell them that they wanted to register me, but that I could not sign the undertaking, and they asked for discretion to allow me to play.

The first official reaction was to say no, and numerous legal meetings took place, including one with a barrister who advised me on the validity of retrospective legislation. He said that I had a strong case for restraint of trade. There was a small problem – or rather half a million of them, because I was also told that if the TCCB defended the action, the costs could escalate to £500,000.

I couldn't entertain that for obvious reasons, so we kept hammering away at Francis Neate and Slaughter & May for an answer to my request to be registered without signing the undertaking. Firstly, he asked for a copy of the publishers' contract, which they refused to agree to.

It was like a game, but too long-winded for comfort. The first time I knew that the worst scenario was a real possibility was when Rob Bailey called round to tell me that I wouldn't be going on the pre-season tour to South Africa because they didn't want to waste a place on an unregistered player. Again we pressed the TCCB for an answer, but they just dragged their heels.

I could have gone to the Cricketers' Association for advice, but it rankled with me that not once did they offer me any help or advice in the ball tampering case in 1992. Of course I broke my contract by writing in the *Mirror* without clearance, but the issue went wider than that as proved by the fact that my fine was reduced by so much on appeal. The Cricketers' Association is the body who represent the cricketers on all matters, including discipline and registration, and in the 1970s did a great deal to redraw the rules of registration, yet nobody ever picked up a telephone to me, so I had no confidence in approaching them this time.

It was put to me that I could have quietly signed the undertaking and then sustained a convenient injury when the book was published before the end of the 1996 season. Or claimed that I hadn't read the small print and gone ahead and published. Northants really made that difficult by writing to the Board at the beginning of the year, but I would never have done that anyway. I had read the small print. I did know what the consequences were, and anyway, how could I play until mid-August and then pull out, especially if the club was going well and in the running for one or more titles? I have been accused of many things, but never of being devious. Yes, I always have an eye open for opportunity. Yes, I have always made sure that A J Lamb has always looked after A J Lamb when it comes to the commercial and contractual side of cricket. But nobody can ever claim that they did not know where they stood with me in negotiations.

Cricket is a short career, even one lasting 24 years as mine did, but life has to be lived and worked at after the age of 40, and that is why I have always driven the hardest possible bargain. There was another factor to consider if I had signed and played until the publication of the book. The publishers wanted the book to come out before the end of the season and were not prepared to agree to defer it until October when I would be out of contract. They said that if I tried to publish before the end of the season and quit playing, the Board could get an injunction and prevent publication, so everyone would lose out.

It was a mess, but one which was not all down to me. I know it is my book, but I don't see why I should be prevented from putting my side of things, even if it happens to upset those TCCB officials who always settle for a quiet life. It is not a matter of having my cake and eating it. I made a full commitment to English cricket and I am proud of everything I have done for county and country.

We made one last effort. I asked the publishers on 10 March to delay serialisation, but they said that would miss an important part of the market, and refused. They did agree finally to send the copy of the contract to Francis Neate and that went on Friday 12 March – a full month before I needed to sign the undertaking.

Lindsay and I talked it through in the next few days. Irrespective of what the Board did – or more likely, didn't do – my legal fees were rising like a thermometer in a heat wave, so it came down to three alternatives. I told Lindsay that either we knocked the book on the head, or came out with one like Noddy, or I packed in playing and thus freed myself to write exactly what I wanted.

The Board still dawdled, and that is when I heard how Tony Brown asked whether I wanted to be a cricketer or an author. The Northants players had gone to South Africa and I already felt as though I was being forced more and more on the outside of a game I had played with love and passion for well over half my life.

Every time I convinced myself that I had to retire, I would give myself another day to see if a miracle of common sense would happen. It didn't, which is why on Friday 12 April I went to the club offices and told Steve Coverdale that I was going to accept the inevitable and suffer a retirement that I believe was forced on me from Lord's. They can argue all they like, but it can't be natural justice to make me break a contract with my publishers that I signed well before they changed their rules in the player's undertaking. I always believed you can't move the goal posts in legal matters, but the TCCB did just that with me.

By now, I had signed to do a weekly column in the *Sunday Express* and I made my official announcement on 31 March. To sum up my thoughts and feelings about the corner I was forced into, I feel bitter and angry that I have left the game as a player because of petty authority. The heart of the issue is not only whether I could publish this book. It is whether English cricketers should be forced by the TCCB to sign contracts that turn them into slaves.

The English game is crying out for open debate. It is blindingly obvious that the game is in crisis and that the men who run it have no idea what to do.

It is an insult to our intelligence that their scope and power is without parallel in any other major sport. The TCCB wants to own English cricketers lock, stock and barrel, but I refuse to be owned by anyone. I had hoped to finish my playing career on a high note, but because the Board was so frightened of what I would say, it didn't happen. In England, you cannot play cricket and write openly about the game, and the TCCB believes that is a good thing.

And what about the wide-ranging attacks that the Chairman of the Board, Dennis Silk, made about the state of the English game? If a player had done that he would have been carpeted, yet I understand that his public pronouncements were brought to the notice of Eddie Slinger, head of the Disciplinary Sub-committee. Nothing happened of course. One law for some and one for the rest of us.

I wanted to play cricket in 1996 in my testimonial year and plan for my future, including the publication of this book, just as many other cricketers have done. I was denied this. I knew that I would be snowed under with calls when the news broke, so Lindsay and I went skiing in Austria for a week. Lynn Wilson told me to clear off and leave everything to him, and it was good advice, because his telephone never stopped.

That week settled my mind enough to be able to deal with everything when I got back. I did a stack of interviews on radio and television, and I made sure that the local media got all the facts, so that the Northamptonshire members and supporters knew the background behind my decision.

Northamptonshire paid many generous tributes to me, and at least I left them on good terms. Steve Coverdale made public the fact that he had 'spent many hundreds of hours trying to broker a deal with the TCCB'.

Everyone tried, except the men at Lord's.

24
Imran Court Case

Wednesday 31 July 1996 is a day I will never forget. All my life I have been able to cope with bad news. Life is full of disappointments and failures, and I've had my share of both. Also injustices, because these are part and parcel of playing sport for a living. You learn to take what cards are dealt and play them accordingly. I can think back over my life to body blows, shocks and unexpected things I never saw coming, but nothing has ever devastated me as much as when the foreman of the jury stood up in Court 13 and announced they were finding for Imran Khan.

For the 13 days of the case, plus the few weeks before it started, when I realised that Imran was not going to withdraw, I never gave one thought to the possibility of losing. Every bit of advice Ian Botham and I were given was positive and encouraging. Only when the jury was out for so long on that Wednesday, did Lindsay start to worry. She had had a terrible month, much worse than I did because it was her second court case. She was also very wound up about the effect on Katie-Ann and Richard, with both of us out of the house by 6.30 am each morning and not back until after 9 pm.

She had given evidence in support of a gynaecologist friend of ours, who was found guilty of sexual harassment. He delivered both our kids and we knew him well, so Lindsay naturally offered him support when he asked for it. There again, the legal view was that he would win, but Lindsay soon sniffed what was happening when the jury was out for so long.

I tried to reassure her while we waited, but I couldn't calm her down. When they filed back in, I tried to guess from their faces, but

I couldn't. All I knew before the foreman stood up was that Imran and his team believed they were down.

The result shocked me so much that I'm struggling to remember my reactions, even now. I know I felt cold, icy cold. I know I grabbed Lindsay's hand, and said we had to be strong. I can remember just staring at the ceiling – maybe to check if it was going to fall in on us to complete the day.

We had waited over four hours and now this. I suppose the writing was on the wall when the jury came back to ask two questions, but I still didn't see how we could lose.

I believe Imran had called me a racist and 'of lower class'. Never mind that his defence was that he had been misquoted. My name had been defamed, and I assumed – wrongly as it turned out – that natural justice would put it right. British justice. Ironic, really, that I had taken out citizenship and done everything possible to show people that I was a wholly committed Britisher.

'Both', Kath, Lindsay and I sat in court for as long as it took to clear, and then we were escorted out through a side door by the police. We faced the cameras, because we had nothing to hide, and then we walked over to the offices of Swepstone Walsh, our solicitors. As we walked though the crowds of cameramen and reporters, all I could think of was the closing line of George Carman's summing up on behalf of Imran. He said that if the jury found that the claims failed in law, then nobody had accused Botham and Lamb of cheating and racism.

Yet, my kids had come home from school and wanted to know why 'Daddy didn't like black men any more?'

I've spoken a lot about my kids and how they were affected, but what about my folks back in South Africa? The same with Both's parents, Les and Marie. God knows, all four had given us a great upbringing to the best of their ability, and now they were accused of being lower class. I read somewhere next day that, because we objected to that, we must be snobs. All I can say is that when the crap starts to fly, you hear the greatest rubbish imaginable.

After a chat and a glass of wine with our solicitors, Lindsay and I cabbed it to my sister, Brenda, in Roehampton, who had been looking after the kids that day. More tears there before we drove back home and arrived at 9.45 pm. Lindsay was beside herself, and I just felt numb, but we had to try to put a face on everything for

Katie-Ann and Richard. They knew we were upset, but couldn't really understand the case or the consequences of losing.

We were both completely exhausted, but we didn't sleep. I lay in bed, thinking over and over again about the two and a half weeks of the trial. I tried to think of one reason why we lost. Just one reason, even if I didn't agree with it, but I couldn't. As far as I was concerned, it was up to Imran to prove he did not say those things, or to apologise for saying them. His entire defence was that he had been misquoted and taken out of context.

Well, here is what he wrote in May 1994 with Shekhar Gupta, Senior Editor of *India Today*, and Imran has never suggested this was a misquotation. He was asked why he had admitted to his biographer, Ivo Tennant, that he cheated in a county match by using a bottle top. He said: 'The reason I raised the issue is that ever since Wasim and Waqar, two great bowlers, destroyed the English batting line-up, they have faced this abuse that they cheat. Even after the World Cup in 1992 there were snide remarks. Why did the umpires not catch them? The only two cases where players have been caught tampering involved Derek Pringle and Phil Tufnell, a spinner who was doing it for the fast bowlers. And remember John Holder, the umpire who caught him, has never stood in a Test match again. You know why? He is black.'

I assume Imran is referring to The Oval Test against the West Indies in 1991 when Holder and Merv Kitchen warned the England captain, Graham Gooch, that the ball had been tampered with and he had better crack down on his fielders, or else. That incident took place, although the TCCB still refuse to confirm it. But what a statement that Holder has never stood in a Test since because he is black.

And I'm supposed to be the racist.

If anyone wants to see how Imran shifts his ground to suit his argument, what about the next question, which was why he had resigned from the International Cricket Council.

'I never thought I was guilty. I did something illegal, admitted it in good faith and was not guilty because once in 21 years is no big deal.' If we all lived our lives according to that philosophy, nobody would ever be convicted of a first offence, be it dangerous driving or whatever. Think about what Imran said, 'Yes I did something illegal, but no, I am not guilty.'

Then comes the real give-away, the real chip on Imran's shoulder. The race issue again. He was asked why the English media and a section of cricketers blew the issue of ball tampering out of all proportion. He replied:

'There is a lot of racism here. When Bob Willis or Fred Trueman were tearing the heart out of Indian or Pakistan batsmen, we never heard an outcry about short-pitched bowling. How come the noise started when the West Indies and the Pakistanis began winning matches with their fast bowlers? How come we never heard about slow over-rates until the West Indies fast bowlers came along? Australians can get away with anything because they are white. There is a lot of racism in this society. Look at people such as Lamb and Botham making statements like, "Oh, I never thought much of him anyway, and now it's been proved he is a cheat."'

He then followed up with that Oxbridge quote, which he attempted to justify in court by calling most of the people he named as witnesses. He was asked about his view that English cricket suffers from a class problem. 'Yes, look at Tony Lewis, Christopher Martin-Jenkins, Derek Pringle. They are all educated Oxbridge types. Look at the others. Lamb, Botham, Trueman. The difference in class and upbringing makes a difference.'

Not much there to take out of context or misquote, because the entire theme of what is nearly a 2,000 word article is the same. He even had the cheek to say that the TCCB are racist because Holder never stood in a Test after The Oval 1991 because he was black. I know I've criticised the Board about many things, but never that. As for his claim that English cricket is full of racism, I'm not having that at any price. I would not disagree that there have been problems on some grounds with the spectators, but I have never come across it in a dressing-room.

I still can't take it in that Imran could utter stuff like that and get away with it, saying he was misquoted when it came to references to Both and me. He also said that he dissociated himself from the Tennant book, but only spoke to Ivo because he was promised a donation to his hospital project. In which case, if his involvement was so small, why was he sent a list of some 80 alterations to be made to the book by Ivo Tennant, marked 'changes made by Ivo Tennant at Imran's behest'. For example, one of those alterations concerned Imran's admission that he had used a bottle top to tamper with a cricket ball. The original wording was 'he tampered with the ball on occasion, scratching the side and lifting the seam and once, playing for Sussex against Hampshire in 1981, asking the twelfth man to bring on a bottle top.' Imran told Ivo Tennant that he wanted that sentence to be prefaced with the words 'although in other respects a fair sportsman'. So he knew what he was doing was wrong and unfair.

I remember Imran well in the 1992 World Cup in Australia and New Zealand. When he asked to have a substitute fielder for Inzamam-ul-Haq in the Final against us, I was batting and objected. I told him that Inzamam hadn't fielded in the semi-final in New Zealand either, and it wasn't on. He argued the other way, so I told him straight, 'Imran, if that's the way you want to win the World Cup, do it, but don't bullshit me. You've got to live with yourself.'

There's another thing – how he chose to fight the court case on two fronts, which neither I nor Both would do. The court kept hearing references to his charity work, and I'm not knocking that. But Both would not be drawn into trying to compete with who did what for which charity, and nor would I. I doubt whether any sportsman in the world has put so much time and effort into charity work as Both. Other people might have raised more money, but Both had chosen to raise money for leukaemia the hard way, by putting himself on the line in those long walks that showed what phenomenal strength of mind and body he has. I do my bit for Cystic Fibrosis, but that is a matter of organising events to produce money. The point is that we chose not to mention our efforts, while Imran and George Carman played the sympathy charity card as often as they could.

The other huge difference in how our cases were fought was the dirt angle. Both was crucified by Carman, including going back to the England tour of New Zealand in 1983/84, the so-called sex, drugs and rock 'n' roll tour. Kath had to sit there and listen to the dirt being dished all over again, knowing that their children are now much older and having to consider the effect it would have on them, particularly Becky who is now ten years old.

The law can turn dirty when it wants to, and I know I have been no angel, but I was honestly shocked when Imran's side started down that particular road.

Lindsay said to me right from the start that we could have played it dirty, just like Imran, but why put his wife Jemima through the same sort of wringer? I know as a single man he was a free agent, but we could have resurrected the story about his love child, only we didn't.

You don't need a crystal ball to work out why Imran and his team did it, but I am proud that we didn't stoop so low. I am told by our lawyers that the only way such attacks on Both could be introduced at all was because of the Defence of Justification that Imran introduced four days before trial began. He produced some two-minute video footage, of a couple of Tests played in 1982, which he claimed showed Both tampering with the ball in the presence of David Gower and myself. Then, nine days into the trial, Imran withdrew this charge and publicly apologised in the witness box for having made it in the first place. But, of course, Mr Carman had by then completed his muck-raking before the jury.

Which brings me to why I sued. Imran's article appeared in May 1994, and once Alan Herd, acting on behalf of Both and me, wrote a letter demanding an apology, I thought that would be the end of it. It was not a matter of trying to get some easy money. In fact that subject was never discussed once, either between Lindsay and me, or with 'Herdy' and our other legal advisers. All my life, I have been aware of racism, initially in the first 20-odd years of my life when I lived in the Cape, and then when I came to England and could never shake off the South African tag.

I've come across racism as I know it in every cricket-playing country in the world. You won't find anything more bitter than between the Afros and the Indians in the West Indies. Viv Richards was nearly stoned in Guyana for remarks he made about the strong African influence in the West Indies side, compared with cricketers from Guyana and Trinidad.

The Aussies with the Aborigines, the New Zealanders with the Maoris and the caste system in both Pakistan and India. You name it, they've got it. It is the way of the world, but Imran's charges were more sinister. They concentrated on black versus white, which is different from one nation against another. I know some Welshmen who say they hate everything and everyone connected with England, and the Scots and Irish are not far behind. But that stems from history, whereas Imran's charges are in the present time, with his constant harping on the colour issue.

Things seemed to be moving the way we wanted when Imran

offered in July of that year to write a letter to *The Times* clearing everything up. But we couldn't accept what he wanted to say: namely, that he hadn't said the attributed remarks. However he wrapped it up, he refused to apologise for something he claimed he never said, and seemed more concerned about the distress he was suffering. In his proposed letter to *The Times* Imran said his motives were to get the ICC to clarify the laws about ball tampering. In court Both described this as a smoke-screen. I agree. The Laws of Cricket couldn't be clearer.

I forgot about the case for some time, because I still never thought it would go to court. The lawyers kept working away to try to avoid a big, expensive case, but because we were always told that we were as cast-iron certainties to win as you can ever get in law, we never had a second thought about going all the way if we had to.

I read after the trial from people like Frances Edmonds that we should have found a simpler way of settling it, and there were many views expressed in the national press that it was sad and silly that three sportsmen should fund the legal system for 13 days on a matter of who said what and when. Frances happens to be good friend of Imran, and she did quite well out of the trial. Somehow she managed to sell a story after the verdict to two tabloid newspapers on the same day. Nice one. I'll show you one thing to prove how Imran's racist remarks got to me. In April 1996, I was told I had a strong case against the TCCB for restraint of trade after their refusal to register me unless I signed the players' undertaking, which would bring me into contractual dispute with my book publishers.

That was also a point of great principle, but I backed off when I was told that if the Board defended strongly and I happened to lose, the costs could approach £500,000. But this time, I went to court soley on a matter of principle – in fact, the greatest matter of principle in my life as far as I was concerned. My character and reputation had been muddied by Imran, and his remarks had been read by millions of people in India and England.

If I'm guilty of anything, it is being so proud, and Imran might say the same thing. That is why I sued, and that is why people who are not in the public eye to the same extent might think it was all unnecessary. For some reason, the fact that you are a sportsman seems to make a difference. It doesn't. We are human beings who have the same feelings as people in other walks of life.

What I was to find out was that the laws of libel in my country are a lottery. You are in the hands of the jury, more than in the hands of the counsels and the judge. Remember also that the final verdict was a majority one, not unanimous, and two significant things happened immediately afterwards. A couple of the jurors were in tears, and Mr Justice French left the court at a rate of knots after only bowing to the jury in the briefest way, but not thanking them. His summing-up seemed to point our way, although Mr Carman caused a few ripples when he got up and queried the summing-up on some 20 counts.

George Carman is a top man in his job. Sometimes, you never know where he is leading to, and then he pounces. The jury were out of court when he stared to query Mr Justice French's summing-up on various matters of fact. The arguments went on for a couple of hours, in which time the jury were told not to start considering their verdict. That did us no favours, with them sitting twiddling their thumbs for two hours while Mr Carman objected on matters of fact and misdirection on matters of law. Strong stuff, but that's what he is paid for.

Right up to the start of the trial, on Monday 15 July, there were efforts to settle, particularly from the businessman Jim Slater, who is a good friend of James Goldsmith. He offered to meet most of the costs already incurred if we would shake hands on the steps of the court and call it quits. Our line was the same. If Imran withdrew and apologised for his remarks, then we were happy. He would not, and so the pin was pulled. We also wanted something in damages, but nothing silly. Imran's lawyers made it clear to our team that even £5 was out of the question.

Now I sit down and think of our daily routine, I can hardly believe how we got through the next 17 days. Lindsay and I would leave home just after 6 am to drive to Kettering station and we would arrive at Herdy's office around 8.30 am. Then to court and back to the office for a few sandwiches at lunchtime to discuss how the morning had gone. Back there again after the end of the day's proceedings, with Both insistent that the odd bottle of Chardonnay was opened. Then to St Pancras for the trip back home and the kids. Sometimes it was quite late when we walked in, but they always wanted to wait up and ask us if we had won or lost.

The press, as usual, were not always spot on with their facts. For instance, as we left the court by a back door on the first afternoon, they took photographs which appeared next day of 'Ian Botham and his wife Kath' and 'Allan Lamb with wife Lindsay'. Fine, except I was pictured with Paul Downton's wife, Ally. As Lindsay said when she saw it on the train the next morning, 'I've heard of quickie divorces, but this is ridiculous!'

Looking back on the 13 days in court now, I realise that if Both had done his case separately from mine, my one on the racism aspect would probably have lasted a couple of days at the most. But everything became blurred from the time when Imran decided to introduce video footage of what he claimed was Both tampering with the ball.

That decision alone wasted nearly nine days of time and money, as well as the terrific inconvenience it caused the cricketers and ex-cricketers he called, such as John Emburey, Mike Atherton, David Lloyd and all the former players now in the commentators' box.

Emburey was already playing in the Northamptonshire match against Middlesex, and missed chunks of play in a game Northants lost by 26 runs. He batted at no. 3 in the first innings because he knew he would be in court later, and only bowled 16 overs on a turning pitch on which Phil Tufnell and Paul Weekes bowled 47 and 28 overs respectively and shared eight wickets.

Atherton and Lloyd were called on the Wednesday morning before the Thursday start of the Lord's Test against Pakistan, and missed the morning practice session. I know that cricket has to come second where the law is concerned, but what an unnecessary waste of time it proved to be for everyone when Imran withdrew his justification plea the following week. At least he had to pay a proportionate part of the costs, but even that doesn't compensate for the hassle he caused everybody.

A bit of fun and a few laughs came out of it, with Brian Close and Geoffrey Boycott airing some private grievances against each other. Yorkshiremen are a different breed, if that's not too racist a remark. 'Closey' would not answer a question put to him about 'Mr Boycott being an honest man', and 'Boycs' referred to Closey as an embittered man.

Boycott put up an astonishing performance which must have brought him close to a charge of contempt of court. First, he had the neck to turn up in court without a jacket and apologise because he had had no time to grab one once the call came to him in the commentary box to go to court.

But he was able to make sure he was wearing a shirt with the Wills World Cup logo on the left breast, and he also somehow found time to pick up a Reebok boot, which he brought into the witness box to try to make some point or other. He was stopped from doing that, but he made sure that every photograph taken – and there were plenty – showed the logo and the boot. He also found time to hold an impromptu press conference right outside the Court doors for reasons that will never be apparent to me.

The split of the cricketing witnesses were: called by Imran – Boycott, Derek Pringle, David Lloyd, Mike Atherton, Tony Lewis and Christopher Martin-Jenkins; interestingly all called by subpoena, not one volunteering. Those called by us were Robin Smith, Brian Close, Gladstone Small, David Gower, Bob Taylor, John Emburey and Don Oslear – all of whom volunteered. Just like in my court case against Sarfraz, the jury had no chance of understanding the mechanics of reverse swing. But they spent hours listening to what constituted ball tampering, and what was acceptable in cricket for bowlers in giving Mother Nature a helping hand.

It all confused what, as far as I was concerned, was a simple case of the accusation against me of being a racist and from the lower classes. I sat there each day thinking what waste of everyone's time it was.

And money, too, in my case. For instance, our rail fares were over £100 each day, and then there was the time I lost on my benefit functions. A lot of people reckon that my benefit would be much bigger once I stopped playing and therefore could spend all my time organising things. I don't agree with that, because an ex-player never gets the same support as a current player, no matter how good a career he might have had.

The biggest problem I had during the case was on the second Tuesday, when I had a big golf day at The Buckinghamshire, organised and supported financially by Hewlett Packard and Front Line. John O'Leary, the former top golfer, helped to run the day, and if I had not attended for the start of play in the morning, it would have meant a big loss of income.

I was in no trouble at court, except for one important thing. Sod's Law decided that the morning I was excused attendance at court would be the very time when Lindsay would give evidence. I should have known better, because I knew how worked up she had been from day one, but I let her persuade me to go to the golf, and so not be in court when she went into the box. Not many wives would have done that, and I know now it was a mistake. You are on your own in the box, but it is a small court-room, and it helps when you can look at someone for reassurance.

I put her on the early train at Kettering, and tried to tell her she would be all right. She was in a terrible state when she was called. She told me later that she could hardly control her legs to walk into the box and she was very emotional in her evidence. She said how she taught the children and me some Xhosa phrases so we could talk to the black people on her mother's farm, and then she brought the house down without meaning to when she complained she was fed up about listening to nothing but balls for four days.

When the laughter started, she put her foot in it by saying that of course she meant cricket balls. Rhory Robertson, one of our legal team, told me later she was in tears when she finished her evidence, and he had to hold her hand and try to calm her down when she sat by him. At least Mr Carman backed off and didn't cross-examine her.

I've always known what a strong person she is, and the few weeks before, during and after the case proved it over and over again. What a trouper! I don't yet know what the long-term effects of the case will be on our lives, but I do know that we are even stronger as a family, and no rotten verdict is going to finish me. As she said, 'I'll stack shelves at Sainsbury's if I have to', and she would. I have always been careful with money, but only to give my family and myself a good lifestyle. If that has to change, then so be it. In the end, you have to take what life gives to you and make the best of it. But what a year 1996 was for me. Not to be able to play my last season with Northants was a body blow, but nothing like as hurtful as the Imran case.

The more I think about those 'racist' claims of Imran, the more I could spit. I remember him accusing the England selectors of racism by not picking the Sri Lankan batsman, Gehan Mendis, when he qualified as English, playing for Sussex and Lancashire. But Imran's defence that he was misquoted was accepted by the jury.

You could punch holes through that defence, and Charles Gray did just that, yet the jury accepted it and that is something I will never understand for the rest of my life. If only I knew one good reason why the majority went with Imran.

My own evidence was patchy. The first day I was called was in the afternoon, and I finished off the next day. I started slowly and nervously, but I was better the next morning, even if I did get confused between the words 'condone' and 'condemn' when I was asked my feelings on ball tampering.

Whatever happened throughout the trial, the summaries of Mr Carman and Mr Gray were crucial, and even more so was that of Mr Justice French. He was last, of course, and finished about 10.20 am on the final morning. Just as the jury were about to go out to consider their verdict, up pops Mr Carman, saying that he wishes to raise several points in the Judge's summing-up, both facts and misdirection.

The jury were then told to go, but not to consider their verdict until they were told to. For the next 90 minutes, Carman had a real go. He accused the Judge of not summarising some of the witnesses' evidence – for instance that of the England captain, Atherton. He also made a lot of what was called 'qualified privilege'.

It had been explained to me that Imran could plead qualified privilege in his remarks about Both and me if it was ruled that our articles about him in the *Sun* and the *Mirror* were unjustified. I didn't see how, on the one hand Imran, could claim he had never made the reported accusations of racism and class about me, but, on the other hand, also claim that his remarks were made as a response to attacks made in the press by me.

Mr Gray quickly made the point that all we had done was to nail Imran on his own admission of ball tampering; therefore the articles were justified. Therefore, qualified privilege could not be used by Imran. That seemed straightforward, but Carman ploughed on and even mentioned the possibility of demanding that the jury be discharged and a retrial ordered. The Judge wasn't keen on that, and said to remember that the court was dealing with people of limited resources, and it would be best all round if the various points could be resolved.

The jury were called back at about 12.15 pm, but matters only got more confused when Mr Justice French seemed to make a hash of explaining the point about qualified privilege.

I don't know whether Carman had got him ruffled or not, but in the first place he told the jury that Imran could plead qualified privilege if our articles were justified. Both Carman and Gray got up to tell him he meant the opposite; namely, that only if our articles were unjustified could Imran claim qualified privilege. All in all, it was a messy ending to the proceedings before the jury finally were allowed to retire and come to their verdict.

They came back at 3.15 pm to tell the judge that it was unlikely they could reach a unanimous verdict, so he told them that, reluctantly, he would accept a majority verdict of either 10–2 or 11–1. Even then, I wasn't worried, because I thought the voting was the other way. I know the Imran camp had given up, and that is why it was as big a shock for them as it was for us when they came back and the foreman announced that they had found for the defendant on both counts.

Lindsay went into total shock. That just about topped things off for her, especially as, at one time, I thought she would become involved in a third court case in a few weeks. But she'd better tell the story herself.

I can still hardly believe what happened on the late-night train back to Kettering at the end of the second week of the trial. Lamby and I were totally knackered, and bought first-class tickets and a bottle of wine so we could sit in comfort and unwind.

The train from St Pancras didn't take off for nearly after an hour after we boarded, so we sipped and supped on our own and started to feel a bit better. I wanted to go to the toilet, but it was occupied. I remember leaning out of the open window in the corridor and taking a look up and down the platform.

The next thing I knew was that I was well and truly groped from the back – not just a pinch but a complete handful of the Lamb chump chop. That did it. I snapped, after the ten days I'd had, plus the frustrations of daily attendance at court when most of the business only concerned Both. The little guy who did it just happened to pick on the wrong person at the wrong time in the wrong place. I went berserk. I grabbed him by the collar, stuck him up against the wall and was just about to pummel all my frustrations and anger into him when Lamby heard my language and came running.

He took over – pulling me off the guy, not the other way around – and told him to piss off. By this time the police had arrived, and I thought to myself, 'Things are supposed to go in threes. Now what's going to happen? I've been in court for my gynaecologist, and I'm still in court for Lamby. Here's the hat-trick. What the hell is a simple country girl from the Eastern Cape doing late at night at St Pancras station on the verge of beating up a guy who had tried to take a handful of what wasn't his?'

I said later I felt that the two and a half weeks in court left me feeling violated – even raped – by all that happened, and I suppose that train incident was part of it. I don't know how long it will take for some of the scars to heal. Maybe never, but we'll survive. We survive for the kids and for each other, because we are each other's lives, and no legal system can spoil that. Not even that verdict, which makes me feel that it wasn't the cricket balls that were scuffed, scrambled and tampered with, it was the brains and minds of the jury.

I knew we had many good friends, but never how many. I can't count the messages and offers of help we've had – simply because people know we were right, and the jury was wrong.

My only regrets are what I put Lindsay through. I never dreamed it would be like that, or that it would drag out for so long. Otherwise, I did what I have always done in life: gone with my instinct and gut reaction to a libel that called me a racist. That is why I confined my remarks about Imran afterwards, in front of the camera, to his ability as a cricketer. I can live with myself in how I brought the case and how it was fought on my behalf.

Postscript

In my last three years, the England set-up went soft. We came close in the West Indies in 1989/90 to getting things right, but after that it seemed to me that the selectors and the management made things up as they went along. What planning there was was too rigid and there was little attempt to be flexible in adopting different treatment towards different players. In other words, man-management was non-existent and, until that is put right, England's Test team will not improve.

Because of our failure to throw overboard the old methods, the English game has fallen behind that of every other country. We have to change dramatically, and at least we made a start with the appointment of David Lloyd as England coach. He is bright and bubbly which is a useful start. Illingworth must have been a fine cricketer and a good captain, but whatever he says, the age gap finally swallowed him up. Also, I'm not convinced that he was as firm as he says he was when it came to push and shove. Otherwise, we wouldn't have drifted so badly from one crisis to another at the end of the South African tour and then the World Cup. Even a bit of homework in Pakistan would have helped, but we were still in a mess in our final game against Sri Lanka.

It didn't need a genius to realise that Sri Lanka had so many left-handers in their top-order, yet we left out Neil Smith and ended up with Phil DeFreitas bowling off spinners against them, because Richard Illingworth had been slogged out of the attack.

On the broader front, the new English Cricket Board – and what a shambles there has been to get that up and running – has got to reactivate cricket at grassroots level. Kids at school have little chance because of lack of facilities and the willingness of the teachers to help out. Whatever it costs to remedy that will be well spent, but money thrown at more advanced stages is often wasted.

South Africa proved that when they started their township development programme. They had to start from scratch in a way no other country has ever known. They concentrated on the under-12s and they will be proved right now that the first few kids are starting to came through.

The county staffs should be cut to under twenty. There is so much dead wood, with most of the clubs having several youngsters who have no chance. There should be divisional competitions for the kids – just as there is in New Zealand rugby. That is the way to tackle it. Make the kids competitive from the time they start playing. I know it is not the English way, but the rest of the world is passing us by. If we want to keep up with them, we must change.

County coaches must also be involved at club level around the country. I know that some counties have a good talent spotting system, but it is invariably hit and miss. That is why there are players coming on to playing staffs who will never make the grade. Make a place on the club staff something to be prized and earned after coming through a divisional system of competition.

Also, we have to relax the registration rules to stop counties being able to tie up youngsters they have found and developed, but to whom they can't give first-team cricket. I know it is rough on a county which spends time and money on a youngster, but then loses him, and I know that some counties are not well organised and therefore live on poached scraps from elsewhere. Perhaps a compensation scheme would help.

We had a youngster at Northants, David Sales, who played when he was sixteen against Essex in 1994. He made 70, but we still didn't play him much in 1995, and that was my responsibility as much as anyone's. The trouble is that when you are trying to win every match, it is difficult to ignore the short term and persevere with a youngster like David Sales. Somehow, the whole English game needs opening up.

I know it now – and that is half the trouble. It is only when you leave the game that you get a wider view of it. I am definitely in favour of a two-divisional championship. Originally I had my reservations, but now I think the advantages outweigh the disadvantages. Never mind the traditional fixtures that have to go; widen promotion and relegation to three or even four per division of nine, and the turnover of clubs moving up and down would soon concentrate a few minds. More matches would be tougher. The players would become harder, and the whole county scene would change for the better.

As for the rules, the most damaging change was the one limiting the number of bouncers per over. Take it out and make the umpires do their jobs properly by warning against intimidation, but allow genuine hostile bowlers to reap the rewards they deserve.

Cricket is such a great game that players, umpires and administrators alike must make every effort to get the most out of it. We are all to blame that the game in England has gone soft. The future now lies with the English Cricket Board, and I hope it will have the guts to do whatever is necessary. The biggest stumbling block of all they must get rid of is the selfish attitude of the county clubs.

Since they took over the running of the first-class game in England nearly thirty years ago, standards of play have declined, and that is no coincidence. Every club preaches the gospel of a strong England side and then blocks the progress to that at every turn. The game should be bigger than any club or individual player. Until the clubs learn that lesson, English cricket will suffer.

Career Statistics

MILESTONES IN FIRST-CLASS CAREER

1972-73	First-class debut: Western Province v Eastern Province at Cape Town (January 12)
1976-77	First first-class hundred: 109 Western Province v Rhodesia at Bulawayo
1978	Debut for Northamptonshire: B&H Cup match v Middlesex at Lord's (April 29)
	First-class debut for Northamptonshire: v Pakistanis at Northampton (May 10)
	Championship debut: v Nottinghamshire at Northampton (May 24)
	First hundred for Northamptonshire: 106* v Essex at Northampton (July 27)
1979	1000 runs in season (1) at average 67.19
1979-80	Passed 5000 first-class runs during season
1980	1000 runs in season (2) at average 66.55
1981	1000 runs in season (3) at average 60.26 (Only time in career 2000 runs/season)
1981-82	Passed 10000 first-class runs during season
1982	First Test: v India at Lord's
	First Test hundred: 107 v India at The Oval
	1000 runs in season (4) at average 46.50
1982-83	First overseas tour with England to Australia
1983	1000 runs in season (5) at average 56.00
1984	1000 runs in season (6) at average 40.30
	Passed 15000 first-class runs during season
1984-85	Took first Test wicket: M. Prabhakar at Calcutta
1986	1000 runs in season (7) at average 59.08
1987-88	Debut for Orange Free State v Eastern Province at Bloemfontein (December 17)
	Scored his highest score (294) in this match
	Scored 50th hundred: 133 Orange Free State v Natal at Bloemfontein
	Passed 20000 first class runs during season
1988	Recalled to Test team
	1000 runs in season (8) at average 52.86
1989	Appointed captain of Northamptonshire
	Broke finger fielding at Leicester on July 20 and did not play again in the season
1989-90	Took over the captaincy from Gooch, whose hand had been broken by E A Moseley in the third Test at Port-of-Spain. The first match was against Barbados, followed by the fourth and fifth Tests
	Scored 119 in the first innings of the Bridgetown Test, the second instance of an England captain scoring 100 in his first match as captain against West Indies
1990	Scored his highest score for Northamptonshire: 235 v Yorkshire at Headingley (April 27-28)
	1000 runs in season (9) at average 63.84
1990-91	154 and 105 v Tasmania at Hobart (November 16-19)
	December 21: injured calf muscle while jogging back to hotel in Ballarat after scoring 143 against Victoria. This meant he missed the second and third Tests against Australia, for which he might have been captain, as Gooch had been operated on for a septic hand
	Passed 25000 first-class runs during season
1991	1000 runs in season (10) at average 38.60
	Best bowling figures: 2-29 v Lancashire at Lytham

Continued opposite

1992	Played last Test at Lord's v Pakistan (June 18-21)
	209 and 107 v Warwickshire at Northampton (July 21-23)
	1000 runs in season (11) at average 60.83
1993	1000 runs in season (12) at average 40.44
	Passed 30000 first-class runs during season
1995	1000 runs in season (13) at average 56.22

Note: Allan Lamb has never bagged a pair.

MILESTONES IN TEST CAREER

1982	Test debut at Lord's v India
	First Test hundred: 107 v India at The Oval
1983	Reached 1000 Test runs in 15th Test
1984	First player to score three Test hundreds v West Indies in an English season
	First player to score four Test hundreds in the same season since D C S Compton in 1947
1984-85	Took first Test wicket at Calcutta (M Prabhakar)
1985	Reached 2000 Test runs in 33rd Test
1986-87	50th Test v Australia at Melbourne
	Took 50th catch (D McD Wellham at Sydney)
1988	Tore calf muscle in right leg in fourth Test v West Indies at Headingley
	Batted in second innings with a runner, but missed the fifth Test
1989	Reached 3000 Test runs in 57th Test
1989-90	Took over captaincy from G A Gooch (injured)
	Captained fourth Test at Bridgetown and scored 119, the second instance of an England captain scoring a hundred in his first Test as captain against West Indies. This was his 6th Test hundred against West Indies, equalling M C Cowdrey
1990	Record partnership England v India: 308 3rd wicket with G A Gooch in the first Test at Lord's
1990-91	Captained England for the third and last time (Gooch had been operated on for a poisoned hand)
	Passed 4000 Test runs in 68th Test
1991	"Celebrated" his 37th birthday by scoring only 1 v West Indies in second Test at Lord's
1991-92	75th Test v New Zealand at Christchurch
	Scored his highest Test score: 142 in the second innings v New Zealand at Wellington in the second Test
1992	Played his last Test at Lord's v Pakistan

SUMMARY OF ALL FIRST-CLASS MATCHES

		M	I	NO	HS	Runs	Av	100	50	Ct	O	M	R	W	Av	BB
1972-73	WP	2	3	0	58	96	32.00	-	1	2	-					
1975-76	WP	9	17	2	83	421	28.06	-	3	8	-					
1976-77	WP	8	14	2	109	618	51.50	2	5	4	-					
1977-78	WP	8	12	1	109	428	38.90	1	2	8	-					
1978	Nh	17	27	8	106 *	883	46.47	2	5	10	3.5	0	13	2	6.50	1-1
1978-79	WP	9	17	2	107	473	31.53	1	2	6	-					
1979	Nh	21	34	8	178	1747	67.19	4	11	19	6	1	15	1	15.00	1-13
1979-80	WP	8	13	2	99	594	54.00	-	7	2	-					
1980	Nh	23	39	12	152	1797	66.55	5	6	11	5	0	27	1	27.00	1-26
1980-81	WP	8	15	2	130	578	44.46	1	5	6	1.3	1	1	0	-	-
1981	Nh	24	43	9	162	2049	60.26	5	14	20	8	1	35	0	-	-
1981-82	WP	9	14	3	106 *	472	42.90	1	3	11	-					
1982	Nh/Eng	18	30	2	140	1302	46.50	5	4	6	2	1	1	0	-	
1982-83	Eng in Aus	9	18	0	117	852	47.33	2	5	6	1	1	0	0	-	
1983	Nh/Eng	17	29	7	137 *	1232	56.00	5	3	19	1	0	1	0	-	
1983-84	Eng in NZ/Pak	9	15	0	51	307	20.46	-	1	5	-					
1984	Nh/Eng	18	34	4	133 *	1209	40.30	5	5	14	1	0	6	0	-	-
1984-84	Eng in SL/Ind	10	14	2	67	441	36.75	1	4	13	2	1	6	1	6.00	1-6
1985	Nh/Eng/MCC	19	26	4	122 *	903	41.04	2	5	14	4	1	17	0	-	
1985-86	Eng in WI	8	16	1	78	438	29.20	-	4	5	0	0	1§	0		
1986	Nh/Eng	18	27	4	160 *	1359	59.08	4	8	14	2	2	0	0	-	
1986-87	Eng in Aus	10	18	1	105	534	31.41	1	3	11	1	1	0	0	-	
1987	Nh	23	34	4	101 *	982	32.73	1	5	19	2	0	18	1	18.00	1-18
1987-88	OFS	6	12	2	294	878	87.80	3	3	5	1.5	1	4	0	-	
1988	Nh/Eng	16	27	5	155	1163	52.86	5	5	7	4	0	19	0	-	-
1989	Nh/Eng/MCC	11	15	1	171	733	52.35	3	2	11	-					
1989-90	Eng in WI	7	12	0	132	549	45.75	2	1	9	-					
1990	Nh/Eng	17	29	4	235	1596	63.84	6	5	9	-					
1990-91	Eng in Aus	8	14	1	154	757	58.23	3	4	10	-					
1991	Nh/Eng	19	30	2	194	1081	38.60	3	5	21	3.4	0	29	2	14.50	2-29
1991-92	Eng in NZ	5	8	2	142	563	93.83	1	5	3	1	0	6	0	-	-
1992	Nh/Eng	18	28	4	209	1460	60.83	6	5	12	-					
1992-93	WP	5	10	1	206 *	636	70.66	3	1	3	-					
1993	Nh	18	28	1	172	1092	40.44	2	6	13	-					
1994	Nh	15	22	1	131	908	43.23	2	5	17	-					
1994-95	Nh in Zim	1	2	0	72	134	67.00	-	2	3	-					
1995	Nh	16	26	4	166	1237	56.22	3	6	15	-					
TOTALS		467	772	108	294	32502	48.94	89	166	371	50.5	11	199	8	24.87	2-29

§ bowled one no-ball in first Test at Kingston 1985-86

FIRST-CLASS CAREER

	M	I	NO	HS	Runs	Av	100	50	Ct	O	M	R	W	Av	BB
Western Province	66	115	15	206*	4316	43.16	9	29	50	1.3	1	1	0	-	-
Orange Free State	6	12	2	294	878	87.80	3	3	5	1.5	1	4	0	-	-
Test Matches	79	139	10	142	4656	36.09	14	18	75	5	2	23	1	23.00	1-6
Championship Matches	265	427	70	235	19204	53.79	53	96	203	26.4	5	116	6	19.33	2-29
Nhants v Touring Teams	14	19	3	100*	485	30.31	1	2	7	13.5	1	49	1	49.00	1-8
Nhants v Oxford Univ	3	3	1	140	287	143.50	2	-	2	-					
Nhants v Cambridge Univ	1	1	0	18	18	18.00	-	-	3	-					
Nhants v Mashonaland	1	2	0	72	134	67.00	-	2	3	-					
MCC	2	2	2	122*	189	-	1	1	-	-					
England in Australia §	14	25	1	154	1390	57.91	6	6	14	-					
England in New Zealand §	5	9	2	88	372	53.14	-	4	1	1	0	6	0	-	-
England in Sri Lanka §	1	1	0	53	53	53.00	-	1	2	-					
England in India §	4	6	1	34	147	29.40	-	-	2	1	1	0	0		
England in West Indies §	6	11	1	83	373	37.30	-	4	4	-					
TOTALS	467	772	108	294	32502	48.94	89	166	371	50.5	11	199	8	24.87	2-29

§ excluding Tests

COUNTY CHAMPIONSHIP

	M	I	NO	HS	Runs	Av	100	50	Ct	O	M	R	W	Av	BB
1978	16	26	8	106*	883	49.05	2	5	9	2	0	5	1	5.00	1-1
1979	20	32	6	178	1614	62.07	3	11	19	6	1	15	1	15.00	1-13
1980	22	37	12	152	1720	68.80	5	5	10	4	0	26	1	26.00	1-26
1981	21	38	8	162	1962	65.40	5	13	17	5	1	22	0	-	-
1982	10	17	1	140	882	55.12	3	4	5	-					
1983	13	21	5	119	840	52.50	3	2	9	1	0	1	0	-	-
1984	11	21	3	133*	693	38.50	1	5	10	-					
1985	11	17	2	111	525	35.00	1	4	6	1	1	0	0	-	-
1986	14	20	4	160*	1261	78.81	4	8	12	2	2	0	0	-	-
1987	23	34	4	101*	982	32.73	1	5	19	2	0	18	1	18.00	1-18
1988	9	15	2	155	731	56.23	3	3	4	-					
1989	8	12	0	171	537	44.75	2	1	10	-					
1990	10	16	3	235	1040	80.00	4	3	5	-					
1991	14	23	2	194	993	47.28	3	5	13	3.4	0	29	2	14.50	2-29
1992	15	23	4	209	1350	71.05	6	5	11	-					
1993	17	27	1	172	1046	40.23	2	6	12	-					
1994	15	22	1	131	908	43.23	2	5	17	-					
1995	16	26	4	166	1237	56.22	3	6	15	-					
TOTALS	265	427	70	235	19204	53.79	53	96	190	26.4	5	116	6	19.33	2-29

FIRST-CLASS HUNDREDS: 89

1.	109	Western Province	v Rhodesia	Bulawayo	1976-77
2.	105	Western Province	v Natal	Durban	1976-77
3.	109	Western Province	v Natal (2)	Durban (2)	1977-78
4.	106 *	Northamptonshire	v Essex	Northampton	1978
5.	+100	Northamptonshire	v Glamorgan	Cardiff	1978
6.	+107	Western Province	v Rhodesia (2)	Cape Town	1978-79
7.	+118 *	Northamptonshire	v Nottinghamshire	Trent Bridge	1979
8.	+100 *	Northamptonshire	v Indians	Northampton (2)	1979
9.	140 *	Northamptonshire	v Derbyshire	Burton-on-Trent	1979
10.	178	Northamptonshire	v Leicestershire	Leicester	1979
11.	+113 *	Northamptonshire	v Gloucestershire	Bristol	1980
12.	149 *	Northamptonshire	v Worcestershire	Northampton (3)	1980
13.	112	Northamptonshire	v Middlesex	Lord's	1980
14.	+117	Northamptonshire	v Lancashire	Southport	1980
15.	+152	Northamptonshire	v Leicestershire (2)	Leicester (2)	1980
16.	130	Western Province	v Transvaal	Cape Town (2)	1980-81
17.	+133 *	Northamptonshire	v Lancashire (2)	Northampton (4)	1981
18.	+102 *	Northamptonshire	v Sussex	Northampton (5)	1981
19.	162	Northamptonshire	v Gloucestershire (2)	Northampton (6)	1981
20.	159	Northamptonshire	v Middlesex (2)	Northampton (7)	1981
21.	117	Northamptonshire	v Essex (2)	Northampton (8)	1981
22.	106 *	Western Province	v Eastern Province	Port Elizabeth	1981-82
23.	140	Northamptonshire	v Oxford University	Oxford	1982
24.	102	Northamptonshire	v Leicestershire (3)	Leicester (3)	1982
25.	107	ENGLAND	v INDIA	OVAL	1982
26.	140	Northamptonshire	v Hampshire	Northampton (9)	1982
27.	106	Northamptonshire	v Essex (3)	Chelmsford	1982
28.	117	England	v Queensland	Brisbane	1982-83
29.	108	England	v Victoria	Melbourne	1982-83
30.	108	Northamptonshire	v Surrey	Oval (2)	1983
31.	+107 *	Northamptonshire	v Yorkshire	Northampton (10)	1983
32.	+102 *	ENGLAND (2)	v NEW ZEALAND	OVAL (3)	1983
33.	+137 *	ENGLAND (3)	v NEW ZEALAND (2)	TRENT BRIDGE (2)	1983
34.	119	Northamptonshire	v Glamorgan (2)	Cardiff (2)	1983
35.	+110	ENGLAND (4)	v WEST INDIES	LORD'S (2)	1984
36.	100	ENGLAND (5)	v WEST INDIES (2)	HEADINGLEY	1984
37.	100 *	ENGLAND (6)	v WEST INDIES (3)	OLD TRAFFORD	1984
38.	107	ENGLAND (7)	v SRI LANKA	LORD'S (3)	1984
39.	+133 *	Northamptonshire	v Worcestershire (2)	Worcester	1984
40.	122 *	MCC	v Australians	Lord's (4)	1985
41.	111	Northamptonshire	v Essex (4)	Northampton (11)	1985
42.	+157	Northamptonshire	v Sussex (2)	Hastings	1986
43.	+160 *	Northamptonshire	v Middlesex (3)	Northampton (12)	1986
44.	+117	Northamptonshire	v Middlesex (4)	Lord's (5)	1986
45.	159	Northamptonshire	v Derbyshire (2)	Derby	1986
46.	105	England	v South Australia	Adelaide	1986-87

47.	101 *	Northamptonshire	v Kent	Northampton (13)	1987
48.	294	Orange Free State	v Eastern Province (2)	Bloemfontein	1987-88
49.	+101	Orange Free State	v Western Province	Bloemfontein (2)	1987-88
50.	133	Orange Free State	v Natal (3)	Bloemfontein (3)	1987-88
51	101 RH	Northamptonshire	v Oxford University (2)	Oxford (2)	1988
52.	+113	ENGLAND (8)	v WEST INDIES (4)	LORD'S (6)	1988
53.	117	Northamptonshire	v Gloucestershire (3)	Bristol (2)	1988
54.	+140 *	Northamptonshire	v Glamorgan (3)	Wellingborough School	1988
55.	155	Northamptonshire	v Essex (5)	Chelmsford (2)	1988
56.	+148	Northamptonshire	v Leicestershire (4)	Leicester (4)	1989
57.	171	Northamptonshire	v Surrey (2)	Northampton (14)	1989
58.	125	ENGLAND (9)	v AUSTRALIA	HEADINGLEY (2)	1989
59.	132	ENGLAND (10)	v WEST INDIES (5)	KINGSTON	1989-90
60.	119	ENGLAND (11)	v WEST INDIES (6)	BRIDGETOWN	1989-90
61.	235	Northamptonshire	v Yorkshire (2)	Headingley (3)	1990
62.	135 *	Northamptonshire	v Sussex (3)	Northampton (15)	1990
63.	139	ENGLAND (12)	v INDIA (2)	LORD'S (7)	1990
64.	+109	ENGLAND (13)	v INDIA (3)	OLD TRAFFORD (2)	1990
65.	134	Northamptonshire	v Essex (6)	Northampton (16)	1990
66.	+165	Northamptonshire	v Essex (7)	Chelmsford (3)	1990
67.	154	England	v Tasmania	Hobart	1990-91
68.	+105	England	v Tasmania (2)	Hobart (2)	1990-91
69.	143	England	v Victoria (2)	Ballarat	1990-91
70.	125	Northamptonshire	v Lancashire (3)	Lytham	1991
71.	194	Northamptonshire	v Surrey (3)	Northampton (17)	1991
72.	109	Northamptonshire	v Yorkshire (3)	Northampton (18)	1991
73.	+142	ENGLAND (14)	v NEW ZEALAND (3)	WELLINGTON	1991-92
74.	101	Northamptonshire	v Worcestershire (3)	Worcester (2)	1992
75.	109 RI	Northamptonshire	v Glamorgan (4)	Luton	1992
76.	209	Northamptonshire	v Warwickshire	Northampton (19)	1992
77.	107	Northamptonshire	v Warwickshire (2)	Northampton (20)	1992
78.	160	Northamptonshire	v Hampshire (2)	Bournemouth	1992
79.	+122 *	Northamptonshire	v Leicestershire (5)	Leicester (5)	1992
80.	+206 *	Western Province	v Northern Transvaal	Cape Town (3)	1992-93
81.	134	Western Province	v Transvaal (2)	Johannesburg	1992-93
82.	121	Western Province	v Eastern Province (3)	Cape Town (4)	1992-93
83.	172	Northamptonshire	v Somerset	Luton (2)	1993
84.	162	Northamptonshire	v Leicestershire (6)	Northampton (21)	1993
85.	+131	Northamptonshire	v Hampshire (3)	Southampton	1994
86.	114	Northamptonshire	v Essex (8)	Chelmsford (4)	1994
87.	124	Northamptonshire	v Glamorgan (5)	Cardiff (3)	1995
88.	166	Northamptonshire	v Surrey (4)	Northampton (22)	1995
89.	115	Northamptonshire	v Nottinghamshire (2)	Northampton (23)	1995

*   Not out

+   In 2nd innings

RH   Retired hurt

RI   Retired ill

FIRST-CLASS WICKETS

1.	Wasim Bari	Northamptonshire v Pakistanis	Northampton	1978
2.	P N Kirsten	Northamptonshire v Derbyshire	Derby	1978 +
3.	Sadiq Mohammad	Northamptonshire v Gloucestershire	Bristol	1979 +
4.	J C Balderstone	Northamptonshire v Leicestershire	Northampton	1980 +
5.	M Prabhakar	ENGLAND v INDIA	Calcutta	1984-85 +
6.	I Redpath	Northamptonshire v Essex	Ilford	1987 +
7.	G Fowler	Northamptonshire v Lancashire	Lytham	1991
8.	G D Lloyd	Northamptonshire v Lancashire	Lytham	1991

+ Denotes 2nd innings

HUNDREDS IN DOMESTIC LIMITED-OVERS MATCHES: 14

Gillette Cup

1.	101	v Sussex	Hove	1979

NatWest Trophy

1.	103	v Suffolk	Bury St Edmunds	1989
2.	124 *	v Essex	Chelmsford	1993
3.	129 *	v Middlesex	Uxbridge	1994

Sunday League

1.	127 *	v Worcestershire	Worcester	1981
2.	104 *	v Essex	Chelmsford	1982
3.	125 *	v Hampshire	Northampton	1985
4.	132 *	v Surrey	Guildford	1985
5.	120	v Sussex	Tring	1992

Benson & Hedges Cup

1.	106 *	v Leicestershire	Leicester	1983
2.	106	v Leicestershire (2)	Northampton	1986
3.	116	v Nottinghamshire	Trent Bridge	1987
4.	126 *	v Kent	Canterbury	1987
5.	108 *	v Lancashire	Northampton	1992

BENSON & HEDGES CUP

	M	I	NO	HS	Runs	Av	100	50	Ct
1978	4	4	0	34	98	24.50	-	-	2
1979	4	3	1	77	154	77.00	-	2	2
1980	7	7	1	72	117	19.50	-	1	3
1981	3	1	0	54	54	54.00	-	1	-
1982	4	4	0	95	264	66.00	-	3	1
1983	5	4	1	106 *	143	47.66	1	-	3
1984	4	4	1	92	258	86.00	-	3	2
1985	5	4	1	20	30	10.00	-	-	1
1986	5	5	0	106	220	44.00	1	1	2
1987	7	7	2	126 *	398	79.60	2	1	2
1988	4	3	0	19	33	11.00	-	-	1 §
1989	4	4	2	87 *	220	110.00	-	2	2
1990	1	1	0	34	34	34.00	-	-	-
1991	5	5	0	48	150	30.00	-	-	2
1992	4	4	1	108 *	214	71.33	1	1	2
1993	3	3	1	60	145	72.50	-	2	-
1994	1	1	0	25	25	25.00	-	-	-
1995	3	3	0	41	79	26.33	-	-	1
TOTALS	73	67	11	126 *	2636	47.07	5	17	26

§ Bowled 1-0-11-1 v Minor Counties in 1988

SUNDAY LEAGUE

	M	I	NO	HS	Runs	Av	100	50	Ct
1978	11	10	1	31	147	16.33	-	-	3
1979	15	15	3	77	433	36.08	-	4	4
1980	15	15	3	68 *	342	28.50	-	1	2
1981	15	15	1	127 *	551	39.35	1	2	2
1982	9	8	2	104 *	360	60.00	1	1	2
1983	10	10	0	72	217	21.70	-	1	1
1984	9	9	2	99	446	63.71	-	4	4
1985	8	7	4	132 *	463	154.33	2	2	2
1986	10	10	1	97	340	37.77	-	3	4
1987	12	11	0	68	311	28.27	-	2	3
1988	6	5	0	79	215	43.00	-	2	1
1989	5	5	1	80 *	121	30.25	-	1	-
1990	9	9	0	70	248	27.55	-	1	2
1991	11	11	0	61	177	16.09	-	1	4
1992	13	12	2	120	347	34.70	1	-	4
1993	16	15	3	96 *	384	32.00	-	3	9
1994	12	11	1	78	304	30.40	-	2	2
1995	2	2	0	48	82	41.00	-	-	1
TOTALS	188	180	24	132 *	5488	35.17	5	30	50

GILLETTE CUP AND NATWEST TROPHY

		M	I	NO	HS	Runs	Av	100	50	Ct	
1978	Gillette Cup	1	1	0	5	5	5.00	-	-	-	
1979		4	4	0	101	214	53.50	1	1	-	
1980		1	1	0	8	8	8.00	-	-	1	$
1981	NatWest Trophy	4	4	1	28 *	53	17.66	-	-	1	
1982		2	2	0	42	53	26.50	-	-	-	
1983		3	3	0	76	151	50.33	-	2	2	
1984		4	4	0	65	142	35.50	-	1	2	
1985		2	2	0	42	49	24.50	-	-	1	$$
1986		1	1	0	80	80	80.00	-	1	-	
1987		5	5	0	88	230	46.00	-	2	-	
1988		1	1	0	27	27	27.00	-	-	-	
1989		2	2	0	103	107	53.50	1	-	-	
1990		5	5	1	68 *	195	48.75	-	3	2	
1991		4	3	0	31	84	28.00	-	-	1	
1992		5	5	1	69	153	38.25	-	1	1	
1993		3	3	1	124 *	199	99.50	1	1	2	
1994		3	3	1	129 *	142	71.00	1	-	1	
1995		3	3	0	63	103	34.33	-	1	2	
TOTALS		53	52	5	129 *	1995	42.44	4	13	16	

$ Bowled 1-0-8-0 v Surrey 1980

$$ Bowled 0.2-0-4-1 v Shropshire 1985

SUMMARY OF DOMESTIC LIMITED-OVERS MATCHES

	M	I	NO	HS	Runs	Av	100	50	Ct	O	M	R	W	Av	BB
Benson & Hedges Cup 1978-1995	73	67	11	126 *	2636	47.07	5	17	26	1	0	11	1	11.00	1-11
Sunday League 1978-1995	188	180	24	132 *	5488	35.17	5	30	50	-					
Gillette Cup/ NatWest Trophy 1978-1995	53	52	5	129 *	1995	42.44	4	13	16	1.2	0	12	1	12.00	1-4
Totals	314	299	40	132 *	10119	39.06	14	60	92	2.2	0	23	2	11.50	1-4

SUMMARY OF ALL TEST MATCHES

		M	I	NO	HS	Runs	Av	100	50	Ct	O	M	R	W	Av	BB
1982	India	3	5	1	107	207	51.75	1	-	-	-					
	Pakistan	3	6	0	33	48	8.00	-	-	1	-					
1982-83	Australia	5	10	0	83	414	41.40	-	4	5	1	1	0	0	-	-
1983	New Zealand	4	8	2	137*	392	65.33	2	1	10	-					
1983-84	New Zealand	3	4	0	49	82	20.50	-	-	1	-					
	Pakistan	3	5	0	29	78	15.60	-	-	4	-					
1984	West Indies	5	10	1	110	386	42.88	3	-	3	-					
	Sri Lanka	1	1	0	107	107	107.00	1	-	1	1	0	6	0	-	-
1984-85	India	5	7	1	67	241	40.16	-	3	9	1	0	6	1	6.00	1-6
1985	Australia	6	8	1	67	256	36.57	-	1	7	1	0	10	0	-	-
1985-86	West Indies	5	10	0	62	224	22.40	-	1	3	-§	-	1	0	-	-
1986	India	2	4	0	39	65	16.25	-	-	2	-					
	New Zealand	1	1	0	0	0	-	-	-	-	-					
1986-87	Australia	5	9	1	43	144	18.00	-	-	6	1	1	0	0	-	-
1988	West Indies	4	8	2	113	254	42.33	1	1	-	-					
	Sri Lanka	1	2	0	63	71	35.50	-	1	1	-					
1989	Australia	1	2	0	125	129	64.50	1	-	-	-					
1989-90	West Indies	4	7	0	132	390	55.71	2	-	7	-					
1990	New Zealand	3	5	1	84*	129	32.25	-	1	2	-					
	India	3	6	0	139	364	60.66	2	1	2	-					
1990-91	Australia	3	6	0	91	195	32.50	-	2	2	-					
1991	West Indies	4	7	0	29	88	12.57	-	-	7	-					
1991-92	New Zealand	3	5	0	142	338	67.60	1	2	2	-					
1992	Pakistan	2	3	0	30	54	18.00	-	-	-	-					
v INDIA		13	22	2	139	877	43.85	3	4	13	1	0	6	1	6.00	1-6
v PAKISTAN		8	14	0	33	180	12.85	-	-	5	-					
v NEW ZEALAND		14	23	3	142	941	47.05	3	4	15	-					
v WEST INDIES		22	42	3	132	1342	34.41	6	2	20	-	-	1	0	-	-
v SRI LANKA		2	3	0	107	178	59.33	1	1	2	1	0	6	0	-	-
v AUSTRALIA		20	35	2	125	1138	34.48	1	7	20	3	2	10	0	-	-
TOTALS		79	139	10	142	4656	36.09	14	18	75	5	2	23	1	23.00	1-6

§ 1 no-ball

TEST CAPTAINCY

1989-90	v West Indies fourth Test*	Bridgetown	Lost by 164 runs
	v West Indies fifth Test	St John's	Lost by an innings and 37 runs
1990-91	v Australia first Test	Brisbane	Lost by ten wickets

* Won the toss and elected to field

RECORD TEST PARTNERSHIPS

| 308 | 3rd wicket v India with G A Gooch | Lord's | 1990 |
| 87 | 6th wicket v Sri Lanka with R M Ellison | Lord's | 1984 |

TEST MATCHES IN ENGLAND

		M	I	NO	HS	Runs	Av	100	50	Ct	O	M	R	W	Av	BB
1982	India	3	5	1	107	207	51.75	1	-	-	-					
	Pakistan	3	6	0	33	48	8.00	-	-	1	-					
1983	New Zealand	4	8	2	137*	392	65.33	2	1	10	-					
1984	West Indies	5	10	1	110	386	42.88	3	-	3	-					
	Sri Lanka	1	1	0	107	107	107.00	1	-	1	1	0	6	0	-	-
1985	Australia	6	8	1	67	256	36.57	-	1	7	1	0	10	0	-	-
1986	India	2	4	0	39	65	16.25	-	-	2	-					
	New Zealand	1	1	0	0	0	-	-	-	-	-					
1988	West Indies	4	8	2	113	254	42.33	1	1	-	-					
	Sri Lanka	1	2	0	63	71	35.50	-	1	1	-					
1989	Australia	1	2	0	125	129	64.50	1	-	-	-					
1990	New Zealand	3	5	1	84*	129	32.25	-	1	2	-					
	India	3	6	0	139	364	60.66	2	1	2	-					
1991	West Indies	4	7	0	29	88	12.57	-	-	7	-					
1992	Pakistan	2	3	0	30	54	18.00	-	-	-	-					
TOTALS		43	76	8	139	2550	37.50	11	6	36	2	-	16	0	-	-

TEST MATCHES OVERSEAS

		M	I	NO	HS	Runs	Av	100	50	Ct	O	M	R	W	Av	BB
1982-83	Australia	5	10	0	83	414	41.40	-	4	5	1	1	0	0	-	-
1983-84	New Zealand	3	4	0	49	82	20.50	-	-	1	-					
	Pakistan	3	5	0	29	78	15.60	-	-	4	-					
1984-85	India	5	7	1	67	241	40.16	-	3	9	1	0	6	1	6.00	1-6
1985-86	West Indies	5	10	0	62	224	22.40	-	1	3	-	-	§1	0	-	-
1986-87	Australia	5	9	1	43	144	18.00	-	-	6	1	1	0	0	-	-
1989-90	West Indies	4	7	0	132	390	55.71	2	-	7	-					
1990-91	Australia	3	6	0	91	195	32.50	-	2	2	-					
1991-92	New Zealand	3	5	0	142	338	67.60	1	2	2	-					
TOTALS		36	63	2	142	2106	34.52	3	12	39	3	2	7	1	7.00	1-6
Tests in England		43	76	8	139	2550	37.50	11	6	36	2	0	16	0	-	-
TOTAL TESTS		79	139	10	142	4656	36.09	14	18	75	5	2	23	1	23.00	1-6

§ Bowled 1 no-ball in Kingston Test

SUMMARY OF LIMITED-OVERS INTERNATIONALS

		M	I	NO	HS	Runs	Av	100	50	Ct
1982	India	2	2	1	99	134	138.00	-	1	-
	Pakistan	2	2	0	118	145	72.50	1	-	-
1982-83	WSC	10	10	1	108 *	326	36.22	1	1	3
1983	World Cup	7	6	2	102	278	69.50	1	1	6
1983-84	New Zealand	3	3	1	97 *	146	73.00	-	1	-
	Pakistan	2	2	0	57	76	38.00	-	1	-
1984	West Indies	3	3	0	75	86	28.66	-	1	-
1984-85	India	5	5	2	59 *	153	51.00	-	1	-
	World Champ	3	3	0	81	147	49.00	-	2	1
1985	Australia	3	3	1	25	34	17.00	-	-	-
1985-86	West Indies	4	4	0	30	80	20.00	-	-	1
1986	India	2	2	0	45	45	22.50	-	-	-
	New Zealand	2	2	0	33	61	30.50	-	-	-
1986-87	Perth Challenge	4	4	0	71	216	54.00	-	2	-
	WSC in Aus	10	10	3	77 *	243	34.71	-	1	4
1987	Pakistan	3	3	0	61	101	33.66	-	1	1
1987-88	World Cup	8	7	2	76	299	59.80	-	2	2	§
1988	West Indies	3	3	1	30 *	44	22.00	-	-	2
	Sri Lanka	1	1	0	66	66	66.00	-	1	-
1989	Australia	3	3	1	100 *	135	67.50	1	-	-
1989-90	Nehru Cup	6	6	0	91	214	35.66	-	2	4
	West Indies	6	4	1	66	152	50.66	-	2	-
1990	New Zealand	2	2	0	18	22	11.00	-	-	1
	India	2	2	0	56	59	29.50	-	1	-
1990-91	WSC in Aus	6	6	0	72	189	31.50	-	1	2
	New Zealand	3	3	0	61	136	45.33	-	1	2
1991	West Indies	2	2	0	62	80	40.00	-	1	-
1991-92	New Zealand	3	3	0	40	77	25.66	-	-	-
	World Cup	4	4	0	31	79	19.75	-	-	1
1992	Pakistan	5	5	0	60	144	28.80	-	2	-
v INDIA		15	15	4	99	556	50.54	-	4	2
v PAKISTAN		22	22	2	118	830	41.50	1	5	3
v AUSTRALIA		23	23	4	100 *	710	37.36	1	4	5
v NEW ZEALAND		28	28	2	108 *	921	35.42	2	3	9
v SRI LANKA		6	4	0	76	247	61.75	-	4	6
v WEST INDIES		26	24	4	75	711	35.55	-	6	5
v ZIMBABWE		1	1	0	17	17	17.00	-	-	1
v SOUTH AFRICA		1	1	0	19	19	19.00	-	-	-
TOTALS		122	118	16	118	4011	39.32	4	26	31

§ Bowled 1-0-3-0 v Sri Lanka in 1987-88 World Cup

FIFTIES IN LIMITED-OVERS INTERNATIONALS: 30

1.	99	India	Oval	1982
2.	118	Pakistan	Trent Bridge	1982
3.	108 *	New Zealand	Sydney	1982-83
4.	94	Australia	Melbourne	1982-83
5.	102	New Zealand (2)	Oval (2)	1983
6.	53	Sri Lanka	Taunton	1983
7.	97 *	New Zealand (3)	Auckland	1983-84
8.	57	Pakistan (2)	Lahore	1983-84
9.	75	West Indies	Old Trafford	1984
10.	59 *	India (2)	Bangalore	1984-85
11.	53	Australia (2)	Melbourne (2)	1984-85
12.	81	Pakistan (3)	Melbourne (3)	1984-85
13.	66	Australia (3)	Perth	1986-87
14.	71	West Indies (2)	Perth (2)	1986-87
15.	77 *	Australia (4)	Sydney (2)	1986-87
16.	61	Pakistan (4)	Oval (3)	1987
17.	67 *	West Indies (3)	Gujranwala	1987-88
18.	76	Sri Lanka (2)	Peshawar	1987-88
19.	66	Sri Lanka (3)	Oval (4)	1988
20.	100 *	Australia (5)	Trent Bridge (2)	1989
21.	52	Sri Lanka (4)	Delhi	1989-90
22.	91	India (3)	Kanpur	1989-90
23.	66	West Indies (4)	Kingston	1989-90
24	55 *	West Indies (5)	Bridgetown	1989-90
25.	56	India (4)	Headingley	1990
26.	72	New Zealand (4)	Sydney (3)	1990-91
27.	61	New Zealand (5)	Christchurch	1990-91
28.	62	West Indies (6)	Old Trafford (2)	1991
29.	60	Pakistan (5)	Lord's	1992
30.	55	Pakistan (6)	Lord's (2)	1992

Index

281

205–206, 221, 228, 230, 232, 233, 235, 237, 241, 249–262
Botham, Kath 124, 250, 253
Boyce, Keith 163
Boycott, Geoff 'Boycs' 82–83, 85, 233, 257–258
Brache, Frank 39
Bradman, Sir Donald 55
Bramhall, John 183, 189
Branson, Richard 217
Brassington, Andy 52
Brearley, Mike 93
Brewer, John 168
Briers, Nigel 88
Broad, Chris 143, 195
Bromage, Peter 196
Brown, Laurie 150, 171
Brown, Tony 132–133, 137–138, 140, 180, 182–184, 207–209, 244, 247
Bruce, Stephen 78, 80
Bruyns, Andre 20
Bucknall, Tony 11, 123, 125
Burdett, Les 104
Burt, Jack 25, 30
Bing, Fritz 31, 96

Cairns, Lance 112
Caldecott, Andrew 217–230
Callaghan, Dave 148
Cambridge University 44
Capel, David 153, 156–158, 169, 173
Carlstein, Peter 24
Carman, George 250–262
Carr, Donald 72, 138, 182, 184, 186, 244
Carter, Bob 159, 181
Cattell, Liz 111, 144
Cawdry, Tony 183
Chamberlain, Frank 153, 192–193, 196, 212
Chappell, Greg 101, 106–107, 239, 241
Chappell, Ian 31
Chatfield, Ewen 112, 143
Cheetham, John 27
Chevalier, Grahame 27, 30
Childs, John 157
Chist, Alan 69
Claremont (team) 30
Clarke, Sylvester 25, 44, 147–148, 236
Clift, Paddy 23, 26, 78–80
Close, Brian 239, 257–258
Constant, David 97
Cook, Geoff 62, 63, 77, 85, 92, 101, 142,

152, 155, 162, 183–184
Cook, Jimmy 81–82, 95
Cook, Nick 88, 152, 155, 157–158
Cottam, Bob 158
Coverdale, Steve 152, 177, 196, 244–245, 247–248
Cowans, Norman 'Flash' 106–107
Cowdrey, Chris 220–221
Cowdrey, Sir Colin 15
Crafter, Tony 145
Crank, Sue 122
Cresta Run 165–167
Cricketers' Association 76, 183, 198, 246
Croft, Colin 237
Crowe, Martin 240
Crystal, Jonathan 217–230
Cudmore, Harold 119
Cumberbatch, Clyde 169
Curran, Kevin 157–158, 238
Currie Cup 27, 33, 37, 38, 39, 47–49, 55, 64, 65, 70, 77, 78, 81, 147–148, 240
Curtis, Tim 164

D'Oliveira, Basil 39, 48, 91
Daily Mirror 176–177, 185, 190–191, 202, 206, 209, 214, 245, 260
Dakin, Geoff 29
Daniel, Wayne 44, 52
Datsun Trophy 78, 82, 102
Davis, Percy 45, 60, 62
Davis, Winston 128, 131, 153, 157
Davison, Brian 48, 68, 71, 88
de Silva, Aravinda 133
DeFreitas, Phil 145, 155, 163, 195, 263
Derbyshire 27, 43–45, 50, 57, 67, 77, 155
Dexter, Ted 15, 94, 163, 167, 172, 185, 202
Dilley, Graham 90, 143–144, 150, 194
Donald, Allan 241–242
Donnelly, Paul 114
Doshi, Dilip 90
Downton, Ally 124, 256
Downton, Paul 256
Drourgh, Roy 48
du Plessis, Morne 69
du Preez, Jacky 26
Dudleston, Barry 193–194, 205, 215
Dujon, Jeffrey 129
During, Albie 20
During, John 78
Dye, John 220
Dyson, John 104, 109

INDEX